Crosshairs on the Capital

Crosshairs on the Capital

Jubal Early's Raid on Washington, D.C. July 1864
Reasons, Reactions, and Results

JAMES H. BRUNS

CASEMATE

Philadelphia & Oxford

Published in the United States of America and Great Britain in 2021 by
CASEMATE PUBLISHERS
1950 Lawrence Road, Havertown, PA 19083, US
and
The Old Music Hall, 106–108 Cowley Road, Oxford OX4 1JE, UK

Hardback Edition: ISBN 978-1-63624-011-4
Digital Edition: ISBN 978-1-63624-012-1

A CIP record for this book is available from the British Library

Printed and bound in the United States by Sheridan

Typeset in India by Lapiz Digital Services.

For a complete list of Casemate titles, please contact:
CASEMATE PUBLISHERS (US)
Telephone (610) 853-9131
Fax (610) 853-9146
Email: casemate@casematepublishers.com
www.casematepublishers.com

CASEMATE PUBLISHERS (UK)
Telephone (01865) 241249
Email: casemate-uk@casematepublishers.co.uk
www.casematepublishers.co.uk

Contents

For Chris, Don, Dan, Mandy, Joe, and James

Preface

This book focuses on the reasons, reactions, and results of Confederate Lieutenant General Jubal Early's raid on Washington, DC, in 1864. These three aspects have been overlooked in many of the earlier narratives of the raid, works that have tended to concentrate on the battles and leaders. And, unlike all the other narratives of this kind, this work highlights the forgotten naval role in the 1864 scheme to free Confederate prisoners at Point Lookout, Maryland, and its implications.

Welcome to Civil War-era Washington. The District of Columbia had been the seat of government since 1790, and for much of its early existence it was considered a relatively sleepy Southern town that in 1860 had a population of roughly 75,000. The city was unbearably hot and humid in the worst of summer. Manure-laden dust storms and its swampy location made it prone to typical Southern seasonal diseases. In the heights of winter, it was icy and windswept, with streets that could resemble rivers of thick, frosty, gumbo-like muck. The city's heavy-eyed character changed dramatically with the onset of the Civil War. Almost overnight the district was transformed from a quiet community into a massively important centralized hub of bureaucratic and public activity that was needed to sustain the war effort. The population at times swelled to as many as 200,000 inhabitants. Overcrowding and a lack of adequate housing and sanitation were major problems. Cleanliness suffered as the city witnessed an intensity of military, civil, and bawdy activities at a previously unknown scale.

As the center of Union management of the war, Washington's safety was seriously threatened several times, including in 1862, when the Confederacy's Army of Northern Virginia invaded Maryland, culminating with the battle of Antietam, and again in 1863 with that same Rebel army's invasion of the North, resulting in the battle of Gettysburg. In each of these instances, the Federal city wasn't the target. That changed in 1864. And the third time wasn't a charm. It was considered a serious threat. Or at least that's what we've been led to believe for 155-plus years. But was it?

While many previous books on the subject of Jubal Early's raid on fortress Washington have focused largely on the military aspects of that incursion, this book concentrates more on the feelings, fears, and facts of the region's civilian population, its causal connections, and its results. Because misinformation was rampant, this book examines the civilians' thoughts, anxieties, and frustrations over the lack of accurate news regarding their safety and their keen—and perhaps morbid—curiosity with what was going on at the nearby killing fields about them.

President Abraham Lincoln was one of those who was drawn to the battlefront like a moth to a bright flame that steamy summer. On several occasions he visited the frontlines and was even reportedly deliberately shot at by Confederate sharpshooters. If true, that made him only the second chief executive known to have faced enemy gunfire while in office (the other was James Madison at the 1814 battle of Bladensburg, which took place only a few miles away to the east from where Lincoln reportedly faced enemy fire).

But I believe that the stories about Lincoln thoughtlessly facing gunfire at Fort Stevens and nearly being shot have been greatly overblown over time. The nature of the Confederate raid on Washington, I believe, has also been greatly misinterpreted. While there were various important goals each time the Confederates invaded the North, Jubal Early's maneuvers were in fact only the latest in a series of annual Southern food raids. The Confederacy had made such incursions in September 1862, culminating with the battle of Antietam; in July 1863, ending with the battle of Gettysburg; and now, again, in July 1864, climaxing with the standoff in front of Fort Stevens. Each time, foraging for food was a major aspect of these operations.

As early as 1862, General Robert E. Lee was intrigued with the idea of attacking Washington, but he accepted the limitations of his situation. As he told President Jefferson Davis, "I had no intention of attacking (the enemy) in his fortifications and am not prepared to (besiege) them. If I possessed the necessary munitions, I should be unable to supply provisions for the troops."[1] That opinion wouldn't change in 1864. Instead, in 1862 and 1863 Lee would merely threaten Washington, while gathering food and supplies for his needy army. In addition to provisions, Lee's army in Maryland and Pennsylvania in 1863 also rounded up large numbers of runaway slaves and herded them back South. July was the perfect month for such maneuvers. It cleared the Shenandoah Valley of bluecoats during the Southern harvest season, and it coincided with low water levels on the Potomac and other river gateways to the North.

The Northern territory that was plundered was always the same, including what became West Virginia in 1863, western Maryland, and southern

Robert E. Lee took Richard "Old Baldy" Ewell's command of the Second Corps away from him in the spring of 1864 and gave it to Jubal Early. Ewell, a native of the District of Columbia, was given command of the defense of Richmond until its fall in April 1865. (Library of Congress)

Pennsylvania, all largely pro-Union regions, but in 1864 Jubal Early's force would pillage deeper into the heartland of secessionist Maryland. The pastures he plundered were largely productive pro-Southerners' farms.

In this regard, the Rebel army in the North was like a biblical plague of locusts. In 1862 the Rebels made off with large quantities of food, fodder, and supplies. One Maryland resident complained that after the Confederates arrived, "The farmers didn't have no chickens to crow..." and, according to Union medical officer William Child, the assistant regimental surgeon with the 5th New Hampshire Infantry, the farms around Antietam Creek were completely picked clean. "The man with whom I stop has not an apple, peach, sweet or Irish potato left," he noted, adding, "he would have had great quantity of each had no army passed this way."[2] In advance of the Rebels marching into Maryland in 1862, many farmers fled north with their horses and livestock, but their crops were left up for grabs. Harvests already put up in barns were hastily taken, as were any remaining animals. The following summer, the Rebels returned, again hoping to abscond with more food and animals.

Mid-to-late summer were the perfect months for conducting food raids. Except for the heat, Summer wheat was typically harvested in July, and by mid-month large quantities were either awaiting milling or already milled. In July gristmills were a prime target. By September wheat and corn flour saved for the winter had already been put up. In September, barns were a principal objective.

In July 1863, Robert E. Lee cautioned his soldiers to behave well when it came to Northern private property, saying, "no greater disgrace could befall the army, than the perpetuation of the barbarous outrages upon the unarmed and defenceless [sic] and the wanton destruction of private property that have marked the course of the enemy in our own country," but the pent-up hostility of seeing so much damage inflicted by Northern troops was always hard to suppress.[3] In 1863 Lee also planned to pay for what his army took from Northern farm folks. On 23 June 1863 he told Jefferson Davis,

> In addition to the supplies that we have been able to gather in Fauquier and Loudoun [Virginia] Counties, in the Shenandoah Valley, and west of the Alleghany, we have collected sufficient north of the Potomac for the support of Ewell's corps to the 30th instant; and 1,200 barrels of flour are on hand in Maryland for the rest of the army. I hope we shall get enough for the subsistence of our men. Forage is very scarce, and we have mainly to rely on grass for the animals. From the reports I receive, I believe we shall obtain enough salt for our purposes while north of the Potomac, for which we are paying 75 cents a bushel. The flour that we have purchased in Maryland costs $6.50 per barrel; beef, $5 per hundred gross. We use Confederate money for all payments. I shall continue to purchase all the supplies that are furnished me while north of the Potomac, impressing only when necessary.

The use of Confederate paper money wasn't really quite true in 1864. To Northern farmers, receiving Southern paper money in payment was pretty much worthless. Besides, Early's units and his individual soldiers weren't always obedient to the need for purchasing what otherwise could easily be pillaged. Additionally, Early insisted he expected to use the gold ransom payments he extorted from Northern towns instead of Confederate paper money to pay for purchases. How much gold was actually paid out is unclear. Early was pleased with his plunder. After the war he said, "beside the money levied in Hagerstown and Frederick, which was very useful in obtaining supplies, we brought off quite a large number of beef cattle, and the cavalry obtained a large number of horses, some being also procured for the artillery."[4]

During that invasion of Pennsylvania in 1863 J. E. B. Stuart was able to capture 125 wagons loaded with fodder and supplies at Rockville, Maryland, while he was AWOL as Lee's eyes and ears. Those wagons slowed Stuart's movements and likely cost Lee the battle of Gettysburg, which he hadn't really wanted to fight. Lee's principal target was expected to be Harrisburg, Pennsylvania, the relatively unprotected state's capital. By the time Stuart and his 5,000 horsemen finally arrived at Gettysburg on 2 July, the opposing forces were already locked in deadly combat at one location. The opposing forces were drawn there as if by a giant vacuum, initially predicated on a search for shoes.

A few days earlier, Dick Ewell's Rebel units, including Jubal Early's division, had been northeast of Gettysburg at York and Carlisle, Pennsylvania, plundering farms for food and probing around Harrisburg. Drawn to the developing battle, Early's men had converged on Gettysburg by 1 July 1863 to help lead the way through that small town in the rapidly escalating fight. This gave Early an added sense for what street-by-street fighting was like, reinforcing what he had learned from the house-to-house fighting at Fredericksburg, Virginia, in December 1862.

Because of the previous food raids in 1862 and 1863, perhaps someone in the War Department in Washington should have anticipated another raid in 1864, but obviously no one had given the pattern much thought.

Things would be different in the summer of 1864. By then Lee couldn't march his entire army onto the verdant Northern farmlands for the food his men so desperately needed. Because of the draught during the summer of 1864, and the devastation caused by Union forces in the Shenandoah Valley, and the need to protect the Confederate capital, Richmond, Lee's men around Petersburg had to stay put, despite their hunger. So, in 1864, he dispatched a small, yet ample band led by a well-respected and overly aggressive Union hater to the closest places he knew were capable of filling his empty Rebel bullies—the fields, farms, and mills just across the Potomac River. In attacking Washington, Lieutenant General Jubal Early would have four divisions under his command. His divisional commanders were Major Generals John C. Breckinridge, Robert Rhodes, John Brown Gordon, and Stephen Dodson Ramseur. And, even with fewer men in 1864 than had been with Lee in 1862 and 1863, Early's divisions would still do all right for themselves bumming off fertile Northern farmlands again.

Before crossing the Potomac River, Early advised Lee that his "provisions were nearly exhausted" and that he intended to take the fastest pathway to Northern food. This was the traditional route used in the past, hopscotching from Harpers Ferry to Shepherdstown, West Virginia, and crossing the Potomac at Boteler's Ford into Maryland. (There once had been a bridge there, but Stonewall Jackson had ordered it to be burned in June 1861 to keep it from becoming a convenient Union causeway into the South.) Not only would Early take abundant provisions for his men from the enemy's countryside, but he'd carry away sufficient supplies to feed Lee's famished forces at Petersburg for a time.

What was needed most was livestock and milled flour. The need for food was obvious, even to Arkansas slave Shepherd Rhone. Interviewed for the Federal government's Slave Narratives Project in the 1930s, Rhone's opinion was that "the only reason the Yankees whipped the South was (because) they starved them."[5] Gus Brown agreed. He served as a Confederate soldier even though he was a slave from Alabama. He told a slave project interviewer,

"We want beaten, we wuz starved out! Sometimes we had parched corn to eat and sometimes we didn't have a bite o' nothing because the Union mens come and tuck all the food for their selves."[6]

In 1864 the typical Confederate soldier was eating far less than his Federal counterparts, as much as 1,500 calories less a day. The average daily Confederate consumption was between 2,000 to 2,500 calories. That level of intake was slowly starving the South's soldiers. Rhone's and Brown's observations are a premise of this book. Southern soldiers were being starved into defeat and Jubal Early's raid into the North was in large measure a desperate scramble for food to sustain the fight.

This book also highlights how some of the region's everyday civilians fought back, and how so many simple citizens, often scared witless, rallied to defend their homes and the Union. Clearly the arrival of battle-tested Federal troops from Petersburg saved the day, but for a brief period of time, everyday citizens, including many African Americans, stood on the frontlines, shoulder to shoulder with a small number of 100-day militiamen, invalid soldiers, government workers, and active-duty troops to defend the nation's capital. These were accompanied by a few trained regiments of heavy artillerymen. They all were prepared to save the Federal city, come what may.

This book is about what life in Washington, DC, and Maryland was like for those on the ramparts and in the city's rifle pits during that hot July in 1864, and how Federal leaders reacted to the crisis.

An ambrotype of an unidentified Confederate soldier in relatively rag-tag condition. His appearance was similar to those who accompanied Jubal Early in 1864. His canvas haversack held his grub, which might have included several hardtack crackers, a handful or two of corn, a small bag of coffee, and, if he was lucky, a twisted rag containing a small amount of sugar and maybe a bit of meat. (Library of Congress)

It also corrects some of the thinking about Early's raid, including the reason behind his orders from General Lee to cross the Potomac and the thoughts behind the proposed raid on Point Lookout and the role of the Confederate navy in that failed effort. It presents a perspective different from what has been taken before in explaining Jubal Early's raid on Washington—rather than focus on what happened, as so many books of this type do, this work highlights why things happened as they did in 1864. It identifies the cause-and-effect connections that are truly the stuff of history. It reveals some of the critical background links that are often ignored or overlooked in reading books dominated by battles and leaders. In effect, it recognizes that *why* something was done is as important as understanding *what* was done.

Much of the information cited here is from Volume 37, Part II, of the War of the Rebellion: A Compilation of the Official Records of the Union and Confederate Armies, published by order of the Secretary of War in 1891. This volume includes hundreds of orders, reports and correspondence covering operations and actions in Northern Virginia, West Virginia, Maryland and Pennsylvania by both sides from 1 May to 3 August 1864.

Introduction

Not counting the domestic assault on the Capitol building in January 2021, the nation's capital has come under direct attack by hostile forces twice in our history. The first time was in 1814, when British forces succeeded in capturing and burning the city. That attack was payback for the destruction of York (now Toronto) in 1813, when American forces captured the capital of Upper Canada and hauled off the king's royal standard, a rare flag that is still held as a war trophy by the US military. The second time was 50 years later, when forces under the command of Confederate Lieutenant General Jubal Early attacked the outer perimeter of the city's defenses, fortifications left vulnerable by the withdrawal of troops to General U. S. Grant's attempt to break the siege at Petersburg, Virginia, and capture Richmond. Grant's army was like a giant magnet when it came to military manpower. It was forcefully pulling in all available soldiers to Petersburg. By the spring of 1864, the force of that deadly attraction left Washington practically defenseless.

Jubal Early was expected to exploit that weakness. His primary mission was to clear the Shenandoah Valley of Union forces, thus ensuring the ability of the Confederates' breadbasket to once again feed Lee's struggling army. Early was also to cause enough chaos to ensure that significant Union forces would be withdrawn from the Petersburg campaign to deal with his rampage, thus relieving the crushing pressure the Army of Northern Virginia was battling under, delaying or eliminating the risk of losing Richmond, and stalling any Union summer offensive. These two primary tasks could be accomplished in Virginia.

While those objectives alone were sufficient reasons for unleashing the Second Corps from its defensive positions in Virginia, Robert E. Lee gave Jubal Early additional goals to accomplish while his force was on its tear. The Potomac River was going to be Early's Rubicon. If he crossed it, he was obligated to another set of tasks, and Lee was banking on this happening, so much so that he set in motion a secret plan that would significantly impact Early's operations, one Early would be told about only after he was on Maryland soil. The concept was explained in a secret message to Confederate marine Major William Norris from a Rebel agent in southern Maryland, codenamed "DARST," written on 9 June 1864, which observed, "We think it all important that a diversion should be made, either to capture or release our prisoners at Point Lookout or a raid upon Washington with a view to the destruction of the military supplies…." Either way, this implies that Early's actions in Maryland were meant as a distraction, not a serious attack on either place. Among Early's other implied or specific tasks were to invade Maryland, Pennsylvania, and West Virginia in the hope of capturing large quantities of Northern livestock and foodstuffs, yields that were desperately needed by the South; to ransom as many Northern towns as possible for cash and/or commodities, under the threat of burning them to the ground; to encourage secessionists in Maryland to rally to the Southern cause, possibly leading to a popular uprising in pro-Southern portions of the "Old Line State;" to attract eager recruits to the Confederate army; to destroy Northern canals, rails, and telegraph lines wherever possible, especially around Washington, thereby disrupting communications and transportation and potentially causing panic throughout the North; to adversely impact the Northern presidential election of 1864 such that Lincoln might not be reelected; and to encourage European support for the Southern war effort. There were also the pie-in-the-sky dreams of possibly capturing President Lincoln and taking possession of all the gold deposits and greenbacks in the vaults of the Treasury Department, if by some measure of good fortune Washington could come within Early's crosshairs. Because Early's force was accompanied by Major General John C. Breckenridge, who had served as vice president of the United States from 1857 to 1861, there were even joyful, if unrealistic, thoughts of possibly enthroning him once again in the Capitol, where he had previously served as the presiding officer of the Senate.

Many of these ideas seemed to be fanciful sugarplums dancing around in wishful Southern minds, but Jubal Early's raid would prove to be remarkably adept in achieving many of them.

One last task would be sprung on Early later. This was the secret part of his mission, and it came as a last-minute surprise. Early was to coordinate with and assist Brigadier General Bradley Tyler Johnson's 1st Maryland Mounted Infantry, a regiment that was known as "the Maryland Line," that, in conjunction with the Confederate navy, would attempt a possible prison breakout at Point Lookout, a large Union prisoner-of-war camp in southern Maryland. Bradley Johnson was promoted to Brigadier General on 28 June 1864, to give him the rank he'd need for such an operation.

The big questions in any book such as this is: Could Early possibly have succeeded in capturing Washington in July 1864? And was the prison break at Point Lookout an actual operation, and if it was, did it have a realistic chance of success?

In retrospect General Grant thought capturing Washington was perhaps possible, noting that the Confederates might have pulled it off "if Early had been but one day earlier." But Early arrived late. One of his division commanders, Major General John Brown Gordon, thought so too. "Undoubtedly we could have marched into Washington," Gordon would later write. He insisted, "I myself rode to a point on those breastworks at which there was no force whatsoever. The unprotected space was broad enough for the easy passage of Early's army without resistance."[1] When Gordon returned to urge the men of his division to rush forward, this window of opportunity closed. Early was trying to prod his men into action, too, but he and Gordon were up against a force they couldn't overcome—fatigue. Other Confederate commanders disagreed with the desirability of a headlong military breakthrough. Major Henry Douglas, leading the famed Stonewall Brigade, thought it was ill-advised. He believed that if Early had rushed his available forces at Washington, it would become his quicksand. "If he had I am sure he would never have gotten out again," noted Douglas. His opinion was that no one, not even Early, ever really expected to take the capital city. The view of others, such as Early's chief of artillery, Brigadier General Armistead Lindsay Long, was that they really didn't have to punch a hole in Washington's defensive ring to prove a point. Just threatening the city was good enough.

Late in life, even Early agreed with that assessment. Writing to the editors of *Century* magazine in 1888, he admitted, "if you will read Barnard's 'Defense of Washington,' you will see that it would have been impossible for me to have entered Washington at any time with my force. Before I got in front of the

Brigadier General Armistead Lindsay Long. (Library of Congress)

works, there were not less than 15,000 in the trenches in that front, before the arrival of Wright's troops." Early confirmed to *Century*'s editors that General Lee never expected his troops to enter Washington. The fact is, he said, Lee was satisfied with him merely threatening the Federal city. According to Early, Lee said capturing it "would be impossible."[2] As for a prison break at Point Lookout, it appears to have been planned as payback for a similar raid perpetrated on the South a short time earlier.

CHAPTER 1

The Confederates Turn the Tables

Besides the obvious need for food, Robert E. Lee got the idea for one aspect of Jubal Early's raid on Washington in July 1864 from the Union. None of the authors who have written about Early's raid before this have pointed out the similarities between the mission Union forces carried out only a few months earlier, but undoubtedly that mission was clearly on Lee's mind at the time. In effect, Lee opted to become a copycat, mimicking what the Union tried, yet failed to achieve, in the winter of 1864. However, instead of copying the whole Federal playbook, he compensated for much of the Federal shortfalls in timing, manning, and planning.

The Union's raid was principally the result of a secret message from Elizabeth Van Lew to Union General Benjamin Butler on 30 January 1864, telling him that for security reasons the Confederate government was going to send the prisoners-of-war held in the hellholes in Richmond to Georgia's newly opened Andersonville Prison and other places. She urged that a raid be conducted to thwart that possibility. Van Lew was a 43-year-old widow who was more than just a kind-hearted and sympathetic Unionist. Although she was ostracized for her "assiduous attentions to the Yankee prisoners" and was frequently threatened by her neighbors, she volunteered to nurse the Union prisoners held in various locations in Richmond, which she described as "unsurpassed in wretchedness and squalid filth."

During her prison visits, Van Lew brought food, medicines, books, bribery money, and war news. The food she smuggled in was never enough. The men were forced to survive on one-quarter of a loaf of corn bread in the morning and one-third of a loaf at night, with half a pint of black beans, the latter often wormy and unfit to eat. The bread was underbaked and the

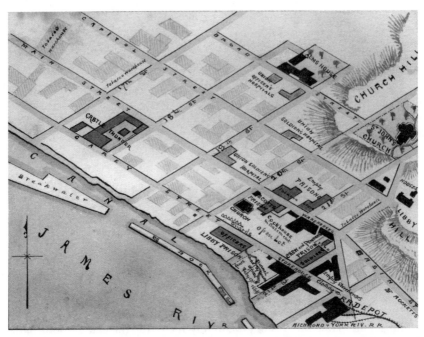

This is the plan of the portion of Richmond below Church Hill, from the canal to Broad Street and from 17th to 21st Streets, that included Castle Thunder and Libby Prison and the Union officers' and soldiers' hospitals, as drawn in 1863. Elizabeth Van Lew visited all these wretched places to comfort the inmates, all the while learning about and passing along secrets to the Union. (Library of Congress)

prisoners believed it was concocted to produce irritation and sickness instead of sustain life. She also hid messages in some of the books she furnished and received books back that contained messages written in pin pricks. She bribed the guards to furnish better treatment and even snuck prisoners out of the camps and conducted them safely to Union lines. She also served as a nurse at Confederate hospitals, where she overheard countless confidential conversations. "The men in the hospital have nothing much to do, so they talk," she recalled. Since December 1863 she was the fearless head of a highly effective Union spy ring in Richmond.

Reportedly code named "Babcock," Van Lew passed secrets on to Major General Benjamin Butler and later to General Grant, both of whom forwarded her messages to Secretary of War Edwin Stanton for action. That was the case with the message concerning the need for a prison break.

Northerners were reading accounts in their local newspapers written by exchanged Union prisoners who had been held at Richmond's Belle Isle and Libby Prisons. These described deplorable conditions and brutal treatment. The prisoners told of arriving with next to nothing. Immediately upon being

Elizabeth Van Lew's mansion in Richmond, Virginia, circa 1900. (Library of Congress)

captured they said they were stripped of everything of value by their immediate captors, including their overcoats, watches, and boots, if they were in good condition. Upon arriving at Libby or Belle Isle they were further searched by the guards for anything else they might have, including money or other valuables, such as wedding rings. These were all confiscated. According to W. S. Toland, a sergeant in the 9th Regiment of the New York State Militia, in a letter to Secretary of War Stanton on 23 April 1863 that was also sent to the *New York Times*, "On entering Libby Prison we were closely searched by the rebel authorities, and most of the prisoners robbed of whatever money they had, not one cent of which they ever saw again." The republished letter noted,

On the 14th of November about 100 of us were taken from the Libby and marched to Belle Isle, reaching there about 9 a.m. The prisoners collected on the bank on all sides of the inclosure to meet us, and such a collection of woe-begone, miserable, starving men I never beheld. We were marched inside of the gate and turned loose like so many cattle, to find a resting place where we could; shelter there was none. The whole inclosure does not comprise more than four acres, and within it more than 8,000 prisoners were at one time confined. The only shelter was tents, generally worn out and leaky; and during the whole winter hundreds, and sometimes more than a thousand men, were obliged to sleep in the open air on the ground and in ditches. The coldest winter days, the thermometer down to 5 or 8, from 200 to 500 men were invariably sent over from Libby Prison, where they had been all winter under shelter and had sold their clothing to procure food. Some walked the weary night, some laid down and died, some went raving mad.

Unmoved by such stories of privation, Jubal Early's opinion was that Federal soldiers were overfed and when they became captives, they expected the same amount to eat that they had enjoyed before captivity. He reasoned that prior to becoming prisoners the bluecoats were spoiled. "No army that ever took the field was so well supplied in all that was necessary, and much that was superfluous."[1] To him, "the prisoners taken by their valor, and who had been so well pampered in their own country, thought proper to regard, when furnished them, as evidence of a disposition to starve them," he wrote in his *Memoirs*.[2] As it was, Early believed that Union prisoners were eating better than his own men, who were often reduced to subsisting on roasted ears of green corn or mere pieces of cooked bacon. He thought that grossly unfair. "Now, I ask, in the name of all that is sacred, did they expect that the men who had come down to make war upon a people so reduced by their

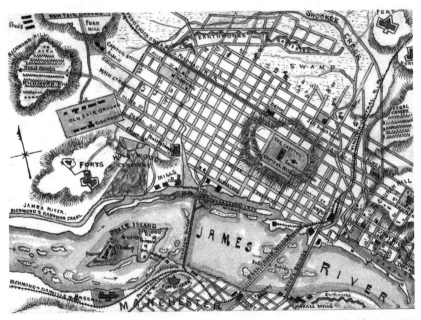

This map of Richmond was drawn in 1863. It designates Belle Isle as holding 10,000 Union prisoners. In comparing this map with the previous one it is clear that the ill-planned Richmond prison break wasn't likely to succeed because of the 2.6-mile separation between Belle Isle and the prisoner compounds where Libby Prison was located further to the southeast. Another barrier was the Rebel forts and earthworks on the Manchester side of the James River that covered the approaches to the bridges the prisoners would have to cross initially to gain their freedom. (Library of Congress)

barbarous acts to the very verge of starvation and nakedness should, when taken in battle, be fed and clothed better than the men who, sacrificing all mere personal considerations, were so bravely meeting their foes in deadly strife, while their wives, children, mothers and sisters were starving?"[3] Even General Lee, who Early considered "the foremost commander of the age," was forced at times to subsist on meager food. One of the General's dinners consisted entirely of hard crackers, fried fat back, and a brewed concoction of substitute coffee without sugar. If Lee could eat this way, he reasoned, why couldn't Federal prisoners? Early wasn't moved by the prisoners' rags either. Of his own men he said, "I have seen commissioned officers often, marching on foot with their pantaloons out behind, their coats out at the elbow and their toes sticking out of their shoes, with but a pretence [sic] for a sole, while they had but the shirt that was on their backs as their whole supply of linen."[4] Early rationalized that if Federal officials were really so concerned with the plight of their POWs they'd agree to exchange more of them for Confederate captives.[5]

Some paroled Union prisoners talked about defensive conditions in the Confederate capital. One account by Corporal John F. White of the 83rd New York Infantry, published in the *New York Sunday Mercury* on 13 September 1863, noted, "our Government ought and can take Richmond any day, if they have a mind to; no soldiers around there nearer Fredericksburg. The city militia does not amount to anything, and the people of Richmond will help us as soon as our forces near the city." Uncle Sam's army would indeed attempt just that within a matter of months.

Two months later the newspaper admitted that the island had to be temporarily evacuated to allow it to undergo "fumigation for purification purposes." By January 1863 Bell Isle's POW camp was back in business. By May it was again emptied out, only to be refilled a short time later. In August the Union furnished 150 tents just to shelter the prisoners held at Belle Isle adequately. As fall approached the island was expected to hold 14,000 hungry mouths, which the *Richmond Examiner* called "the 'azure-stomached' race." The paper demanded to know what was to be done with the prisoners, who "like the locusts of Egypt…eat up our subsistence." Fed up with their conditions, Belle Isle prisoners attempted an unsuccessful prison break in early November 1863.

In December 1863 the *Richmond Sentinel* told its readers that Belle Isle's prisoners were going to be moved to Georgia, "where no difficulty will be encountered in supplying their wants." Fears of another prison riot simmered, with the *Richmond Whig* reporting on 10 February 1864,

> There has been a good deal of talk recently of an apprehended outbreak among the Yankee prisoners on Belle Isle. It is true that the prisoners manifested some exultation, last Sunday, when the signal bells were summoning the local

troops to their rendezvous; and it is also true that one or two anonymous notes have been received by the authorities warning them of a plot to effect the escape of the prisoners; but, beyond these developments, there is no ground for apprehension of a Yankee insurrection on Belle Isle. The military authorities, however, have very properly strengthened the guard on the island, and made other arrangements for promptly quelling any insubordination among the prisoners that may arise. Let the Yankees attempt to escape, and but few of them will ever get back to the land of onions, wooden nutmegs and steady habits.

Miss Van Lew was carefully reading such accounts and listening to every bit of street gossip, and one reoccurring bit of talk was that "Three regiments of cavalry [were] disbanded by Lee for want of horses." She immediately passed this along to her bluecoat contacts. Initially, nothing was done about it, but the accuracy of this tidbit of intelligence would ring a bell with the army's secretary when Early's raiders began rounding up herds of Northern horses in July 1864.

Whether Secretary of War Edwin Stanton gave Brigadier General Hugh Judson Kilpatrick the idea for the raid on Richmond or somehow Kilpatrick was clairvoyant is unclear, but in either case Kilpatrick was summoned to Washington in mid-February 1864 to explain the proposed prison raid to President Lincoln.

Stereoscopic view of the railroad bridge and the Diamond Iron and Nail Works on Belle Isle, circa 1865. (Library of Congress)

On 12 February 1864, Lincoln met with Kilpatrick, who outlined the daring plan to attack Richmond and free its Union prisoners. Lincoln liked what he heard and sent Kilpatrick to see Secretary of War Stanton to hash out the details. Of course, Stanton already knew the basics, having likely formulated them in the first place based upon Elizabeth Van Lew's intelligence. Still, Kilpatrick claimed the credit, which seems to have been fine with Stanton, because it maintained Van Lew's cover and personally protected himself, especially if the whole thing went sour.

Kilpatrick was given too few men to accomplish the mission. There were also issues with its timing. The mission was launched at the height of winter in the mid-Atlantic, the worst of all possible times of the year for such a fast-moving offensive operation to free ill-dressed and underfed prisoners. And, worst of all, there was no well-coordinated plan of action for after the elements of the raiding party reached Richmond. Oddly, Lee didn't specifically address the issues of food and clothing in his plan for Jubal Early during the summer of 1864, either. It must be assumed that

The plan to relocate the prisoners held in Richmond's Libby Prison to Georgia prompted a successful prison break. Prisoners dug an escape tunnel in a basement area of the old tobacco factory and warehouse building known as "Rat Hell." This section of the basement was so infested with rats that guards avoided it. Working with pocketknives, spittoons, tin cups, and makeshift tools, the prisoners spent 17 days creating their escape tunnel under Cary Street. On the night of 9 February 1864, 109 of them staged a breakout. The escapees were gone about 12 hours before they were missed. Forty were later rounded up, but the others got away. The decision to move the remaining prisoners to the newly opened Andersonville Prison and other camps prompted the Kilpatrick-Dahlgren raid weeks later. (Library of Congress)

Union prisoners awaiting their rations at Andersonville on 17 August 1864. At Camp Sumter at Andersonville, Union prisoners died at an alarming rate. Twenty-nine percent of those held there perished. (National Archives and Record Administration)

he envisioned the prisoners simply stripping their guards and raiding the camp's commissary and kitchens.

Corporal Samuel J. Gibson of the 103rd Pennsylvania Infantry Regiment was one of those imprisoned at Andersonville in 1864. He arrived there on 3 May and in just a matter of months he had aged greatly. He noted in his pocket diary for 6 August 1864, "I am 31 years old to day; but I am more broken down & my joints are stiffer than they ought to be at 60; It is a hard place to celebrate a birth day; in a military prison where a man cannot call his life his own; to day [sic] I saw one of the guards shoot a man through the head killing him instantly; O cruel enemy; your turn may come sooner than you think." A few days later Gibson wrote of his miseries: "Passed a restless night; clothes all wet & disagreeable; & this morning is still very disagreeable; add to this a hungry Belly for our merciless captors seize on every pretext to cut off the rations; & yesterday's rain caused one good enough for the breakfast consisted of corn mush & water."[6]

Death became so commonplace that Gibson began to question his own fate. On 12 August, he expressed his doubts in what he was doing. "I don't know for whom I am keeping this Diary; I still have hope that I will yet outlive this misfortune of being a prisoner but I am not made of <u>iron</u>; still I consider myself pretty tough: I have got the better of the scurvy again & am now in tolerably good health, & will try to keep my head <u>above water</u>; but I

Five Confederate prisoners from Camp Douglas in Chicago, circa 1862, in front of their barracks, showing no signs of significant deprivation. (Library of Congress)

am seeing my dream verified every day; by seeing scores of my fellows carried out dead." In a rare letter to his wife while being held, Gibson downplayed the Hell he was living through, but in his journal he admitted that, "If this is not Hell itself, it must be pandemonium; which is only Hell Gate. Heaven forbid I should ever see a worse place." Corporal Gibson survived Andersonville. He died in 1878, far from the place he considered in his diary to be "this Hell-upon-earth of a Prison."

Union officers were moved to Camp Oglethorpe at Macon, Georgia. One of those sent to Macon was Lieutenant Lucius Dwight Hinkley of the 10th Wisconsin Infantry. He wrote his brother on 6 June 1864 that he actually preferred Libby Prison to the military prison at Macon because he felt better there, but admitted that the food was a bit better in Georgia. "Our rations do very well in quantity, and consist of corn meal, pretty fair bacon & hams, a few beans and a little very poor rice."

When Ulric Dahlgren, the son of Rear Admiral John Dahlgren, learned of Kilpatrick's plan to raid Richmond and free its Union prisoners, he wanted in on it. President Lincoln liked the elder Dahlgren; in fact he was Lincoln's favorite naval officer. And the president was particularly fond of young Ulric, too. The young man had proven to be a model army officer in every respect. Like Lincoln, "little Ully" had studied law[7] and was driven by the same ambitions that drove his father—the search for glory and fame.[8] Ulric asked for permission to join Kilpatrick's enterprise and his request was swiftly granted. Kilpatrick was ordered to include Dahlgren in on the scheme on 23 February 1864. Now it was "the Kilpatrick-Dahlgren raid" and the scheme seemed simple. With all the fighting going on around Petersburg, the Confederate capital wasn't expected to be heavily defended. The thinking was that it might at best be guarded by a force of home guardsmen composed of factory workers, shopkeepers, and government clerks. That would make the prospects of successfully attacking the city fairly high.

The plan got the green light on 27 February. The raiding party, to be commanded by Kilpatrick, was to include 3,500 horsemen of the 3rd Cavalry Division, plus a smaller contingent of 460 men under the command of Colonel Dahlgren, who had lost part of a leg in an engagement with Rebels following the battle of Gettysburg the year before. The plan was for both Union groups to converge on Richmond from two different directions and in a coordinated attack, take the city. The Union raiding parties were to also attempt to liberate the thousands of Union prisoners held at Belle Isle and Libby Prisons—Libby held officers, while Belle Isle, located on an island in the James River, housed lesser ranks, in overcrowded tents. This tent city was ripe for disease and exposure. Roughly 25 prisoners-of-war reportedly died daily.

From the start in 1862 Belle Isle was said to be plagued with prisoner-on-prisoner violence and thievery. According to the *Richmond Examiner*, "They are the most inveterate thieves, and on every opportunity depredate upon one another. For one to take off his shoes, or a piece of his garment, and fall to sleep, is to invite a theft from his comrades, and every day complaints are made to the commanding officer of the guard of such depredators. Numbers have lost their shoes and pieces of their clothing, and go about barefooted, or in their stocking feet, and half naked." Stealing continued to be a problem. The theft of food and blankets became a way of life, with the men characterized by prisoner John Ransom in his diary on 11 February 1864 as "just like so many hungry wolves penned together."

To help alleviate the suffering the US Sanitary Commission was able to obtain somewhat accurate lists of Union prisoners at prisons like Libby, and the lists were used to send personally addressed care packages to the POWs. There was a bit of subterfuge behind these mailings to ensure that the packages reached the men as intended. Each package had to be wrapped differently so it didn't look like the packages came from a single source. Each had to be a different size. Each had to be mailed from a slightly different location. Each was to be packed as if by a personal friend or family member of the intended recipient. Each had to contain different things so that no two were exactly alike, and items such as canned pork was to come in different cans so it didn't appear that they all came from a common purveyor. And only a few parcels were to be sent at one time; the maximum safe number was thought to be 15 or 20 packages.[9] These precautions were due to the fact that Confederate authorities held a great deal of animosity towards the Sanitary Commission, believing it to be meddlesome do-gooders. Generally, the packages were to contain canned meats, coffee, sugar, crackers, bandages, shirts, and pants. According to doctors associated with the Sanitary Commission, canned pork was preferred over beef. The food was critical to supplement the prisoners' meager diets, which consisted largely of wormy boiled beans and cornbread or mushy corn meal. A little pepper was also to be included in several parcels. Whenever possible the packages were to go to wounded soldiers, because without proper food and bandages they were likely to die in confinement. The typical mortality rate at the "better" Southern prisons was about 15 percent.[10]

The Sanitary Commission was allowed to furnish small quantities of writing paper, and the officers at Libby Prison were allowed to write letters via the exchange point at Fort Monroe, but they were limited to just six lines. Captain Charles Thayer wrote to his mother on 2 April 1863 on Sanitary Commission stationery to say,

> I arrived this 6 P.M. from Gordonsville (Va).
> Wounded through fleshy part of right thigh—doing well
> 10 Privates of my reg't are with me. A Flag of truce boat is
> here & will take them off tomorrow—no chance for Officers
> to be Paroled or exchanged. 2 from my reg't are here before me
> I can write only 6 lines—write soon all of you—goodbye love to all.[11]

Confederate prisoners had the same limits. Another letter from Confederate prisoner F. B. Bear to his father, brother, or cousin mailed on 12 January 1865, reads,

> I have been in prison for some time, and I am very much in need of
> Sum [sic] money and would be under many obligations to you if you would be
> so kind as to send me a small amount of money.
> And I will certainly pay you when ever [sic] I am released from prison.
> Please write to me soon direct your letter to F.B. Bear, Co. H, 5th Division
> Prison Camp Pt Lookout, M.d. and oblige your friend.[12]

Given the deplorable condition Union prisoners in Richmond apparently were living under, Lincoln endorsed the overall escape plan, however, details of how the prison break was to be managed were somewhat sketchy, and there was no real plan for arming, feeding, or organizing the famished and ragtag prisoners if the breakout was successful. There were many other obstacles too, including the fact that, unfortunately, as with so many of Kilpatrick's schemes to garner glory, once the raid began much of the operation would be ad hoc. During the fast movements, the Union forces were to set fire to any buildings of military value. They were also to destroy any Southern railroad property and any other transportation infrastructure they found, including canal barges and locks. This was going to be somewhat hard to do while swiftly operating on the fly.

The combined Union raiding party started out on 28 February 1864, moving South from Culpeper, Virginia, until reaching Mount Pleasant, where Kilpatrick's force continued due south to attack Richmond from the north, while Dahlgren's force veered west to loop around along the James River towards Richmond in order to attack the city from the west.

The scheme began falling apart when men of Colonel Bradley Johnson's Confederate 1st Maryland Mounted Regiment intercepted a dispatch from Colonel Dahlgren at Yellow Tavern asking Kilpatrick what time his unit should attack so that both prongs of the Federal assault would arrive simultaneously.

Belle Isle's POW cemetery photographed in 1865 by Thomas Sullivan. In 1862 Southerners were told that Union prisoners at Belle Isle were "sheltered from the sun in excellent tents, and supplied with all the games of pastime and sport that their inclinations suggest." None of that was true. (Library of Congress)

Member of the 1st Maryland Mounted Regiment at the start of the war. (Library of Congress)

To Kilpatrick's way of thinking the combined Union attacks were timed to take place on 1 March at 10:00 a.m., but Dahlgren was clearly in the dark regarding this point. Johnson's men dogged Dahlgren every step of the way, attacking him at Beaverdam, about 25 miles north of Richmond, and trailing him all the way to Tunstall's Station, about 15 miles east of Richmond. Because of Johnson's tenacity in tracking Dahlgren, Major General Wade Hampton, the senior Confederate commander in the area, commended the Marylander in a communiqué to General Lee. Hampton told Lee that in his opinion, "the enemy could have taken Richmond, and in all probability would have done so, but for the fact that Colonel Johnson intercepted a dispatch from Dahlgren to Kilpatrick...." Dahlgren and his men had inadvertently done more damage than that. Upon learning that Confederate Brigadier General Henry Wise was visiting his daughter's family only a few miles away, Dahlgren decided to make a quick detour to pay an unannounced visit to Eastwood, the stately home of the Hobson family, to capture the general. Fortunately for Wise, he was warned of Dahlgren's approach. While the women of the household detained the bluecoats, including Annie Jennings Wise Hobson and her sister, Ellen, with pleasant small talk, their father, the general, visiting on furlough, and his son-in-law raced off to Richmond with word of the raiding party's advance on the city. Their alarm saved the city, allowing time for Richmond's home guard to mobilize.

By then some in Washington had gotten wind of the planned raid. Secretary of the Navy Gideon Welles recorded in his diary on 2 March, "From what I learn, Kilpatrick, with a large cavalry force, is to make a raid upon Richmond with a view of capturing the place. He is sanguine that he will be successful. I have my doubts...."[13] By the time Welles wrote this in his diary, the raid was already over.

Kilpatrick's units had the shortest distance to travel and arrived outside Richmond pretty much right on time. Swollen streams, rainstorms, and intermittent sleet and snow delayed Dahlgren's detachment. Near Richmond, 100 of his men were sent off to operate as a true raiding party, with orders to burn anything of benefit to the South. They dutifully torched six gristmills and burned well-stocked barns, stables, coal works, sawmills, and houses. They also did some looting and horse stealing along the way. This segment of the detachment survived the raid.

With Dahlgren and the remainder of his troop about 15 miles away from the others at Manakin, Virginia, Kilpatrick commenced his attack on Richmond. Upon arriving outside Richmond, Kirkpatrick's bluecoats advanced to the city's defenses before they were met by the forewarned and determined force of roughly 3,000 Rebel home guard, plus cavalry commanded by Major General Wade Hampton and Colonel Bradley Johnson's mounted Marylanders. By late afternoon Dahlgren's troops still hadn't arrived at the rendezvous point,

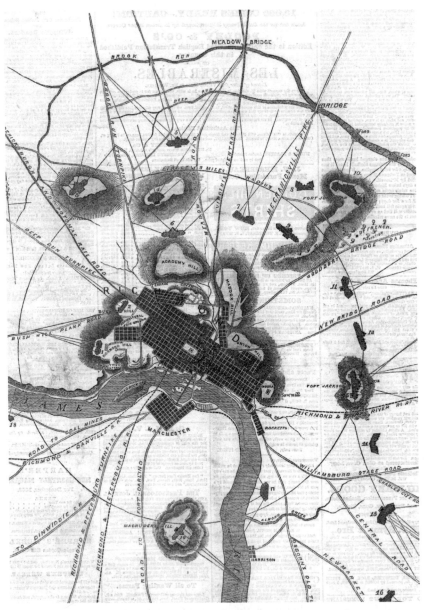

Harper and Brothers 1862 map of Richmond showing its fortifications. (Library of Congress)

prompting Kilpatrick and the remainder of the force to withdraw to the southeast towards New Kent Courthouse.

Dahlgren's force wasn't as lucky. By the time his troop was within range of a point of attack, Kilpatrick's units were long gone. Unsupported by Kilpatrick and unable to link up with the Union's main body, Dahlgren and his men fled too, heading northeast towards the Mattaponi River. Once across the river at Aylett's they turned southeast towards the King and Queen Courthouse, fleeing for the protection of the Union's lines. Dahlgren's men were hotly pursued by a small body of horsemen of the 9th Virginia Cavalry led by Lieutenant James Pollard, plus men of the home guard. In rushing to outrun the Rebels, Dahlgren rode into a Confederate ambush at Walkerton on 2 March at about 11:30 p.m. Dahlgren charged at the Rebel pickets, demanding that they surrender. He attempted to use his pistol and it misfired, prompting the Rebels waiting in ambush to open fire. The area was immediately blanketed with lead shot. In an instant Dahlgren was hit multiple times. Ninety-two of his men were ultimately taken prisoner. Worse still, their commander's bullet riddled body was stripped and partially mutilated. The papers and memoranda reportedly found on his body contained what was said to be "indisputable evidence of the diabolical designs of the enemy." One document was said to be an order to his soldiers to find and hang Jefferson Davis and the Confederate cabinet. The following address to the officers and men of his command was written on a sheet of paper, with "Headquarters Third Division, Cavalry Corps, —, 1864" printed on an upper corner:

OFFICERS AND MEN:

You have been selected from brigades and regiments as a picked command to attempt a desperate undertaking—an undertaking which, if successful, will write your names on the hearts of your countrymen in letters that can never be erased, and which will cause the prayers of our fellow-soldiers now confined in loathsome prisons to follow you and yours wherever you may go. We hope to release the prisoners from Belle Island first, and having seen them fairly started, we will cross the James River into Richmond, destroying the bridges after us and exhorting the released prisoners to destroy and burn the hateful city; and do not allow the rebel leader Davis and his traitorous crew to escape. The prisoners must render great assistance, as you cannot leave your ranks too far or become too much scattered, or you will be lost. Do not allow any personal gain to lead you off, which would only bring you to an ignominious death at the hands of citizens. Keep well together and obey orders strictly and all will be well; but on no account scatter too far, for in union there is strength. With strict obedience to orders and fearlessness in the execution you will be sure to succeed. We will join the main force on the other side of the city, or perhaps meet them inside. Many of you may fall; but if there is any man here not willing to sacrifice his life in such a great and glorious undertaking, or who does not feel capable of meeting the enemy in such a desperate fight as will follow, let him step out, and he may go hence to the arms of his sweetheart and read of the braves who swept through the city of Richmond. We want no man who cannot feel sure of success in such a holy cause. We will have a desperate fight, but stand up to it when it does come, and all will be well. Ask the blessing of the Almighty, and do not fear the enemy.

U. DALHGREN,
Colonel, Commanding.

The following special orders, written on similar paper and on detached slips, reportedly described the diabolical plans for the expedition, particularly the killing of President Davis and his cabinet and the burning of the city:

Guides.—Pioneers (with oakum, turpentine, and torpedoes), signal officer, quartermaster, commissary. Scouts and pickets. Men in rebel uniform. These will remain on the north bank and move down with the force on the south bank, not getting ahead of them, and if the communication can be kept up without giving an alarm it must be done; but everything depends upon a surprise, and no one must be allowed to pass ahead of the column. Information must be gathered in regard to the crossings of the river, so that should we be repulsed on the south side we will know where to recross at the nearest point. All mills must be burned and the canal destroyed, and also everything which can be used by the rebels must be destroyed, including the boats on the river. Should a ferry-boat [sic] be seized and can be worked, have it moved down. Keep the force on the south side posted of any important movement of the enemy, and in case of danger some of the scouts must swim the river and bring us information. As we approach the city the party must take great care that they do not get ahead of the other party on the south side, and must conceal themselves and watch our movements. We will try and secure the bridge to the city, 1 mile below Belle Isle, and release the prisoners at the same time. If we do not succeed they must then dash down, and we will try and carry the bridge from each side. When necessary, the men must be filed through the woods and along the riverbank. The bridges once secured, and the prisoners loose and over the river, the bridges will be secured and the city destroyed. The men must keep together and well in hand, and once in the city it must be destroyed and Jeff. Davis and cabinet killed. Pioneers will go along with combustible material. The officer must use his discretion about the time of assisting us. Horses and cattle which we do not need immediately must be shot rather than left. Everything on the canal and elsewhere of service to the rebels must be destroyed. As General Custer may follow me, be careful not to give a false alarm. The signal officer must be prepared to communicate at night by rockets, and in other things pertaining to his department.

The quartermasters and commissaries must be on the lookout for their departments, and see that there are no delays on their account.

The engineer officer will follow to survey the road as we pass over it, &c.

The pioneers must be prepared to construct a bridge or destroy one. They must have plenty of oakum and turpentine for burning, which will be rolled in soaked balls and given to the men to burn when we get in the city. Torpedoes will only be used by the pioneers for destroying the main bridges, &c. They must be prepared to destroy railroads. Men will branch off to the right with a few pioneers and destroy the bridges and railroads south of Richmond, and then join us at the city. They must be well prepared with torpedoes, &c. The line of Falling Creek is probably the best to work along, or as they approach the city Goode's Creek, so that no re-enforcements can come up on any cars. No one must be allowed to pass ahead for fear of communicating news. Rejoin the command with all haste, and if cut off cross the river above Richmond and rejoin us. Men will stop at Bellona Arsenal and totally destroy it, and anything else but hospitals: then follow on and rejoin the command at Richmond with all haste, and if cut off cross the river and rejoin us. As General Custer may follow me, be careful not to give a false alarm.

Dahlgren was said to have also had the following penciled timetable in his possession when he died:

Saturday—Leave camp at dark (6 p.m.). Cross Ely's Ford at 10 p.m.
Twenty miles—Cross North Anna at 4 a.m. Sunday. Feed and water one hour.
Three miles—Frederick Hall Station 6 a.m. Destroy arts 8 a.m.
Twenty miles—Near James River 2 p.m. Sunday. Feed and water one hour and a half.
Thirty miles to Richmond—March toward Kilpatrick for one hour, and then as soon as dark cross the river, reaching Richmond early in the morning (Monday).
One squadron remains on north side and one squadron to cut the railroad bridge at Falling Creek, and join at Richmond; 83 miles.
General Kilpatrick—Cross at 1 a.m. Sunday; 10 miles.
Pass river 5 a.m. Resistance.
Chilesburg—Fourteen miles; 8 a.m.
Resistance at North Anna; 3 miles.
Railroad bridges at South Anna; 26 miles; 2 p.m. Destroy bridges, pass the South Anna, and feed until after dark; then signal each other. After dark move down to Richmond and be in front of the city at daybreak.
Return—In Richmond during the day. Feed and water men outside.
Be over the Pamunkey at daybreak. Feed and water and then cross the Rappahannock at night (Tuesday night), when they must be on the lookout.
Spies should be sent on Friday morning early, and be ready to cut.

All these documents were suspect. The first was signed "U. Dalhgren." Ulric Dahlgren clearly knew how to spell his last name. Equally odd, he was never known to use only his first initial in signing anything.[14] The faulty spelling of his last name was attributed at the time, in the South, to a distortion created by repeatedly folding and unfolding the original paper. None of that mattered in the South, where Dahlgren was said to reign in "eternal infamy" as a willful and determined assassin. In reporting his death the *Daily Richmond Examiner* assured its readers that "in the years to come defenseless women and innocent children will peruse, with a sense of shrinking horror, the story of Richmond's rescue from the midnight sack and ravage led by Dahlgren."[15]

Colonel Dahlgren's body was initially buried in the field. It was later exhumed and brought to Richmond, where it was briefly displayed and unceremoniously buried again. Writing about Dahlgren's death, Elizabeth Van Lew observed, "A Coffin was made, and the body of Dahlgren placed in it and buried, where he was killed, at the fork of two roads, one leading from Stevensville and the other from Mantua ferry. After a few days it was disinterred by order of the Confederate government, brought to Richmond, and lay for a time in a boxcar at the York River Railway station. It was buried, as the papers said, at eleven o'clock at night, no one knew where and no one should ever know." Elizabeth Van Lew knew. Her network included numerous slaves and they apparently did the digging. Slaves were viewed as innocuous in the South, yet they saw, did, and heard far more than their masters ever imagined. Van Lew said her most reliable information was gathered by slaves. One of her Black operatives, Mary Elizabeth Bowser, even worked in the Confederate White House. With the information she possessed, Van Lew had the body covertly disinterred yet again and secreted it away until it could be safely returned to the Dahlgren family. Not knowing anything about the body's removal by Van Lew's agents, Rear Admiral Dahlgren asked for his son's remains back. The Confederate government complied and was flabbergasted to find that the grave was empty. According to the *Examiner*, "Dahlgren had risen...."

No one in Washington owned up to authorizing the attempt to assassinate President Jefferson Davis or any members of the Confederate cabinet, although some scholars believe that such an order was something that Secretary of War Stanton might have concocted. When interrogated, the captured men of Dahlgren's command insisted that they were never ordered to kill anyone. Northern newspapers claimed that the documents were Southern fabrications. The Confederate Topographic Department produced 50 photographic copies of the Dahlgren order as evidence of the Northern aggression. General Lee forwarded one on 1 April 1864 to Union General George Meade, who was technically Dahlgren's commanding officer, with a demand for an explanation. Lee's letter, which took 14 days to reach Meade, read,

> GENERAL: I am instructed to bring to your notice two papers found upon the body of Col. U. Dahlgren, who was killed while commanding a part of the Federal cavalry during the late expedition of General Kilpatrick. To enable you to understand the subject fully I have the honor to inclose photographic copies of the papers referred to, one of which is an address to his officers and men,

bearing the official signature of Colonel Dahlgren, and the other, not signed, contains more detailed explanations of the purpose of the expedition and more specific instructions as to its execution. In the former this passage occurs:

We hope to release the prisoners from Belle Island first, and having seen them fairly started, we will cross the James River into Richmond, destroying the bridges after us and exhorting the released prisoners to destroy and burn the hateful city; and do not allow the rebel leader Davis and his traitorous crew to escape. The prisoners must render great assistance, as you cannot leave your ranks too far or become too much scattered, or you will be lost.

Among the instructions contained in the second paper are the following:

The bridges once secured, and the prisoners loose and over the river, the bridges will be secured and the city destroyed. The men must keep together and well in hand, and once in the city it must be destroyed and Jeff. Davis and cabinet killed. Pioneers will go along with combustible material.

In obedience to my instructions I beg leave respectfully to inquire whether the designs and instructions of Colonel Dahlgren, as set forth in these papers, particularly those contained in the above extracts, were authorized by the United States Government or by his superior officers, and also whether they have the sanction and approval of those authorities.

Meade responded on 17 April that no such orders were ever sanctioned by the Union military. His reply said,

GENERAL: I received on the 15th instant, per flag of truce, your communication of the 1st instant, transmitting photographic copies of two documents alleged to have been found upon the body of Col. U. Dahlgren, and inquiring "whether the designs and instructions of Colonel Dahlgren, as set forth in these papers, particularly those contained in the above extracts, were authorized by the United States Government or by his superior officers, and also whether they have the sanction and approval of these authorities." In reply I have to state that neither the United States Government, myself, nor General Kilpatrick authorized, sanctioned, or approved the burning of the city of Richmond and the killing of Mr. Davis and cabinet, nor any other act not required by military necessity and in accordance with the usages of war.

In confirmation of this statement I inclose a letter from General Kilpatrick....

Meade's protestations of innocence regarding his personal knowledge of the full extent of the plans found on Dahlgren may have indeed been true, but it is somewhat at odds with the fact that in hoping for a long-shot breakthrough of the city's defenses, Meade had placed his entire Army of the Potomac on alert on 2 March so that it could rapidly exploit any crack in Richmond's defenses. That exploitation would certainly have benefited greatly from the chaos caused by the death of Davis and having Richmond in flames at the hands of thousands of rampaging Federal prisoners. Such turmoil would be a crushing blow to the viability of Lee's army, potentially leading to the collapse of the Confederacy. It also would have help cinch Lincoln's reelection.

Meade was ordered to go to Washington in mid-February, and it is likely that he first learned of the administration's desires for a raid on Richmond during that visit, because his frequent letters to his wife prior to that don't mention the raid. On 14 February Meade spent nearly five hours with Secretary Stanton in closed-door discussions. Meade disliked visiting Washington. He despised the intrigues, hair-brained schemes, petty politics, and "great noise" that he endured there.

By 29 February Meade began referring to the planned raid as "My cavalry expedition." By then he clearly believed that he owned it and he was immersed in its planning. "I have been a good deal occupied with the attempt I am about making, to send a force of cavalry into Richmond to liberate our prisoners. The undertaking is a desperate one, but the anxiety and distress of the public and of the authorities at Washington is so great that it seems to demand running great risks for the chances of success," he told his family in February. As part of his planning Meade dispatched George Armstrong Custer with 1,500 cavalrymen, plus two pieces of artillery, towards Charlottesville as a diversion for Kilpatrick's and Dahlgren's raiders. Despite his involvement, Meade always had his doubts about the plan, recording on 6 March, "I did not expect much from it. Poor Dahlgren I am sorry for."

This was a chaotic time for the Union army. Congress had just passed the "Lieutenant General Bill," which made General Grant the army's general-in-chief, leaving Henry Halleck's role in doubt. How command and control within the Union army would work was unclear.

As for Kilpatrick, his riders reached the safety of Union's lines at Yorktown on 4 March. In light of the fiasco, and of the fact that he had abandoned Dahlgren's smaller force, Kilpatrick was demoted by General Grant in short order and sent to serve under General Sherman in Georgia. This got him out of Washington and away from Secretary Stanton and the Northern press.

Up until late April 1864, General Lee was receiving a steady stream of reports regarding the results of the Kilpatrick-Dahlgren raid, so the action was very much fresh in his mind as the summer campaign season began. Two months later General Lee would order Jubal Early to turn the tables, using Kilpatrick's basic plan as a template for a similar raid on Washington. Early's raid would become a worthy payback for the raid on Richmond.

Although the Lincoln administration universally disavowed the assassination-related aspects of the raid, after Richmond fell in April 1865, Secretary of War Edwin Stanton would reportedly order his staff to search through the records of the Confederate War Department to find the original Dahlgren document and burn it. Since the issuance of that burn order, the original has never surfaced. All this has added to the thoughts that Stanton was indeed the chief architect of the raid and its hoped-for diabolical outcomes.

As for the prisoners at Belle Isle, a medical report prepared on 31 March 1864, after an inspection of the site, noted how unsanitary conditions there really were, saying,

> Into the camp containing an area sufficient for the accommodation of about 3,000 men have been crowded for many months past from 6,000 to 10,000 prisoners. To prevent escapes they have not been allowed to visit the sinks at night. These deposits of excrement have been made in the streets and small vacant spaces between the tents. The streets are so greatly crowded during the day as greatly to interfere with the working police parties, so that nearly the whole day is consumed by them in the imperfect removal of the filthy accumulations of the night. The whole surface of the camp has thus been saturated with putrid animal matter. Surrounded by such circumstances the prisoners have been totally careless of personal cleanliness. The rations now consist entirely of bread, rice, and peas or beans. The bread is made of corn-meal, unsifted or bolted. Not separating the bran from the meal tends greatly to cause and continue the two diseases (diarrhea and dysentery) most prevalent among the prisoners. Many of them are badly clad and destitute of blankets, having sold the articles lately furnished them by their Government. Under these circumstances, though they have been furnished with fuel, there has been great suffering from cold during the unusually cold weather of January and February, to which the brutal conduct of the prisoners in expelling their comrades from their tents at night has greatly added.

The South was outraged by such a stinging report, so much so that it initiated its own investigation of camp conditions. Not surprisingly, a joint select committee of the Confederate Congress in March of 1865 concluded that prison conditions in the South were never as bad as had been reported in the North. Northern newspaper coverage during the war was characterized as being far too biased and "sensational." The published photographs of ema-ciated bluecoats were said to be no worse than the condition of some Rebels who suffered in the North but were never photographed. The committee's members concluded that no Southern officer would ever have permitted prison guards to rob prisoners of any personal property. As for prisoner hygiene the committee said that the cause of any personal filth among the prisoners was the result of the poor habits of the Northern men themselves. The committee denied that the South had any policy to intentionally starve or mistreat Union prisoners. On the contrary, the policy of the South, it insisted, was to humanely treat all those who fell into their hands. And, with respect to rations, it insisted that the prisoners ate what their guards ate, and in some cases they received more and better food than their guards. The committee's conclusion with respect to food was that if there were any brief shortages, they were "the result of the savage policy of our enemies in burning barns filled with wheat or corn, destroying agricultural implements, and driving off or wantonly butchering hogs and cattle." The committee's report also denied that any prisoners at Belle Isle ever froze to death because of the Confederacy. According to the committee, "The facts are, that tents were furnished sufficient to shelter all the prisoners; that the Confederate commandant and soldiers on the island were lodged in similar tents; that a fire was furnished in each of them; that the prisoners fared as well as their guards, and that only one of them was ever frozen to death, and he was frozen by the cruelty of his own fellow-prisoners, who thrust him out of the tent in a freezing night because he was infested with vermin." The committee further rejected the notion that Sanitary Commission or personal packages, as well as food parcels from Uncle Sam, meant for prisoners were ever pilfered. All of the harsh critics of the South with respect to prisoner treatments, particularly those held in captivity that said they witnessed the mistreatment, were characterized as "wretched vagabonds, of depraved morals, decrepit in body, without courage, self-respect, or conscience. They are dirty, disorderly, thievish, and incapable." The South's official protestations of being so unjustly slandered was seen by most in the North as utter nonsense.

Mary E. Thropp was one of those Northern non-believers. She was a devoted member of the US Sanitary Commission, who in April 1865 was among four ladies who visited Richmond with supplies for the Union's sick. She arrived in Richmond from her home in Pennsylvania on 14 April 1865 and visited the Belle Isle camp. She saw the shallow graves and the squalid

Captain William H. May of the 23rd Connecticut Infantry Regiment was photographed in New Orleans after being released from a prisoner-of-war camp at Tyler, Texas. (Library of Congress)

remains of the camp. In July, she returned again to help the American Union Commission create several schools for Richmond's children. Writing to her father at Valley Forge on 12 July 1865 about visiting Belle Isle on the Fourth of July, she was struck by how it now held a new meaning for her. She wrote,

> Again, we have been taken to Belle Isle. This time rowed over the James by moonlight—the full moon shining from a cloudless heaven. A more beautiful scene than the now peaceful James, studded with its emerald islets, lying out there in the calm beauty of that exquisite summer night, I have never seen. And yet when I thought of the aching hearts that turned away despairingly from the same solemn beauty less than a year ago, and laid them down to die, my heart grew full to weeping. Since my last visit the Christian Commission has tenderly enclosed the graves. But is not Virginia one vast graveyard of heroes, martyred in the cause of liberty? It has indeed become "sacred soil" forevermore.[16]

Union prisoners elsewhere seemed to have better care.

When units of Early's army reached Martinsburg on 3 July they found a huge amount of Union supplies. A deserter reported that the men had been living off hardtack. Coffee and sugar were no longer being regularly issued. Hunger forced Early's famished troops to go on a feeding frenzy. They wildly devoured the Union's leavings. This disgusted the Lieutenant General who insisted that his men were to be better behaved when they crossed into Maryland. (Library of Congress)

CHAPTER 2

Into the Valley

By the time Jubal Early's force detached from its positions around Gaines' Mill and slipped into the Shenandoah Valley with orders to clear it of the Union scourge, things there were already dire. Earlier that spring a small Union force under the command of Major General Franz Selig had caused havoc in the mid-portion of the valley, which was part of the vital granary for feeding Lee's army. The Confederates needed to sweep the valley clean of this blue-clad menace as swiftly as possible. When Selig moved on New Market on 15 May 1864, a Rebel force comprising units under Major General John C. Breckinridge and Brigadier General John Imboden soundly defeated him. No sooner was Selig out of the way, than Major General David Hunter appeared in the valley with an even greater Federal force. Hunter attacked a small Confederate force, commanded by Brigadier General William E. Jones, and in the ensuing lopsided battle on 5 June 1864 at Piedmont, Jones was killed and the Southern troops fell back on Waynesboro, Virginia. On 12 June Early received verbal orders from Robert E. Lee to move the Second Corps into the Valley and end Hunter's presence. Early was directed to destroy Hunter's force, before crossing the Potomac near Leesburg or above Harpers Ferry and then move on to threaten Washington, DC, *if he chose to do so.*

The irascible, tobacco-spitting Early was also ordered to join forces with John Breckinridge, who would serve as his second in command. This was an odd couple if ever there was one. Early was impulsive and reacted instinctively to situations based largely on his own counsel and intuition. Breckinridge was a deliberative commander who sought a consensus of opinions from his subordinates. Early had a shrill falsetto voice. With his mouth typically full of tobacco, he was often hard to understand, except perhaps when he

John Cabell Breckenridge was the nation's youngest vice president, serving from 1856 to 1859. This image was taken about 1860 when he served as a US Senator. (Library of Congress)

was cussing, which was often. Early dismissed his lack of popularity in his *Memoirs* by claiming that he was never blessed with captivating manners, and as a result, he was often considered haughty or disdainful.[1] Totally absorbed in his thoughts, he would frequently pass friends without acknowledging their presence, giving grave offense. Breckinridge, on the other hand, was an accomplished statesman. He was an eloquent, polite, and polished speaker. His hand was always extended in friendly recognition. Appearance-wise the men were different, too. Early was afflicted with arthritis brought on by his service in the US Army during the Mexican War. This caused him to walk with a bit of a stoop. He also had bouts of painful rheumatism. Breckinridge was ramrod straight. Although Early once cared for fine attire, he didn't by 1864. "My tastes," he admitted, "would always have induced me to dress neatly and genteelly if I could have indulged them," but during the war, "I had no time to get new clothes if I had been able."[2] A contemporary of his, whom he dismissed as not knowing what he was talking about, described his appearance as looking forever as though he were a stagecoach driver.[3] Another described him as habitually appearing to be ready to hitch up a plow. Breckinridge was cut from finer cloth. He dressed the part of a Kentucky gentleman-officer. Early was different in other ways, too. He clearly defied social convention. Although he never married, he maintained a longstanding relationship with Julia A. McNealey, whom he met when she was a teenager. She gave birth to his first child, Joseph Emerson Early, in 1850, when she was 17 and he was 34. They had three more children together, including a daughter and two more sons. Robert Early was born in 1860. The last son, Jubal L. Early, was born in 1864. After the war, while the general was out of the country during a self-imposed exile, Julia took up with another man, named Charles Pugh. Pugh and she had a daughter together in 1867 and they were married in 1871.

By the time Early and Breckinridge joined forces on 17 June 1864, Hunter already held Staunton, Virginia, and a significant part of the valley. At Lynchburg on 18 June, Early engaged his foe. When confronted with the prospects of battling with a sizable combined Confederate force, Hunter opted to back away from the conflict. He maneuvered his force farther and farther backwards, retreating more than 60 miles, each step of the way pursued by Early's force. Such evasion had the unintended consequence of keeping a planned link up with Philip Sheridan at bay. Whenever Early attempted to get ahead of Hunter, the Union general merely sidestepped out of the way. In the end Hunter literally backed out of the valley. When Hunter finally slipped into the mountains of West Virginia on 21 June, Early called off the chase. "As the enemy had got into the mountains, where nothing useful could be accomplished by pursuit, I did not deem it proper to continue it further," Early would later write in his *Memoirs*.[4] Hunter, for his part, told General Grant that he withdrew from his positions because his men were low on ammunition, although Early thought that excuse was preposterous, claiming in his *Memoirs* that Hunter hadn't fought enough to be low on any such thing.

Early rested his troops on 22 June. At this point General Lee advised him either to return to the Army of Northern Virginia or to carry out the second part of his primary mission—threatening Washington.

When Early's Second Corps resumed its march towards Washington on 23 June, it was confronted by the further realities of Hunter's wrath. Everywhere they went, houses had been burned or pillaged by the retreating Federals. Public institutions, including the Lexington Military Institute and Washington College, had been torched or plundered. And civilians had been robbed of their personal possessions and dignity. A Southern gentleman who defended his wife's honor against crude insults from several of Hunter's soldiers was hanged, Early claimed after the war. Throughout the South, such degradations placed Hunter in the pantheon of most despised Union commanders. In the Confederacy there was an understanding that if Hunter or any of his officers was ever caught, they weren't ever to be exchanged. Instead, they were to be kept in the deepest, darkest dungeons until the end of the war.

According to the *Staunton (Virginia) Vindicator*, which had to delay its normal publication until 8 July 1864 because of the fighting in the Shenandoah Valley, Union troops had created havoc in every way and everywhere possible. Businesses and transportation links were a prime target, with the newspaper reporting,

> they commenced that incendiarism and thieving which has characterized this raid of Hen-roost Hunter and makes him as deservedly odious as Beast [Benjamin Franklin] Butler. By Hunter's order the fine mill of J & B F. Walker,

near Mt Meridian, was burned, also, the Woolen Factory of Crawford and Young, the Steam Mill, Steam Distillery Government Workshops, Stables and Forage-houses, the Stage Stables of J. I. A. Trotter together with twenty-six coaches, and the Railroad Depots, (all in Staunton,) and the large mill of W.F. Smith, in the town of Greenville. They destroyed the track of Railroad west of this place, at intervals, to Goshen, burning the bridges at Swoopes, Craigsville and Goshen, and destroyed a number of culverts and small bridges at different points on the road. East of Staunton, they tore up the track, bending the rails, to Christie's Creek, burning the bridge over the same and the Depot at Fishersville. They broke open the stores here, taking whatever they wanted and leaving the rest a prey to an accompanying rabble, cut to pieces and destroyed the machinery of the Shoe Factory, and broke the presses of the *Spectator* and *Vindicator*, throwing the type of the former into the street.

Because of the damage done to the type and equipment of the *Staunton Spectator*, it was not able to resume publication during the war.

Clearly the civility of war had changed. While factories were fair targets, the clear distinction between combatants and non-combatants, assumed to exist in July 1861, had vanished by 1864. Except for random acts of charity or decency by the officers and soldiers on either side—stemming from qualities that by 1864 Hunter and many of his comrades no longer possessed—individuals and families in the valley were made to suffer. The *Vindicator* reported, "By an order from Gen. Hunter to take all the provisions from each family, leaving only three days rations, they robbed the man of means and widow with her mite of whatever their larder contained, leaving but a scanty supply, save where the humanity of some officer, to whom the execution of the order had been entrusted, prevented him from faithfully complying with it, in which few, exceptional cases something more was left. To particularize these robberies would more than fill our columns, hence we deem it sufficient to say that nearly everybody in that part of the county occupied by the enemy, as well as the town, suffered in the same way." By the time this news, perhaps overly exaggerated, was being read in Virginia, Marylanders and Pennsylvanians would be suffering the same fate at the hands of a different enemy. Jubal Early would be taking his revenge for the destruction and thievery inflicted in the South.

Early should have been unforgiving. His temper was up. He had seen the results of Hunter's wrath and he wanted revenge. His greatest reward could have been to see Washington in flames; or he might accept a ransom payment. Ransom became an acceptable alternative to destruction. By 1864 he lacked compassion for his enemy. If he could get $200,000 for not burning Frederick, Maryland, how much more might he get for Washington?

Only one thing could stay his hand from a burning torch—ransom! After the war he refused to call it that. In his *Memoirs* he repeatedly referred to the extorted payments as "contributions," characterizing them by saying, "During the operations at Monocacy, a contribution of $200,000 in money was levied on the city of Frederick..."[5] and "While these operations were going on, Brigadier General John McCausland had occupied Hagerstown, and levied a contribution of $20,000...."[6] These were anything but charitable offerings or gifted donations.

When Early's Second Corps reached Harpers Ferry on 4 July 1864, he refused to allow his men to occupy the town for fear of being shelled by the Union's 100-pound Parrott rifles atop Maryland Heights. He realized that the rain of explosive shells from these powerful garrison guns on the heights overlooking Harpers Ferry would have decimated his soldiers, burying them beneath the rubble of the town's rough stone buildings. Those heavy, 100-pound artillery pieces were the same type of large-size guns that made up part of the defense of Washington.

With Hunter temporarily out of the way, Early sent a part of his force into West Virginia towards Martinsburg to destroy the bridges of the Baltimore and Ohio Railroad. Such destruction was essential in denying the enemy the use of the railroads in moving troops and vital provisions for any further operations in the area. The main Confederate force reached Winchester on 2 July. Provisions were a problem for Early's army, too. His ranks were nearly out of food. Luckily for him, on 3 July his units at Martinsburg brushed

New York State Militia on top of Maryland Heights overlooking Harpers Ferry. (Library of Congress)

The ridge in the background is Maryland Heights, showing how the Union's fortifications there dominated the town of Harpers Ferry. (Library of Congress)

aside skirmishers belonging to Union General Franz Selig, who opted to evacuate the town rather than put up a serious fight. Selig's men left behind a great deal of supplies, provisions Early's men drastically needed. Selig was proving to be as timid as Hunter. During the night Selig slipped his units across the Potomac at Shepherdstown and, rather than attempting to seriously defend Harpers Ferry, took up defensive positions inside his fortifications on Maryland Heights.

Realizing that Maryland Heights was the ideal artillery platform for shelling Harpers Ferry, Early opted not to occupy the hamlet. Instead, under cover of darkness, he had his men collect as much of the Federal stores left there as possible for use by his army. What couldn't be hauled off was burned. The Confederates also burned the great trestleworks across the Potomac and cut all of the telegraph lines in the vicinity before moving on. By 8 July Early's army was in Maryland. That night Breckenridge's and Stephen Ramsuer's men camped near Middletown, Rode's Confederate units slept near Jefferson, and Ranson's Rebel troops occupied Catoctan Mountain. The war had come to Maryland for the third and final time.

Despite what would happen over the next week, Generals Selig and Hunter wouldn't play any significant roles until the two joined forces at Harpers Ferry and took up pursuit of the Early's army, which by 16 July had already retreated back into Virginia.

Union sentries from the 22nd New York State Militia on duty outside Harpers Ferry. Frequent occupation of Loudoun Heights by Confederate forces (the ridge line shown behind the soldiers) threatened Union forces in Harpers Ferry, while Federal possession of Maryland Heights made Confederate occupation of the town equally untenable. For these reasons, Harpers Ferry changed hands multiple times throughout the war. (Library of Congress)

Harpers Ferry from the base of Maryland Heights as photographed by George Stacy in 1860. The bridges were quickly destroyed during the war. (Library of Congress)

Elizabeth Proctor Thomas, affectionately known as "Aunt Betty," owned the property where Fort Stevens was constructed during the Civil War. (Library of Congress)

CHAPTER 3

Defending Washington

With the shelling of Fort Sumter in Charleston Harbor, Union military engineering officers began planning for the defense of the Virginia side of the Potomac River opposite the capital city. The urgency for a Virginia-oriented defensive line came from the realization that Arlington Heights afforded an excellent vantage point for shelling the Federal city if occupied by Confederate forces. The vulnerable Virginia river crossing points, such as the Long Bridge and Chain Bridge, obviously also needed protecting. Additionally, Alexandria, Virginia, needed to be occupied and would then require suitable strong points.

Federal Marines hastily occupied Fort Washington, the abandoned brick casemate fort built after the War of 1812, located on the Maryland side of the river about 12 miles below Washington, across from Mount Vernon.

Until the disastrous Federal defeat at Bull Run in July 1861, little attention was given to fortifying the entire perimeter of the city. The Maryland side was largely ignored.

The first step in better protecting the city centered on constructing suitable forts at key point along the roads into town. These forts were positioned on the most commanding sites available, while still forming an interlocking defensive perimeter when the entire system of fortifications was completed.

By January 1862, 48 forts protected Washington. Although thought to be sufficient at the time, the wisdom of that thinking came into question when Confederate forces invaded Maryland in September 1862.

Following the Rebel defeat at the battle of Antietam, a commission of Union military engineers, headed by Brigadier General John Gross Barnard, the chief engineer for the defense of Washington and one of the founders of the National Academy of Science in 1863, was convened "to examine and

View of the original Fort Stevens's sally port when it was named Fort Massachusetts after the home state of the regiment of soldiers that built it. The name was changed in 1863 and the fort, like many others, was greatly enlarged. The defensive abattis (felled trees) is clearly visible around the perimeter of the earthworks. (National Archives and Records Administration)

report upon a plan of the present forts and sufficiency of the present system of defenses for the city." This group was to come up with a comprehensive plan for rectifying any of the deficiencies and defects in the city's overall defensive plan. The commission spent two months considering every possible approach to protecting the city. The opinion of Brigadier General John Gross Barnard was,

> Numerous gaps existed requiring the interpolation of new works. Ravines or depressions surface, unseen from the works, intersected the line at various points or lay along its front, to control which numerous auxiliary batteries were necessary.
>
> Finally, it was evident that, even with all such improvements, the defenses would yet remain only a system of 'point d'appui' [strategic points] to a line of battle unless they were connected works that would cover the troops occupying the intermediate ground and offer some obstacle to the passage of the enemy.[1]

Barnard's group's deliberations focused on adding forts and constructing rifle trenches between the forts that would be manned by two men per yard in front of a fort's perimeters and one man per yard behind the fort line. The group calculated that 25,000 to 40,000 soldiers were required to man such defensive lines.[2] It also believed that 9,000 artillerists were needed to operate the forts' array of guns. Additionally, they recommended that the city have a permanent cavalry force of 3,000 for reconnaissance purposes. The group's revised plans also called for the addition of field-gun batteries and mortar emplacements between major fortifications. This planning also included replacing the original barbette carriages installed in some of the forts with moveable or pivoting field or siege carriages for larger ordnance whenever possible.

The commission's recommendation for Fort Stevens was that the original work was entirely too small to adequately protect the Seventh Street Turnpike, one of the most important northern routes into the city. The fort needed to be greatly expanded. As part of the makeover, the size was more than doubled and the complement of guns was increased from 10 to 19. As at many of the other forts, a well was dug at Fort Stevens as part of the expansion effort to make it more self-sufficient if attacked.

The planners also considered worst-case scenarios, including the possible temporary occupation of the city. The group believed that only a single day would be required to disperse the government and destroy Federal archives if that happened.

The sentiment of the group was that the 37,000 horsemen, soldiers, and artillerymen, permanently assigned to the defenses of the capital, could reasonably hold off an enemy for at least that long. In July 1864 those estimates would prove woefully inaccurate. In reality, one day wasn't nearly enough time to evacuate the government, and there'd be nowhere near that size force to safeguard the city while any government leaders attempted to flee. In the final report, the engineers did conclude that, "Against more serious attacks from the main body of the enemy, the Capital must depend upon the concentration of its entire armies in Virginia or Maryland."

In the end, Barnard summarized the findings in his 1871 *Report of the Defenses of Washington,*

> Thus, from a few isolated works covering bridges or commanding a few especially important points, was developed a connected system of fortification by which every prominent point, at intervals of 800 to 1,000 yards, was occupied by an inclosed field-fort, every important approach or depression of ground, unseen from the forts, swept by a battery for field-guns, and the whole connected by rifle-trenches which were in fact lines of infantry parapet, furnishing emplacements for two ranks of men and affording covered communications along the line, while roads were opened wherever necessary, so that troops and artillery could be moved rapidly from one point of the immense periphery to another, or under cover, from point to point along the line.

One thing the commission's planners didn't consider was how to compensate the property owners for the confiscation of their lands. Instead, the government merely seized the fort, battery, and trench sites. Some of the landowners waited decades to be compensated for their property. Some were never fully paid for their losses.

Elizabeth Thomas was one of those who waited forever to be paid.[3] Affectionately known in later years as "Aunt Betty," her family moved from neighboring Prince George's County to northwest Washington when she was a child. It settled on about 11 acres on the crest of a prominent hill in the rural northern outskirts of the city and raised cows.

Initially the area was commonly known as "Vinegar Hill," one of the city's initial free African American enclaves. This section of the city had other names over the years, including Chrystal Springs, Cowtown, and Brighton. Ultimately it came to be known as Brightwood. The Thomas family's acreage was strategically adjacent to the original fort site. In 1862 the family's shanty was torn down to expand the fort. The demolition occurred almost before Thomas even realized it. According to the free Black woman's recollections, soldiers from a predominantly German regiment simply showed up and began removing the furniture. She couldn't understand a word they were saying but realized what was happening when they began taking the shanty apart. She was left crying under a sycamore tree amid a pitiful pile of her possessions, with a 6-month-old infant in her arms. After the war she would get her land back, and she lived in the derelict fort, becoming its unofficial caretaker and interpretative guide. She also served as a gracious host to countless veterans returning to the battle site after the war. One of her favorite stories was how, after her house was torn down, she was greatly comforted by a tall, thin man who assured her that her loss "shall reap a great reward." She always insisted that the man who consoled her so sweetly on that dreadful day was President Lincoln. Mary Church Terrel, a prominent African American leader in the District of Columbia, believed that it was Lincoln. In a 22 September 1924 speech at Fort Stevens, given the day before her 61st birthday, she told the audience of veterans, "I fancy I can see now as she looked at the tall, spare form of Abraham Lincoln as he told her he would have to order her home removed so as to use the site for a fort." Indeed, the fortifications erected over the rubble of Thomas's dwelling helped save the city.

Elizabeth Thomas was finally paid for her property in 1916—$1,835 in compensation from the Federal government for the loss of her meager shack shortly before her death at age 96.

In 1861 the Federal government also took possession of the Emory Methodist Church property, which was located to the immediate west of the Seventh Street Turnpike. This served as the footprint for the original fort. The original fortification, begun in October 1861, was initially called Fort Massachusetts, a designation afforded to it because soldiers of the 37th

Massachusetts Regiment had constructed it. The African American Methodist congregation acquired the site in 1856 and erected a brick chapel there the following year. The original chapel was demolished to make way for the fort in 1861. Many of the chapel's bricks were repurposed in building the original fort, including some that were used to create a brick oven for baking bread for the soldiers. Following the war, the congregation got its land back and would build a new church on the former fort site. The current house of worship remains on that site to this day, plus a new housing unit for the elderly.

Ultimately, 37 miles of defensive works, including 68 forts and 93 batteries, protected Washington. These fortifications included 807 guns and 98 mortars.

By 1864 Washington had become one of the world's most fortified cities, except for two things—it had few trained defenders and its nearest commanders were its weakest links. Just how bad things were training-wise was the subject of an inspection tour made by Brigadier General John Barnard's flamboyant assistant, Lieutenant Colonel Barton Alexander, on 6 July 1864. Alexander was shocked by what he found. At Chain Bridge, for example, a major Potomac River crossing about 3 miles above Georgetown, 64 soldiers were assigned to defend this vital crossing point. The defensive works there included Forts Ethan Allen and Marcy, and rifle pits on the Georgetown side. The bridge's planking on the Virginia side could also be removed in case of trouble, making crossing nearly impossible. Additionally, as an added barrier, a large timber stockade, with a gate, protected with boilerplate iron and rifle holes, was installed at the head of the bridge. This gate supposedly could be hastily closed to seal off the span. Unfortunately, Lieutenant Colonel Alexander discovered that, of the dozens of soldiers stationed at the timber-trussed bridge, only one knew anything about cannons, and that knowledge was principally limited to cleaning the guns and stowing ammunition. Additionally, the officer in charge at the time of the inspection assured Alexander that he was well versed in how to blow up the bridge's main support column if it ever came under attack. He said there was a small pipe leading to a powder magazine in one of the main piers that he would drop a lit match down to set off an explosion. Alexander knew this wasn't true. The bridge had never been mined. Alexander concluded that the bridge would probably be secure—if it had a better guard force.

At the Aqueduct Bridge, Alexander discovered that the guard detail on duty couldn't find the bar needed to secure the gate that closed off the bridge and, as a result, the guards couldn't say whether the bar would actually fit. None of them had ever seen the bar—because they never practiced any sort of defensive drills. Once the required bar was found, Alexander witnessed its successful use.

If it was doubtful that Washington was secure, it was equally doubtful that the commanders of troops nearest to the capital were any more prepared.

As a commander, Major General David Hunter couldn't be counted on. He was a major disappointment when it came to holding onto the Shenandoah Valley and coming to the aid of Washington. When confronted by the enemy, he seemed to prefer to move backward rather than forward. (Library of Congress)

Major General Franz Sigel was a "Forty-Eighter." He came to the United States after the failed revolution in Germany in 1848–1849. As a Union officer he had more luck enticing large numbers of German immigrants to join the Union army than he did winning battles. For that success he was kept around as a star recruiter. During the war, more than 170,000 German immigrants fought for the Union. (Library of Congress)

Command-wise, Washington clearly was in no shape to repel a serious attack during the first week of July, despite that Grant had just dispatched about 8,000 troops to the capital on 6 July. Other nearby commanders had shown themselves to be less than stellar performers. David Hunter had thus far proven to be a major disappointment, moving his force towards the enemy, and Washington, at a seemingly glacial pace. Franz Sigel had likewise proved to possess questionable capabilities. Gideon Welles's opinion of Sigel was, "He is always overwhelmed and put on the run," which is perhaps a nice way of saying he was cowardly.[4] By 7 July Grant informed General Halleck, the army's chief paper shuffler in Washington, that he wished to sack Sigel immediately. "I do not feel certain at any time that he will not, after abandoning stores, artillery, and trains, make a successful retreat to some safe place," the newly promoted lieutenant general confided to Halleck.

"Sigel's operations from the beginning of the war have been so unsuccessful that I think it advisable to relieve him from all duty; at least until present troubles are over," Grant wrote. That same day, by order of the president, Albion Howe replaced Major General Sigel as the head of the Military District of Harpers Ferry. As a further demotion, Selig was told to report to David Hunter for his next assignment, but Hunter wasn't long for command either. By then Hunter was nowhere to be found. He wasn't reporting his whereabouts. This infuriated Secretary of War Stanton who finally sent a nastygram during the first week of July to the several places Hunter's army might be. The wire, which found Hunter at Parkersburg, West Virginia, stated, "The rebels have for two days back been operating against Martinsburg, Harper's Ferry, and other points on the line of the Baltimore railroad. These points being within your department you are expected to take promptly such measures as may be proper to meet the emergency." Infuriated, Stanton also insisted on being told where Hunter's forces were and how they were being deployed going forward. Hunter continued to be cryptic on both points.

Tintype of an unknown Confederate private. (Library of Congress)

CHAPTER 4

The Rebels Are Coming

Unbeknownst to most, as early as 4 July General Grant reported the possibility that Confederate forces were heading towards Washington to General Halleck. Grant had gotten information that the Rebel Second Corps was heading north from a Confederate deserter from the 61st Virginia regiment. As a precaution Grant instructed Halleck to hold all the forces available to him for the possible defense of Washington, Baltimore, Cumberland, and Harpers Ferry. Grant believed the deserter's claim because the Second Corps was no longer where it had been. It had disappeared from its assigned position around Petersburg. Such news should have come as no surprise to either Halleck or Stanton. They had been receiving a steady stream of cables regarding sizeable Rebel troop movements from Union commanders in the Shenandoah Valley for days and those Southern troops had to have come from somewhere. Additionally, John Garrett, the president of the B&O Railroad, had been feeding Lincoln, Stanton, and Halleck loads of intelligence gathered from his station managers and ticket agents concerning Confederate movements in that region. By the time Grant sent his cable to Halleck on 4 July Rebel forces were within sight of Harpers Ferry and were closing in on the isolated town.

Grant apparently wasn't all that familiar with Harpers Ferry. He obviously wasn't aware of the common adage about the place. Surrounded as it was on three sides by towering heights, it was said that it was better to attack the town a dozen times than try to defend it once—it was basically indefensible. Before July 1864 it had changed hands a dozen times. Having lost the town multiple times during the war, Union commander Franz Sigel realized the futility of any defense and hastily withdrew his troops to the safety of the fortified 1,400-foot-tall hill-top citadel on Maryland Heights,

Office U. S. Military Telegraph,
WAR DEPARTMENT.

The following Telegram received at Washington, _____ M. _____ 1864.

From _____ 2. _____ 1864.

I trust you can preserve the remainder of the bridge. It is reported the rebels are destroying and burning the track West of Harper's Ferry. Can you not prevent this? Twenty five hundred (2500) re-enforcements, with a battery, will reach you this evening. General Kelly has repulsed attack upon North Anda, South Branch and Paterson Creek bridges. General Hunter is pressing rapidly forward from the West. I trust he will soon be in Communication and aid you in overwhelming the Enemy."

I will promptly Communicate any information of interest I can obtain.

John W. Garrett

D.H.

34297

A 5 July 1864 telegram from John W. Garrett, president of the B&O Railroad, to Abraham Lincoln regarding Confederate troop movements and conditions in West Virginia and Maryland. (Library of Congress)

across the Potomac River, that July. John Garrett confirmed all of this to Secretary Stanton and Halleck at 11:35 a.m. on 4 July, repeating the words of a telegram received from his station agent at Harpers Ferry only a few minutes earlier, which said, "Great excitement here. All citizens leaving. Harpers Ferry is being evacuated by the military."[1]

The Confederate capture of Harpers Ferry had previously served as a preliminary spillway in all of the earlier invasions of the North. That pattern was repeating itself. Selig's ineptitude was showing itself again, too. Selig was the ideal poster child for German Americans. Having fled Germany after the collapse of the 1848 revolution, he was extremely effective at enticing many German immigrants to join the Union army. Halleck, however, disliked him, believing him to be an indecisive bumbler. Despite Halleck's disgust, Selig had been given command of the Military District of West Virginia when West Virginia was admitted to the Union.

Within a few hours of Harpers Ferry's evacuation, a small Southern cavalry force, believed to be Mosby's Rangers, also had crossed the Potomac River west of Point of Rocks, Maryland, south of Harpers Ferry, and begun cutting telegraph wires. John Garrett hastily notified Lincoln, Stanton and Halleck of these unfolding disruptions. That night Frederick, Maryland, was also threatened. Once again the war had come to Maryland. The only question this time was whether the bulk of the Rebel army was heading west, north, east or south.

Cables immediately went out to the Union commanders around Harpers Ferry. By 3:30 p.m. on 4 July word came back from Lieutenant Colonel John F. Hoy at New Creek, West Virginia, that a Confederate deserter from the Second Corps claimed the ultimate target was Baltimore. Logically, Baltimore was never Early's ultimate aim. For an invading army, it was a dead end. If Early moved his entire force to Baltimore, he would paint himself into a corner he'd never come out from. There was simply no way out. Early's only safe escape routes to Virginia were across the Potomac. Baltimore was a minimum of 70 miles from any possible crossing site.

From Washington, however, Edward's Ferry was only about 35 miles while White's Ferry was a further 10 miles. As a diversionary strike, Washington was always the safer of the two targets. Besides, Baltimore didn't have as much to offer. It was largely an industrial and seaport city. And Point Lookout was a great deal farther away from Baltimore. Baltimore was at least 40 miles farther north from Point Lookout, making the entire trek more than 110 miles.

The truth of the matter was that nothing would have been gained by keeping the Federal turtle's head inside its protective shell at Baltimore, while outside Early's Rebel marauders were making off with most of everything Maryland's farms had to offer. But if Early and his men could do that at Washington and get their stolen bounty across the Potomac River as quickly and safely as possible, the raid on Washington would have been considered a stunning success—which is precisely what it was!

Unfortunately, Union leaders weren't thinking logically.

Once across the Potomac in Maryland, Early wisely concealed his initial aim. He did this by dispersing small raiding parties in all directions. He also encouraged his men to lie about their total numbers and intensions. According to a deserter Lieutenant Colonel John F. Hoy caught, the invasion force included 20,000 infantry, 10,000 cavalry, and 60 pieces of artillery, all of which was untrue, as was its ultimate destination—Baltimore.

Pennsylvania's Governor Andrew G. Curtin wasn't waiting to find out whether his state was a primary target. After hastily conferring with Secretary Stanton on 4 July Curtin announced the mobilization of 100-day enlistees throughout the Keystone State. The following day Stanton sent presidential proclamations to other Northern governors, including those of New York, Massachusetts, and Ohio, announcing the call-up of additional 100-day enlistments.

On 5 July General Grant informed Halleck, "If the enemy cross into Maryland or Pennsylvania I can send an army corps from here to meet them or cut off their return south."[2] All Grant asked was that Halleck take charge of arranging for the necessary transportation of his troops from Fort Monroe, Virginia. Within a matter of hours Halleck confirmed that sufficient transports were standing by at the fort, but oddly his response to Grant this time sounded far less urgent than before. "As Hunter's force is now coming within reach, I think your operations should not be interfered with by sending troops here," Halleck told Grant. "If Washington and Baltimore should be so seriously threatened as to require your aid, I will inform you in time." Grant wasn't certain he could trust Halleck's judgment on this, especially since he was now satisfied that Lee had indeed sent his Second Corps northward. Grant advised Halleck of this, saying, "I think now there is no doubt but Ewell's [Early's] corps is away from here." He told the army's chief of staff that, as a precaution, he was dispatching a large contingent of dismounted cavalry from Petersburg and "one good division" of Meade's infantry, with the promise of the balance of that corps if the need arose. Meade's force was underway by 6 July, about the same time the bulk of Early's men were crossing the Potomac into Maryland. Grant was also loath to trust that David Hunter was "coming within reach" of anything. Hunter always moved his men at a snail's pace, except when he was being chased. Almost as soon as Grant's pledged help was on its way, Major General George Meade notified Grant of information received from two deserters that Washington was the real Confederate target. The Federal city was selected, they assured their interrogators, because it was "supposed to be defenseless." That same evening, Halleck equivocated again, begging Grant to send one regiment of heavy artillery to Washington immediately. It apparently had only just dawned on Halleck that the militia forces being called to Washington from the various states likely wouldn't have been instructed in the use of heavy artillery, and they might not arrive in time to be of much help.

Calls for additional troops went out to many different Union commands, too, and most responded favorably. Major General Philip Sheridan was somewhat less supportive. He contributed 2,496 dismounted and unarmed men from his 3rd Cavalry Division, all of which were on his sick list at the time.[3]

For many Washingtonians it was almost as though the Rebels pounced on Washington out of nowhere. On Sunday, 10 July, while Navy Secretary Gideon Welles was at work reading his mail, one of his clerks informed him that the Confederates were on the outskirts of Georgetown, less than 6 miles from where he was sitting. The clerk must have been badly mistaken, thought Welles; that wasn't possible; there had been no alarm. A second clerk confirmed what the first had said. The Rebels were within the district line. Welles immediately requested information from the War Department, but the staff there was as much in the dark as he was. "They were ignorant—had heard street rumors, but they were unworthy of notice—and ridiculed my inquiry," wrote Welles of his efforts to get the facts.[4]

Welles's opinion at that moment was, "Stanton seems stupid, (General) Halleck always does."[5] Welles was no alarmist, but he knew that if the army wasn't prepared to meet the Rebel threat head on, things could spiral out of control, which is precisely what they did!

The rumors had a thousand tongues. The truth was, the Rebels were at the threshold of the capital, and the door was pretty much wide open for them to march in. Many in Washington realized the same thing. Patent Office clerk Horatio Nathan Taft was perplexed over how easy it seemed to be for the Rebels to have managed to slip away from Virginia, cross the Potomac, and "be almost knocking at the gates of the city and [our military leaders] know nothing about it or at least think it is a 'raid' of a few hundred troopers!!"[6] Washington simply wasn't prepared to defend itself.

Lincoln decided to spend the weekend at his summer cottage near the soldier's home. He left the executive mansion on 9 July. Once at the cottage, he received two urgent messages from Secretary Stanton. The first alerted him that his carriage had been followed by a suspicious rider in an unfamiliar uniform: "This induces me to advise that your guard be on <u>alert</u> tonight." The second message was sent at 10:00 p.m. on Sunday, 10 July, reporting on the enemy's rapid advance on Washington. "They are in large force and have driven back our cavalry," he explained in advising the president to return to the safety of the city immediately.[7]

Washingtonians hadn't felt that isolated and defenseless since April 1861 when there were fears that the city might fall victim to native Southern sympathizers, plus attackers from Maryland and Virginia, who might take control of the city. Back then the residents held their collective breath for 10 critical days until sufficient forces could come to the city's assistance. In

1861 many pro-Southerners were divided on the city's fate. Some wanted it captured and transformed into the capital of the Confederacy. Others wanted nothing to do with it. For this latter group, the city was a symbol of the evils of the old government, one it had chosen to abandon.

Lincoln's secretary of the navy, Gideon Welles, had inklings that the Confederates might attack Washington. It made sense, since the soldiers assigned to defend Washington had been siphoned away to support Grant's army in Virginia to a point where only a token force remained. In his diary entry for 6 July 1864 he wrote, "I have sometimes thought that Lee might make a sudden dash in the direction of Washington or above, and inflict great injury before our troops could interfere, or Grant move a column to protect the city. But likely Grant has thought and is prepared for this; yet he displays little strategy or invention."[8] Welles's misgivings proved remarkably timely, coming true within a matter of days. Others sensed it too and had great misgivings about the military's ability to protect the city when the threat came. In his diary entry on 6 July Adam Gurowski wrote, "The Rebels spread over Maryland. Is it a raid or an invasion? Our frightened…Halleck is invested with command and cannot yet find out. Of course not; it is far easier to find a word in a dictionary than to find out the numbers of a roving enemy. If it is an invasion, then it is a brave and desperate attempt of Lee to escape Grant's jaws or to divert his attentions and his forces. Halleck, the brave powder-eater, has doubled the pickets around—his house."[9]

In some ways, conditions inside Washington that July mirrored the way things were in April 1861, when the District of Columbia was nearly undefended. Lincoln's election set off that firestorm. On 12 April 1861, Confederate forces fired on Fort Sumter at Charleston, South Carolina. Immediately, scores of Southern naval officers resigned from the US Navy. Among the few loyal navy officers remaining in Washington, John Dahlgren found himself in command of one of the largest military forces initially capable of defending the District of Columbia from possible secessionist attacks from Maryland and Virginia.

With all the forces he could muster, Dahlgren was expected to protect Washington until Northern regiments could arrive. Dahlgren hastily mobilized all the men available to him—totaling fewer than 350 Marines, sailors, local militiamen, and civilian Washington Navy Yard volunteers—and stationed them around the city. He used some to fortify the navy yard, while others manned picket posts at bridges into the city, including the Washington Navy Yard Bridge. His sailors and Marines also crewed a small naval flotilla to patrol the Potomac River in an effort to ensure unrestricted access to other Northern port cities.

The riverine war around the nation's capital commenced almost as soon as President Lincoln was elected, beginning with the formation of a small flotilla under John Dahlgren's command. One of the flotilla's initial tasks was to clear the Potomac River of Confederate mines and land-based strong points, including Alexandria, Virginia, within sight of the Capitol dome. Dahlgren launched the war's first amphibious operation, landing troops at Alexandria, Virginia, and capturing the city with barely a shot fired.

During these frantic early days of the war, Dahlgren established his command center in his office at the navy yard, using what was described by Lincoln's secretary, John Hay, as "a brain as active as a high-pressure engine" to defend the city.

Among the first Union troops to arrive in Washington were members of the 71st New York Infantry, entering the city on 27 April 1861. The unit was initially housed on the navy yard as Dahlgren's guests. While there, the New York State Militia was subsequently temporarily quartered on a steamboat and later in barracks on the yard from April to July 1861. The unit's officers were housed in John Dahlgren's residence on the yard. Dahlgren moved his bed into his office, where he worked around the clock. To celebrate the breath of relief that accompanied the 71st's arrival, Lincoln was the guest of honor at the yard on 9 May for an afternoon concert of patriotic music, marches, and ballads. Members of the Cabinet and prominent Washingtonians attended the musical program, performed in a decorated storeroom. After the concert, Lincoln was asked to witness a live-fire exercise of Dahlgren's 11-inch gun. John Hay observed in his diary, "The Prest. was delighted."[10]

The New York infantry's arrival allowed Dahlgren sufficient breathing room to direct his creative genius towards other challenges, including producing munitions and making sure naval guns were ready for distribution following the destruction of the Gospoint Navy Yard, which at the time was the navy's largest facility. The loss of the yard at Norfolk, which was burned on 20 April 1861 to prevent its use by Confederate forces, made the Washington Navy Yard the North's most important asset for naval munitions and ordnance.

The end of the crisis in the capital city created a threat to Dahlgren's command. After the initial threats to the capital subsided, and with the arrival of other higher-ranking naval officers, calls came to replace John Dahlgren as the commandant of the Washington Navy Yard with a more senior officer. Lincoln would hear of no such thing, telling Navy Secretary Welles, "The Yard shall not be taken from him."[11] Lincoln's reasoning was simple: Dahlgren had earned it, having taken charge there when no one else could or would, so, with the danger passed, he could stay there as long as he liked.

Lincoln was deeply appreciative of Dahlgren for his efforts in safeguarding Washington. He also valued Dahlgren's advice and what John Hay described as his "wise and witty sailor-talk." Lincoln also approved of his ordnance work and as a result he visited the Washington Navy Yard as often as possible to discuss naval matters and witness Dahlgren's many live-fire experiments. The president's visits became so frequent that many weekends were set aside for what mockingly became known by Dahlgren's military rivals as Dahlgren's "champagne experiments." These weekend visits featured the president and Cabinet members or prominent Union leaders enjoying a champagne lunch and participating in some sort of sophisticated ballistics experiments, with the president often firing the ordnance himself.

Unlike in 1861, by July 1864 Washington had a ring of formidable fortifications to protect it, but just as in 1861, it once again had few trained soldiers to man those bastions.

An early tintype of an unknown Confederate artilleryman in a greatcoat. By 1864 such a coat would have been in tatters. (Library of Congress)

CHAPTER 5

Across the Potomac

Having marched his men over 400 miles in such a short time, having come to the banks of the Potomac River, and having inflicted so much embarrassing damage upon the Union army in the Shenandoah Valley, the typically impulsive Early may not have wished to waste the glimmering opportunity that appeared before him on 6 July 1864 staring at the Potomac River. No matter how slim the chances of success, for a brief instant Early must have thought that *if only* he could punch a hole in Washington's defenses, the whole war might take a critical turn in the South's favor.

Like many postwar memoirs, Jubal Early's contains a number of "if only" glimpses of victory. He was certain, for example, that the battle of Antietam could have been a great Confederate triumph *if only* Lee had more ammunition and troops.[1] He admitted in his *Memoirs* that the needed ammunition was more than 200 miles away and the additional troops were well beyond that, but such realities never seem to stop a dreamer from conjuring up visions of what might have been.

There were many such "if only" moments in the Washington campaign in 1864. If only Early had arrived outside Washington a day early... If only Early's command had been larger... If only the weather had not been so exhaustingly hot... If only Bradley Johnson, the officer responsible for the land-based portion of the Point Lookout breakout, hadn't informed Early on the night of 11 July that he had it from a reliable source that Grant's entire army was in moving towards Maryland and would be there soon... If only! Unfortunately, "if only" isn't the stuff of history. It isn't what happened.

Early had the nerve and the impulsiveness to have attacked in force, and he had good officers. He also had veteran soldiers. He just didn't have enough of them and Mother Nature wasn't on his side. Besides, that wasn't his first order of business. He was to threaten the city, *only if* it was practicable. His was to be a food raid. His actions were also to draw significant numbers of Union troops away from Petersburg by threatening and rampaging through West Virginia, Maryland, and Pennsylvania and in making a show of liberating Point Lookout. His was to be the 1864 version of "shock and awe." The greater the fear factor the better. These things all happened.

General Lee picked his characters thoughtfully. Early was known as Lee's "Bad Old Man," a moniker Lee meant as high praise. Early *was* a grumpy old man. It was hard to like him, and few of his peers did. He could cuss worse than any sailor. He was frequently offensive, occasionally insubordinate, usually unwilling to accept defeat, and always Spartan on discipline.

Confederate cavalry commander Bradley Johnson was a Marylander, as were most of his men. He had been part of the Rebel forces that pursued Kilpatrick's and Dahlgren's raiders a few months earlier, so he knew their playbook and could basically repeat it in the Free State. Additionally, he was born in the town of Frederick, Maryland.

Unfortunately, if Marylanders there thought that his would be a happy homecoming, they were sadly mistaken. The *Washington (County) Union* reported that he was a terrorist. It said that in coming back to town he confronted the man who had legally purchased his former house from the government and demanded back rent payments to the tune of $1,400, or

The presentation of Frederick's ransom demand by Charles Wellington Reed. (Charles Reed Papers/Library of Congress)

else. The home's owner reportedly paid up and then was told he had two hours to get out. He could take whatever he could carry, but he had to go. According to the local newspaper Johnson then burned the house. In reprinting this report, the publisher of the *Alexandria (Virginia) Gazette*, Edgar Snowden Jr., added the following footnote: "We will simply add, that the above story reads very much like a newspaper tale." It was indeed "fake news," but Johnson wouldn't be kind to his onetime fellow residents of the Old Line State.

Frederick's ransom demands. (Frederick County Historical Society/Heritage Frederick)

As for Confederate General John Breckenridge, who was assigned as Early's second in command, he was supposed to be the Second Corps' sophisticated "good cop" who would balance out Early, the Bad Old Man. That wouldn't be an easy role for him to play, because Breckenridge had many close friends in the North and didn't despise all Northerners as Early did.

The threat of burning things become a common threat for Jubal Early and his men. Once across the Potomac, he began demanding steep ransoms in cash and/or supplies from three Maryland towns—Frederick, Middletown, and Hagerstown. He swore that if any failed to pay up, they'd be burned. Middletown, which was ordered to pay $5,000, was actually extorted three times by three different Rebel groups. Frederick was told it had to pay $200,000.

In addition to the money, Early also demanded unreasonable quantities of items that were hard to come by in the South, such as coffee and sugar, but there is no indication that these were ever furnished. Hagerstown was supposed to pay $200,000, too, but a 0 was left off the final demand note, making the amount only $20,000,[2] plus some clothing. Towns in Pennsylvania were also ransomed.

Where money couldn't be had, things were simply taken or destroyed. Without anyone close at hand to pay to protect the Chesapeake and Ohio Canal, portions of the waterway were wrecked. Marooned canal barges were fantastic finds because they often held up to 100 barrels of flour ready for the taking.

Lock and canal barge on the Chesapeake and Ohio Canal near Washington, DC. (Library of Congress)

CHAPTER 6

9 July—Monocacy Junction

"What have you heard about battle at Monocacy to-day? We have nothing about it here except what you say."

TELEGRAM FROM PRESIDENT LINCOLN
TO JOHN W. GARRETT,
PRESIDENT OF THE BALTIMORE & OHIO RAILROAD
AT CAMDEN STATION, BALTIMORE
9 JULY 1864, 5:15 P.M.[1]

By the time John Garrett was handed Lincoln's telegram, the battle of Monocacy Junction was over. Garrett had telegraphed the president frequently during the day, including to advise, "Gen Wallace is now making preparations to defend the point which he will hold up to last possible moment. Enemy are said to be advancing in heavy force down Balt. Pike."[2] Lincoln was aware of Union General Lew Wallace's intentions to fight at the junction.

What Garrett knew from his telegrapher at Monocacy Junction was that fighting had commenced at about 10:30 that morning and was still going on at 1:00 p.m. By 5:00 p.m. Garrett learned from the telegraph operator at Monrovia, Maryland, about 8 miles east of the junction, that "our troops at Monocacy have given way, and that Major General Lewis (Lew) Wallace has been badly defeated."[3]

Garrett conveyed all of this to the president and included that he had heard that 15,000 Rebels were marching towards Baltimore. Garrett also informed Secretary of War Stanton of what he knew via a telegram, sent that evening from Baltimore at 7:35 p.m. General Wallace alerted John Garrett of his situation at 10:40 p.m. Wallace's wire to the president of the B&O Railroad

Alfred R. Waud's sketch of the Monocacy River railroad bridge penciled in 1863. Waud was a renowned Civil War illustrator whose sketches were published in Northern newspapers and periodicals. A version of this rendering was published in the 15 August 1863 edition of *Harper's Weekly*. The bridge was destroyed by Union forces during the battle of Monocacy Junction the following year. (Library of Congress)

The field and area around the Thomas Farm witnessed some of the heaviest fighting during the battle of Monocacy Junction on 9 July 1864. (National Register of Historic Places/Library of Congress)

was remarkably stern: "I did as I promised. Held the (B&O) bridge (over the Monocacy River) to the last. They overwhelmed me with numbers. My troops fought splendidly. Losses fearful. Send me cars enough to Ellicott's Mills (Ellicott City) to take up my retreating columns. Don't fail me."[4] As indicated by his tone, Wallace had acted at the behest of his friend Garrett in protecting

Major General Lew Wallace was the commander of Union forces at the battle of Monocacy Junction. His actions in delaying Jubal Early's raiders, taken at the urging of John Garrett to protect B&O property and with Lincoln's knowledge, are credited with saving Washington, DC, in July 1864. After the war Wallace was the author of *Ben-Hur*. (Library of Congress)

B&O property at Monocacy Junction, where the rail lines to Frederick and Harpers Ferry split from the line to Baltimore. Wallace also intended his little force to serve as a wedge between Baltimore and Washington, an obstruction that might deflect the Rebels from heading in either direction. Garrett transmitted a copy of Wallace's message to Stanton, too, advising that he was arranging for the necessary cars to be sent to Ellicott's Mills as requested, "unless otherwise ordered by you."[5]

Wallace realized his troops had done more than just try to defend the river crossing at Monocacy Junction. They had bought invaluable time. They had succeeded in tying down Jubal Early's Rebels for a full day, time that the military, and Washingtonians and Baltimoreans, desperately needed in preparing to defend their cities. Demonstrating a flare for the dramatic, Wallace claimed that he tried to hold back the Rebels as best he could because he was plagued by thoughts of "President Lincoln, cloaked and hooded, stealing from the back door of the White House just as some gray-garbed Confederate brigadier burst in the front door,"[6] and he wasn't about to let that happen.

Wallace had chosen the battlefield wisely. He positioned his meager force on the eastern side of Monocacy River at the junction of the Washington and Baltimore Pikes, in effect blocking both routes from any immediate Confederate use. Monocacy Junction was nearly equidistant from Baltimore and Washington, roughly 46 miles, which provided both cities about two more days to secure their defensive perimeters if Wallace's troops gave way. The center of Wallace's line of battle was anchored on a B&O Railroad bridge to

Baltimore, which meant his force could get resupplied and reinforced fairly quickly by rail—*if* any additional relief was to be coming his way. A formidable blockhouse protected the western approach to the railway bridge. Wallace's center also controlled a covered road bridge that crossed the Monocacy River. In attacking this position, the enemy's main force would have to advance through an exposed field of corn and newly harvested wheat before crossing the river via the narrow covered bridge. This would constrict the enemy into an ideal killing zone. Wallace wisely placed three howitzers where they could sweep any advance through the exposed fields and across the bridges.

Troop-wise, Wallace's force of 6,600 was outnumbered. Besides a numerical advantage, the Confederates had the advantage of experience—most of Wallace's men were raw home guards and untried 100-day militiamen. Considering this, Wallace positioned these men on his right flank, closest to the railway bridge, which was protected by the river and its steep muddy banks with a deeply wooded area to their backs. His 10 regiments of veteran soldiers and 3 additional cannons were positioned at his center, facing the covered bridge. A light force protected his left flank. A line of Federal skirmishers was put across the river in front of the covered bridge to blunt any Rebel frontal probes.

Jubal Early's men did indeed probe the possibilities of a bridge crossing but quickly realized that a frontal attack was ill-advised. To ensure that, Wallace had the covered bridge set on fire. In the meantime, Early sent out search parties to look for a way to ford the river so he could execute a flanking attack on Wallace's force. A reasonably suitable crossing site was discovered south of Wallace's left flank. A small force of Rebel troops hastily exploited this crossing and engaged Wallace's left flank, but these Rebels were forced back. At this point, there was a brief lull in the fighting. During this lull the majority of Early's corps forded the river. Simultaneously, Wallace redeployed the bulk of his men to his left flank. In fierce fighting, the much larger Confederate force, supported by about 18 pieces of artillery, cracked the Union left flank. Early didn't deploy the rest of his artillery, believing that it would take too much time to unlimber and array the guns for battle. Besides, 18 field pieces were certainly enough to do the trick, considering that Wallace had brought only 6 cannons with him. (Wallace retreated with 8 guns, taking the barrels of the 2 cannons in the railroad bridge's blockhouse with him.)

This Confederate maneuver succeeded in turning Wallace's left flank, forcing the Union troops to make a disorderly withdraw towards Baltimore.

Early's forces didn't chase the bluecoats very far, because Early didn't wish to be burdened with any more prisoners than he already had—600 to 700 unwounded Union prisoners in tow, by his own estimate.

Union casualties amounted to about 1,300 men, while the South suffered about 750 killed or wounded.

On the day of the battle, many in Washington believed that Baltimore was Early's primary target. Baltimoreans believed that too. Their city was already in a state of panic caused by Early's approach. On the evening of July 9, five prominent Baltimoreans deputized by the mayor asked Lincoln for help. "Baltimore is in great peril," the group advised the president. "Can we rely upon the prompt aid of the Government in sending re-enforcements?" Lincoln responded to their pleas, saying, "I have not a single soldier but who is being disposed by the military for the best protection of all. By latest accounts the enemy is moving on Washington. They cannot fly to either place. Lets us be vigilant, but keep cool. I hope neither Baltimore nor Washington will be taken."[7]

Maryland's Governor, A. W. Bradford, wasn't waiting for Lincoln's reply. On 9 July he and Baltimore's Mayor John Lee Chapman issued a joint proclamation calling for volunteers to defend the city. The proclamation to the citizenry stated, "The invading enemy is by the last accounts approaching the city. Men, all the men that can be raised, are wanted, to occupy the fortifications already completed, and to prepare others. It is not important how you should come, but most important that you should come at once." Clearly, Baltimore would have to rely on its own citizens for its much-needed deliverance. And the response was gratifying. Hundreds of Black citizens answered the call, as well as men from every ward of the city. Two of Baltimore's main forts were totally manned by free and emancipated Black citizen soldiers. By 12 July Baltimore was protected by 2,488 regulars of Brigadier General James B. Ricketts' division of the VI Corp, plus about 500 Blacks, 200 sailors, 3,000 militia, and an uncounted array of armed civilians.

Wallace showed that Baltimore wasn't the Rebel's real target. In positioning his troops at the relative junction of the Baltimore Pike and the Washington Pike he could see which way Early's main units went if he failed to stop them. The bulk of the Rebel force headed south towards Washington.

Early proved something, too. In fighting Major General James B. Ricketts and his VI Corps troops at Monocacy, he had accomplished one of General Lee's main objectives for his mission. He had drawn Union troops away from the Petersburg campaign, but this realization presented a quandary: if VI Corps troops had been sent from Petersburg to Baltimore in time to reach Monocacy Junction, what else from the VI Corps might have been sent to Washington, and where were those men now?

CHAPTER 7

9 and 10 July—Taking Shelter

Until it was too late to flee, those that could safely move their possessions into either Baltimore or Washington did so. Wagons loaded with household goods clogged the roads. Others too far from either Baltimore or Washington hid their livestock and valuables. The Rebels were coming.

The general mood within Washington on 9 July was one of growing disgust. In his diary entry for the day, Adam Gurowski, the Polish nationalist and revolutionary who ruthlessly criticized most government officials, captured the sentiments of many when he wrote,

> What blunderings, and ignorance and shame! The military powers, the commanders…are ignorant of the whereabouts of the Rebels, of their number, and allow them to promenade undisturbed from one end of Maryland to another and all under the noses of our mighty ones and within reach of a good telescope! And their commander's blood does not boil to be thus slapped in the face and on both cheeks. It is impossible to decide what is most revolting to witness here. Is it cowardice—is it imbecility? The powers are scared out of their senses. We are taken by surprise, like monks, nuns, or chickens. Eagles we are not, and not bulls. We dare not show either talons or horns, and not even our faces. Oh! What a shame! A man with only the smallest courage would confound these Rebel marauders. It is impossible that they number scores of thousands. Fear sees double.[1]

Gurowski was always critical when it came to the likes of Henry Halleck, and others he disliked. He even devised a rating scheme that judged prominent Union leaders on a three-level leadership scale that included, "Praise," "Half and Half," and "Blame." Halleck was listed under the "Blame" column.

Gurowski's distain for Halleck extended beyond his military incapability's.[2] To Gurowski, who was a professional translator, Halleck was a poor excuse as a military historian, as a translator, and as the general-in-chief of the army. Gurowski was so rude and disrespectful that Lincoln, who was listed under Gurowski's "Half and Half" column as a leader, thought that if anyone was going to try to kill him, Gurowski would be the one. Many of the personal characterizations in his diaries were so demeaning and potentially inflammatory that Washington's district attorney, Edward S. Carrington, threatened to prosecute him for libel if his journals were ever published. They were published in installments. In the first segment, Gurowski, true to form, labeled the president a fool; the secretary of State a knave; the secretary of the Treasury a blockhead; and General Halleck a person beneath all possible contempt.[3] In 1864 *Harper's Weekly* characterized the first installment of his published diaries by saying, "a tornado of abuse whirls through the work from the first page to the last, overwhelming every one except a few arbitrary favorites of the author." The diary entries covering July 1864 were finally printed in 1866, the year Gurowski died. The final section of the published diary contains a highly unflattering page-by-page critique of Henry Halleck's faulty translation of Baron Henri Jomini's work on Napoleon's life.

On 9 July, about all the additional help the War Department knew it could rely on receiving was 3,500 militia from New York, which Secretary of War Stanton directed the state's governor to send by train as quickly as possible, and an unknown number of invalids from Philadelphia's military hospitals. What Stanton needed most was trained artillerymen. Luckily, the New Yorkers included 600 light artillerists and a detachment of the 9th Regiment of New York Heavy Artillery. These artillerymen were crucial because Washington's forts had a large number of pieces of heavy and light artillery, but few who knew how to use them. The opinion of the army's chief engineer in charge of the defense of Washington—Major General J.G. Barnard—to General Halleck was, "The militia regiments now garrisoning the forts scarcely know how to load or fire the guns." How fast these New Yorkers and Philadelphia convalescents could be mobilized and moved was a major question mark. Telegraphers on the B&O Railroad learned from their counterparts at the Philadelphia, Wilmington, and Baltimore Railroad that no troops would be leaving New York until 10 July, despite the fact that time was of the essence.[4]

What Lincoln suspected on 9 July, most Washingtonians learned on Sunday, 10 July. The residents realized something was seriously wrong when influential members of the government noticeably began being called out of church services all around town. After services, congregations began piecing things together, realizing that Washington and Baltimore were in Early's crosshairs.

By late afternoon other people throughout the North began holding their breath, too. Diary entries began filling with the latest war news. New Yorker Charles Willoughby Dayton wrote, "The Rebel Raid has turned out [to be] something after all and they are within 6 miles of Baltimore. Grant it is reported has dispatched part of his army to the defense of Washington."[5]

By 11:00 p.m., Henry Halleck wired Brigadier General Albion P. Howe at Harpers Ferry to link up his forces with those of General David Hunter and head for Washington as fast as possible. Halleck told Howe, "The indications now are that the enemy will attack this place or Baltimore." Taking no chances, at 8:45 a.m. on 10 July the army moved the invalid 10th Regiment of its Veteran Reserve Corps from Washington to Baltimore by B&O railcars. An additional invalid regiment of New Yorkers was sent by rail to Baltimore to help man the fortifications there as well. B&O Railroad President Garrett provided assistance in moving men over his line in special troop trains. This included transporting thousands of men to western Maryland through West Virginia to help pursue Early from the north. Garrett's station agents took control of the chaotic situations. The agent at Ellicott's Mills wired Garrett at 11:15 a.m. on 10 July: "Troops arriving slowly. We propose to load them as they arrive, as there are no officers here in charge of troops."[6] The company's telegraphers and railroad employees also served as the Union army's eyes and ears, furnishing as much intelligence as they could on Confederate troop movements. One report from Ellicott's Mills was that the sounds of gunfire were coming from two directions and that Union forces were being pushed back slowly towards the mill town. Garrett furnished every bit of this information directly to Secretary of War Stanton.

As valuable as these communications were, the two most important telegrams sent on 10 July were one from Lincoln to Lieutenant General Grant and the response. Wiring Grant from Washington at 2:30 p.m., Lincoln suggested that Grant leave a significant part of his army at Petersburg and immediately come to the capital with the rest of his men to take personal charge of the crisis there. He closed his recommendation saying, "This is what I think, upon your suggestion, and is not an order." Eight hours later Grant wired back from City Point, Virginia, saying that he was sending "an excellent officer"—Major General Wright—with a force sufficient to contend with any Rebel threats to Washington. Grant advised the president that Wright and his men would be there by the following evening.[7]

While this was happening, both sides at Petersburg were trying to find out what troops were converging on Washington. General Lee offered extended leave to any soldier who could capture a bluecoat who revealed what forces Grant was sending to relieve the Federal city, while Grant was hoping his men would capture a Rebel or find a deserter who might know how many

Confederates were assigned to Jubal Early. Both sides had trouble finding any answers. General Grant tasked "BABCOCK" with discovering the truth through her network and a steady stream of deserter chatter followed, but nothing significant pertained to Early. She was able to report to Grant that "It was rumored that Longstreet's corps was going to Maryland...."

As 10 July progressed, it was becoming abundantly clear that Early was in fact heading for the District of Columbia and that he was rumored to be at the head of an army of 40,000 to 50,000. This inflated troop count was ludicrous given the fact that Lee had reported in July 1864 that he had roughly 62,000 men fit for service in his entire force defending Petersburg and Richmond, but the Union wasn't sure what Lee's actual troop count was. Despite the absurd numbers being bantered about, many newspapers reported the 40,000–50,000 numbers, making it hard not to believe the misinformation. No one knew for sure what was real and what wasn't. Like the size of the invading army, speculation over its true intension quickly spread. Conflicting opinions ranged the force being merely a punitive raiding party intent on plundering as much as possible to things far more dire. Some believed the plan was for a full-blown attack to capture Washington. Others believed it was to seize the deposits of the Treasury Department, to capture or kill President Lincoln, or to attack with the goal of forcing Grant to pull forces away from Virginia. Washingtonians and other Northern citizens were full of conjecture.

The *Washington Chronicle* would ultimately put the numbers between 6,000 and 50,000 invaders, leaving a huge margin for error.

For some, like Charles Willoughby Dayton, a New York lawyer who was never fond of Abraham Lincoln and hated the idea of emancipation, it was hard to know whether he was happy or sad when he wrote in his diary, "Washington is in imminent danger. Troops are being called out to defend the City. In Baltimore the stores are being closed and disorder reigns in Washington."[8] Dayton was clearly hoping that Early might somehow turn back the clock. This is why he wrote on 13 July, "We have one thing to be thankful for at this very dark hour in the history of the Nation.... We must cheer as for I do wish the restoration of the Union as it was."[9] Dayton would never get his wish. Despite his longing for the past, by 1864 Emancipation was a cornerstone of the Union's war effort.

Washingtonians were indeed seeing the effects of that citywide mobilization.[10] In his diary entry for the evening of 10 July, Horatio Nelson Taft, a 58-year-old clerk with the Patent Office in Washington, wrote, "The street was nearly full of people and soldiers. We met fine Regiments going west or through Georgetown and it was quite an impressive sight to see so many bright bayonets gleaming in the dim gaslight and to listen to the amassed tread upon the pavement."[11] Initially, Taft believed there would be fighting on 11 July, but he thought it would be at Baltimore, but by nightfall on the 10th he accepted that Washington, not Baltimore, was the Rebels' real target. "Considerable skirmishing has been going on just outside of the line of Fortifications north of the City," he wrote. "But as yet there has been no general engagement. It is expected that there will be an attack upon the City tomorrow."[12] As the hours rolled by, Taft worked out why the Rebels were in front of Washington, prophesying, "If they do not attack tomorrow I think it will be because their object is not so much Washington or Baltimore as to obtain Horses, Cattle, and provisions and then they will attempt to slide off over the Potomac into Virginia and escape."[13] To defend the capital city, Taft wrote on 12 July, "The militia of the district has been called out and the clerks in the Department are preparing for duty."[14] On 13 July he concluded, "It has been a great 'scare' for the Country amounting to a great foraging expedition if this is the last of it, and I am inclined to think it is."

Others weren't sure what to think. In his diary entry on 11 July, Captain Edward Hill, an officer with the 16th Michigan Infantry who was on 30-days of leave, believed, "Washington appears to be the real point of the attack having only made a diversion on Baltimore." Hill, who later in the war would receive the Medal of Honor, was struck by the way the entire city was swept up in a combination of great excitement and high anxiety, the latter frame of mind exacerbated by the government's issuance of a proclamation calling for all citizens to take up arms.

That mobilization actually began early on 10 July when the War Department began pulling troops from every possible location based on a tally prepared by Major General Christopher C. Augur, commanding the Military District of Washington.

Augur's head count showed that, excluding civilian volunteers, there were about 12,300 soldiers "north of the Potomac" (on the Maryland side of the

Major General C. C. Augur. (Library of Congress)

river) and an additional 10,300 "south of the Potomac." This count included headquarters staff and hospital guards. Augur's report also included the fact that the army had 484 heavy artillery pieces arrayed around Washington and 29 field pieces, not counting whatever 12- and 24-pound boat howitzers could be borrowed from the Washington Navy Yard. Orders immediately went out to move every available man to Washington. Troops inside the city were consolidated into regiments regardless of whether they were part of the Army of the Potomac. "Use all those fit for duty, no matter where they belong," Major General Augur directed the colonel in charge of the rendezvous area. As soon as these hodgepodge regiments were formed, they were dispatched up 14th Street towards Fort Reno.

Colonel C. R. Lowell at Falls Church was among those who received a notice from headquarters. Lowell's order read, "I am directed by the major-general commanding to direct that you report with the Second Massachusetts Cavalry at these headquarters." Colonel William Gamble, commanding a training camp, was directed to provide 1,000 dismounted men armed as cavalry immediately to Washington, where horses would be provided as soon as they could be procured. This order was almost immediately amended, directing Gamble to send his by-now mounted troopers towards Rockville and Laurel, Maryland, to scout for the enemy. Gamble was told that if his men detected the enemy in force, they were to dispatch a courier to Washington and fall back on Fort Stevens. The army needed these horsemen to determine where the enemy was and in what strength. By 4 p.m. Major William Fry, commanding a unit cavalry of 400 men also sent to the vicinity of Rockville, reported that he expected to be engaged at any moment with Rebel forces. His advice to headquarters was to strengthen the forts in the vicinity of Tenleytown. He reported that the enemy column, which he estimated to include 5,000 horsemen, was moving in that direction and was a mile long, indicating great numbers. (A ploy used to give the impression of larger forces than were really present was to organize columns in groups of two men across instead of four or six men across. This made the overall column longer.)

Tenleytown, guarded principally by Fort Reno, now became the Union's focal point for the perceived attack. Lieutenant Colonel H. H. Wells was instructed to move four of his artillery batteries from the south side of the Potomac to Tenleytown without delay. A regiment of Ohio National Guard from Arlington, Virginia, was also directed to Fort Reno. The concentration of forces at Fort Reno, which was based upon Fry's best guess, was communicated to other field officers. Fry's force was compelled to fall back in confusion towards the fort when it ran low on ammunition. For much of the way, the Rebels pursued Fry's unit, but they broke off the chase about 2 miles outside town.

After marching for 20 miles, Early's force bivouacked just outside Rockville. From a civilian refuge, Major Coe Durland, commanding the 17th Pennsylvania Cavalry, confirmed that enemy cavalry had taken possession of Rockville between the hours of 5:00 and 6:00 p.m., but he also learned that the Confederate vanguard hadn't yet reached Brookeville.

On the tenth of July Federal forces began clamping down on civilian movements within the Federal city. The bridge over the northeastern branch of the Anacostia River was closed to civilian traffic, except where permits were secured from the War Department. If movements into the city were coming to a standstill, Rebel movements outside of town were unchecked everywhere.

A tintype of an unknown noncommissioned officer in the New York State Militia. (Library of Congress)

CHAPTER 8

The Way to Washington

The way to Washington was now wide open. There were only about 20 miles separating Early's troops from Washington, and no serious impediment existed between Rockville, Maryland, and the district line.

Confederate forces approached the Federal city on 11 July, principally from the northwest over two different routes. Brigadier General John McCausland's forces closed in on the Georgetown Pike, while the remainder approached the city via the Seventh Street Turnpike. A cavalry screen preceded each force and horsemen covered the entire army's left flank.

The only serious challenge the Rebels faced was the weather. The July heat was oppressive and the ground was parched from a severe lack of rain, a dry spell that had lasted for over a month and a half. The near 90-degree temperatures were debilitating. Thirst and choking dust made the march on Washington miserable. "While marching, the men were enveloped in a suffocating cloud of dust, and many of them fell by the wayside from exhaustion," wrote Early.[1] The labored progress gave the Federals a bit more time to plan and prepare. For the Rebels, the respite of the tree-lined banks of Rock Creek, Paint Branch, and Sligo Creek, just outside the city, with their much diminished yet cooling spring-fed waters, was a welcome relief as they waited for stragglers and slowly fanned out in front of Washington. Exhausted, some Southern units bivouacked at the farm of John Wilson, in what is now Woodside, Maryland,[2] and on the low bluffs along Rock Creek, the Sligo, and Paint Branch shortly after noon on the 11th.

Immediately, Early posted a thin line of pickets from Robert Rodes's division in the woods along Seventh Street, facing Fort Stevens, with orders to occupy the Federal works if that was at all possible. For Early and

Rodes, the sparseness of the dispersed skirmishers served as a precaution against their coming under heavy fire from the forts. For the Union officers inside the fortifications, the sparseness might also have indicated that the Rebels had only a few forces available, which that morning was indeed the case. Unbeknownst to Federal officers, Early's entire force at Washington numbered about 9,500, *if* he was capable of quickly bringing them all together for a coordinated action. Unfortunately, because of the heat, thirst, and exhaustion, he was incapable of accomplishing that. Robert Rodes commanded about 3,000 soldiers. This was about one-third of the entire Rebel force Early would have at Washington, once they all staggered in. Immediately sending Rodes's men to capture the well-fortified, yet lightly defended city, without the full support of his own artillery and any additional forces assembled in mass to exploit any possible breakthrough, was madness. The defenders, securely ensconced behind well-prepared fortifications, had a distinct advantage. They stood a greater chance of surviving an attack by a numerically superior enemy force, and Early's attacking force was going to be vastly outnumbered, albeit initially by armed civilians, militiamen, invalid soldiers, and an odd collection of military units. The advantage of those ragtag Union defenders was due to their being ensconced behind thoughtfully planned earthworks, fortifications constructed in accordance with Dennis Hart Mahan's 1856 treatise on field defenses. This work, which was prepared principally as a practical reference guide for cadets at West Point for locating, planning, and constructing defensive fortifications, was used throughout the Civil War by both sides. To Mahan's way of thinking, fortifications leveled the playing field for just the type of defenders who were momentarily being called upon to protect Washington:

> To suppose irregular forces capable of coping on equal terms with disciplined troops, is to reason, not only against all probability, but against a vast weight of testimony to the contrary. It is not indeed that discipline confers individual courage; certainly a greater proportion of this essential military virtue will, in all cases, be found among the militia, composed as it must be of men of a higher grade of moral and intellectual qualities, than is to be met with among the common soldiery of any country. But these men, with all the superior advantages that must actuate the volunteer, necessarily want that indispensable element of success, in pitched battles, which results from discipline and habitual training. Called out on a particular emergency, with little or no previous exercise in the services they are required to render, militia cannot have that shoulder-to-shoulder courage, by which men are animated, who have served long together, which begets a reliance on each other, and a confidence in their chiefs, and which is one of the surest guaranties of victory. But place the militia soldier on his natural field of battle, behind a breastwork, and an equilibrium between him and his more disciplined enemy is immediately established....[3]

Additionally, in following Mahan's guidance in laying out the forts, the killing field between the enemy and the fortifications provided the irregular defenders with clear fields of fire and little cover for the seasoned attackers. The aiming instructions for the civilian defenders was based upon the practice of the French: at 110 yards or less, aim for the breast; at 110 to 150 yards, aim from one of the shoulders; and at 150 to 200 yards, aim for the head.

Jubal Early arrived in front of Fort Stevens as Robert Rodes was deploying his skirmishers. At first glance the fortifications appeared to be feebly manned, but the works were exceptionally well laid out. There were earthen strong points every thousand yards or so, artillery placements between the strong points, interlocking rifle trenches surrounding the whole city, and palisades and abattis in front of ditches. Beyond that was a 15-mile-long, half-mile-wide, no-man's-land. This was the ideal killing zone for the use of Union grape and canister shot. In looking at the Union positions Early concluded, "every application of science and unlimited means had been used to render the fortifications around Washington as strong as possible."[4]

The fortifications were also ideally suited for long-range artillery use against smaller Confederate field artillery. The rifling of a Federal 100-pounder gave it superior range and accuracy. Explosive shells from such guns would be effectively used to set fire to several houses being used by Confederate sharpshooters in front of Fort Stevens. The guns could also fire cannister. Cannister was a load of small balls that sprayed towards a target when the

This pair of 4.2-inch (30-pound) Parrott rifles, mounted on mobile siege carriages, are similar to some of what protected Fort Stevens in 1864. They had a maximum effective range of 1.7 miles at a 25-degree elevation. A far more accurate and deadly range was 1,500 yards when the elevation was set at 3.5 degrees. Stacks of explosive shells are shown ready for use. (Library of Congress)

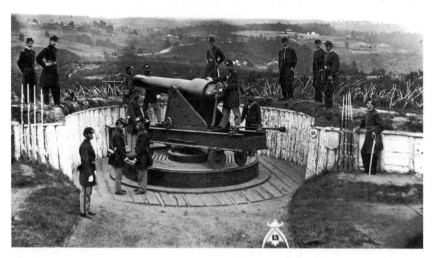

This large, 100-pound pivoting Parrott gun at Fort Totten, to the right of Fort Stevens, was supported by a number of smaller 4.2-inch Parrott rifles that were mounted on siege carriages, as well as fixed-placement 32-pound seacoast guns. The smaller, 30-pound Parrott's were highly mobile. As a result, concentrations of them could be moved from fort to fort to create super batteries if necessary. The defensive entanglement of tree limbs and the degree of the exposed field of fire in front of the fort can be seen beyond the battery. (Library of Congress)

container that held them ruptured during firing. At a 5-degree elevation, the range of explosive shells and canisters fired from a 100-pound Parrott rifle was about 1,700 yards. One soldier wrote to a friend after the battle, swearing that he witnessed 38 Rebels being killed by a single exploding shell. He also said that another shell went completely through a farmhouse and exploded in the backyard, killing a Confederate captain in his tent.

Likewise, a Union prisoner held in Francis Preston Blair's orchard recalled seeing Union artillery fire passing over the fruit trees nearly 2 miles from the fortifications, illustrating their guns' great range.[5]

Jubal Early clearly knew all of this and realized that the moment he organized his soldiers into an obvious line of battle in front of the forts, his men would come under a fierce shelling. It was not uncommon for attacking commanders to form up their men about a half mile from their target. Once organized, they would rapidly move to within one-quarter mile of the enemy to launch their attack. To cover that distance, they'd begin at a fast march and would finally rush at the objective when they were within a few hundred yards. Within 400 yards, the defenders would begin using grape and canister to repulse the attackers. While that distance might take less than 15 minutes

Fort Totten and many other forts had smaller ordnance that had a range of about a mile. (Library of Congress)

to cover, getting past the tangle of fallen timbers in front of the forts would take far longer than that, and at a very high cost. During all this, the carnage from so many large and small guns firing simultaneously would be massive. A trained gun crew could load and fire a 100-pound Parrott rifle with explosive shells in roughly 40 seconds. When manned by a good gun crew, the smaller 4.2-inch Parrott had a somewhat faster rate of fire. This meant that Early's soldiers, and his artillery, were extremely vulnerable within one-third to three-quarters of a mile. And Fort Stevens was well armed with an array of ordnance that July, including four 24-pound fixed-position seacoast guns and six 24-pound mobile siege guns. Using 6 pounds of powder, a 24-pounder's effective range was 850 yards at 1-degree elevation. At 4 degrees with the same charge, it was 1,900 yards. Union requirements called for up to 100 rounds of all types for each gun to be held in the fort's magazines.[6] There were also five 30-pound moveable Parrott guns and a pair of 8-inch siege howitzers, plus a pair of mortars. And there was triangulated and measured fire support from the forts on either side of Fort Stevens.

For these reasons Early had to be extremely cautious about committing his artillery and men to any headlong attack. He knew that as soon as his own smaller guns went into action, the smoke from their discharges would give away their relative positions and the Federal gunners would respond from multiple locations using their more abundant and much larger guns to create a withering counterfire with explosive shells, and the fragments from these explosive shells would have been extremely lethal. Additionally, closer in, grape and canister and double-canister charges from the fort's smaller

This is one of the seacoast guns at Fort Totten, shown in its rolled-back position from its usual forward firing position to accommodate the artillerymen. The range of this smoothbore gun was about 1,920 yards with an 8-pound charge. Each of the northernmost forts—DeRussy, Stevens, Slocum, and Totten—was roughly spaced a mile apart, giving them overlapping zones of artillery coverage. This allowed the forts on either side to shell the flanks of an attacking force, funneling them into the guns of the fort they were facing. (Library of Congress)

Union artillerymen from Massachusetts at Fort Totten in front of a field piece and unharnessed limber. This is the size of field artillery that accompanied Jubal Early's raiders. Clearly his guns were simply no match for the range and destructive power of Washington's heavy artillery. (Library of Congress)

Most of the forts surrounding Washington were on the highest points, such as Fort Slemmer, depicted here, on what is now part of the campus of Catholic University of America. (Library of Congress)

guns would have been used to mow down the advancing Rebel soldiers. If attacked, the Union had an artillery plan to concentrate all cannon fire on sweeping the ground in front of the forts at 600 yards, using double-shotted guns.[7] And concentrated rifle fire would have been added by the soldiers and civilians massed in the rifle trenches forward of and flanking the forts. The final obstacles in any attack were the thick lines of fallen trees in front of the forts and large ditches. The jumble of interlocking branches, which had been sharpened into points, would break up any massed formations that remained, and once any Rebels entered the ditches in front of the fortifications, the defenders were to throw in hand grenades. According to inventories, many of Washington's forts had about 500 hand grenades on hand in their magazines.[8]

Union gunners were instructed to aim wisely. They were cautioned, "A few shots effectively thrown is better than a large number badly directed. The object of killing is to inspire terror so as to deter or drive off the enemy, and precision of fire, and consequently certainty of execution, is infinitely more important in effecting this than a great noise, rapid fire, and less proportional execution." One problem with that order was that the artillerymen had never fired many of the guns defending Washington before, for fear of hitting private property. That July marked the first real live-fire tests for many of Washington's artillery pieces.

While there were no 100-pound Parrott guns at Gettysburg, Union artillerymen in Washington liked the larger Parrott gun because it was considered to be relatively safe and easy for inexperienced crews to operate. A treatise on artillery published in 1865 described this as a gun that could

The ammunition magazine for the 11 guns mounted at Fort Kearny, near Tenleytown, between Forts Reno and DeRussy. (Library of Congress)

be used "without serious risk of damage by exposure and maltreatment in the hands of green artillerists." Those were precisely the kind of gunners who were initially tasked with manning some of the guns at Washington.

Between April 1861 and April 1864, the West Point Foundry at Cold Spring, New York, furnished 444 of its proprietary cast-iron 100-pound reinforced Parrott guns to the Federal army and navy. Some of these big guns protected Washington, particularly at the forts anchoring the defenses along the Potomac River and at strategic high points around the city. Because of their exceptional range, they afforded an excellent degree of protective fire for other forts. While Fort Stevens didn't have a 100-pound Parrott, it was bracketed by forts that did. The single 100-pound Parrott gun at Fort DeRussy, for example, provided fire support for Fort Stevens, shelling Confederate troop movements at a range of up to 4,500 yards. In all, Fort DeRussy, to the left of Fort Stevens, fired 32 100-pound shells at the Rebel raiders. Fort Totten, to the right of Fort Stevens, also had its 100-pounder in action during Early's raid.

As for the prospects of freeing the prisoners at Point Lookout, Early wrote in his *Memoirs* that the prison break was to be attempted "if the attempt [to get into Washington] was successful."[9] The prospects of that were dim. At 4:23 a.m. on 12 July, Major General Alexander McDowell McCook, at Fort Stevens, informed Major General Christopher C. Auger, "Everything is quiet on our front this morning." By noon on 12 July, it was obvious that getting into Washington wasn't ever going to happen. That had to be quickly communicated to Bradley Johnson, who, with his Maryland cavalry, was out marauding around Maryland.

McCook's original "Everything is quiet on our front this morning" message as received by Major General C. C. Auger on 12 July. (Library of Congress)

Another of the question marks surrounding the Early raid and the attempt to free the prisoners at Point Lookout was when Bradley Johnson was advised to wave it off. One historian has claimed that Johnson was advised on 11 July to give up on the raid. This coincided precisely with Jefferson Davis pulling the plug on the naval components of the operation. But this couldn't be, unless Early suffered a brain freeze when he wrote his *Memoirs*. In it he stated that on 12 July, "Johnson had burned the bridges over the Gunpowder, on the Harrisburg and Philadelphia roads, threatened Baltimore, and started for Point Lookout, but I sent an order for him to return."[10] Clearly, the wave-off of the prison raid came on 12 July, not the previous day. This would better account for the time it would have taken to get word to Early, who passed the order along to Johnson.

An additional factor weighing on Early's mind was that on 11 July he clearly lacked the element of surprise in front of Washington. The Federals had known he was coming for well over a week and that likely eliminated the initial premise he was told to act under, which was that the forts would be either undefended or lightly defended. He now had to accept that he'd be attacking well-prepared, fixed fortifications that were heavily armed, if even by thousands of ill-trained civilians and this gave him pause. These circumstances furnished the defenders with a significant advantage, despite potentially having questionable numbers or lesser-trained men. Early knew that in balance, any potential full-scale frontal attack could likely result in a Confederate blood bath, one that might even cost him the bulk of his command. Instead, he opted to create a scare. Early admitted that he'd settled for that, telling Major Henry Kyd Douglas, "Major, we haven't taken Washington, but we scared Abe Lincoln like hell."[11]

Others saw even greater consequences. On the heels of that scare, Charles A. Dana, the Union's assistant secretary of war, believed, "The black and revolting dishonor of this siege of Washington with all its circumstances of poltroonery and stupidity is yet too fresh and its brand is too stinging for one to have cool judgment regarding its probable consequences." That "cool judgment" would indeed be a long time in coming.

* * *

Chances of a successful effort by the city's civilian defenders—many of them farmers, mechanics, merchants, clerks, and professional men—were hard to predict, if they didn't get help. The Rebel odds were unpredictable, too, and about to become even worse. Before any attack order from Early could be carried out, a huge cloud of dust was seen behind the fortifications, indicating the arrival of a large body of Union soldiers moving towards the forts. These new arrivals were veterans. They included men with the most needed military skills—artillerists—to man the guns of the forts. Within minutes of their arrival, Union skirmishers appeared and Federal artillery began firing on the Rebel picket positions. Early now realized that what he had hoped might be a win had just become a miserable impossibility.

Early deployed his forces, with John Bell Gordon and Major General Robert Rodes positioned astride Georgetown Pike on the left of town, and Stephen Dodson Ramseur and Daniel Harvey Hill posted astride the Brookville Turnpike on the right.

Early needed to know what he now was facing. Union commanders needed to know the same about the enemy now confronting them, too. The stare down lasted all that day, punctuated by an occasional pot shot from either side.

The Federal army had the added burden of trying to determine who was actually in command of the defense of the district. There were several contenders for the honor. Lincoln had appointed a commanding officer. Stanton had selected someone else. Halleck had designated a third. And Grant had appointed a fourth. There should have been no debate over who should have command of the field given the fact that Grant had made his choice and he was the army's lieutenant general, a rank originally held by George Washington. Henry Halleck should have had no say in the matter. He had been redesignated the army's chief of staff, an administrative function that meant that he was principally expected to keep the army's necessary paperwork moving. Stanton's opinion was well meaning, but he was perhaps in such a panicked dither that he might not have been thinking clearly about the implications of his choice, either. Navy Secretary Gideon Welles blamed Halleck, Stanton, and Grant for this mix up, believing them all to be "asleep or dumb."

Major General Alexander M. McCook. (Library of Congress)

Luckily, Major General Alexander McDowell McCook was thinking clearly. He adroitly sifted through the egos, political and personal connections, and conflicting orders to come up with a workable leadership structure that seemed to satisfy everyone by giving each contender a significant frontline command. McCook assumed overall command. In this command, he placed himself at the tip of the spear.

Major General Quincy A. Gillmore, in addition to his command and divisional oversight, was given responsibility for all of the northeastern forts, including Fort Lincoln. He was to ensure that all the eastern approaches on the Maryland side of the city were defended. He was a brilliant civil engineer who understood the superior capabilities of earthen fortifications over fixed brick forts. He also had a superb knowledge of siege tactics and the use of rifled artillery.

Montgomery Meigs, newly minted major general and head of the Quartermaster Corps, was given command of Fort Totten.

Brigadier General Martin D. Hardin was given command of the north-western forts flanking the left side of the city facing Maryland. Hardin was a family friend of President Lincoln. He had graduated from West Point in 1859 and received his appointment to brigadier on 6 July 1864.

General Horatio G. Wright and his VI Corps, and about 600 convalescents, served as a reserve force that could be shifted via Military Road, a roadway built by Wright in 1861 to link the forts in Washington to any point that might be threatened by a breakthrough. Wright also was responsible for the frontline pickets and skirmishers.

McCook's cobbled together command structure comprised a mixed bag of abilities and baggage. McCook himself had been given a court-martial hearing because of the Union disaster at Chickamauga in 1863 but was exonerated. Despite being vindicated, he was languishing in Washington without a command as Early approached. Gillmore was highly respected as an artillery officer. He had proven his skills by helping to turn Fort Sumter into a mound of rubble. Commanding the Union army's land campaign on Morris Island, outside Charleston, South Carolina, he had been at odds with his commanding officer and, as a result, was banished to Washington. Gillmore also didn't get along with his naval counterpart at Charleston, Rear Admiral John Dahlgren, and had orchestrated an unsuccessful campaign to have him removed. In September 1863 Welles caught wind of the fact that things weren't right between Gillmore and Dahlgren. He had heard rumors that Gillmore had requested to be relieved of command but brushed it off as mischievous gossip. By then Dahlgren caught on to the backstabbing, and he and Gillmore dropped all pretense of amity. At Gillmore's bidding, two of his officers visited Secretary Welles in October to denounce Dahlgren. They insisted that the naval officer was incompetent and insane, and they shared some of the unpleasant letters exchanged between Dahlgren and Gillmore as evidence. Welles was certain the two officers, Brigadier General Alfred Terry and Colonel Joseph Hawley, were wrong. He realized that because both had strong ties to Connecticut, Welles's home state, Gillmore had deliberately chosen them as his emissaries, expecting they'd receive a sympathetic audience, but the secretary immediately smelled a rat. He recognized that they, and by extension Gillmore, were prejudiced against his naval officer. Dahlgren, he insisted, had no such impediments. Instead, Welles believed Dahlgren was merely enfeebled by bouts of debilitating seasickness, which was true. Following the unpleasant meeting, Welles confided to his diary about Dahlgren, writing that his "cold, selfish, and ambitious nature has been wounded, but he is neither a fool nor insane." This backstabbing effort backfired, turning Welles against Gillmore.

Meigs was the army's principal supply officer. He worked wonders in that capacity but was seen as a military bureaucrat. Few gave him any credit for possessing any tactical or field command capabilities.

Hardin was considered one of Lincoln's favorites, one of his pet wunderkinds.

Wright was Grant's chosen surrogate, and he quickly realized, as his boss had thought, that Washington was going to be a temporary sideshow. His arrival was wildly cheered, and his presence allowed the locals to feel safer. His arrival was met with much rejoicing and a collective sigh of relief. His troops were there to blunt any serious attempts to take the town, but he quickly got the sense that Early's meager showing wasn't a serious attempt to assault the city. The skirmishing throughout the day on 12 July was an indication that Early was just buying time. As a result, Wright rightly figured that once the Rebels had acquired enough booty, it would be Early's turn to make the next move by making a quick exit before getting attacked from multiple sides by the gathering enemy forces. That subsequent pursuit included Wright's VI Corps.

Wright's reserves were positioned behind Fort Stevens and the supporting batteries on land near the farm of Thomas Blagden, a successful lumber merchant and extensive real estate developer in the District of Columbia. Among Blagden's many holdings was the site for what became St. Elizabeth's Hospital. The Blagden family was among the founding families of the Federal city. Thomas's father was one of the city's best stonecutters and served as the chief stonecutter for the Capitol. Thomas Blagden was one of the incorporators of the Washington National Monument Society, which was chartered by Congress in 1859 to raise the funds to build the Washington Monument. His Civil War-era farm was just inside the city's fortified perimeter. It was situated on a prominent plateau overlooking the town and surrounding countryside. Known originally as "Argyle" and later renamed "Crestwood," the farm was purchased by Thomas Blagden from the cash-strapped Russian ambassador to the United States, Count Alexander de Bodisco, in October 1853. The count had used the property as his summer retreat. The area around Crestwood served as the campsite for the labor details assigned to build Fort Stevens. A soldier stationed there in 1861 called it the area a "stinking hole," likely because of the stench of Blagden's bone mill nearby, which crushed rendered animal bones into bone meal. The farmhouse was so near the scene of the conflict that friends were anxious about the Blagden family's safety. The first the Blagdens knew about the approaching Rebels was the news that startled many Washingtonians on coming out of church on Sunday, 10 July. Riding home from that service, they saw an ambulance and some riders coming towards them and supposed

Tintype of an unknown soldier eating an apple. (Library of Congress)

it was a neighboring family that was already fleeing, but on closer approach the family determined that the party consisted of McCook and his staff in search of a place to establish his field headquarters. While Blagden's farmhouse might have proved ideal, it was located a bit off the beaten path. Instead, McCook selected a roadhouse and tavern on the Seventh Street Pike and Missouri Avenue. In just a matter of hours McCook had worked an organizational miracle.

Gideon Welles had no such command and control problems within the navy. During the crises, the navy was prepared for the worst. It had a vessel on standby at the Washington Navy Yard to take Lincoln and the Cabinet away from the capital in case Federal troops failed to repulse Early's force.

CHAPTER 9

The Rebels Take Their Toll

The 9 July edition of the *Alexandria Gazette* announced, "The Market this morning was very well supplied, the country people coming in with a more than usual quantity of vegetables and fruits—but the prices not only keep up, but have a tendency to an increase in some cases." Those increases were a result of the pending Rebel raid, and they were about to get worse. Hoarding and price gouging occurred on 10 July. The sudden price spikes shocked area shoppers. According to the *Bedford (Pennsylvania) Inquirer*, "provision prices became 'panicy [sic]'" in Washington. Although nowhere near as severe as what was being experienced throughout the South, the increases were described as "awful in the extreme" by one Washington shopper. Clearly the true depravities of war, not previously visited upon Washingtonians prior to that July, had arrived. In one day, flour went from $20 to $25 a barrel. Butter went from 50 cents to 75 cents. Rabbits jumped from 35 cents to 40 cents. Mutton went from 30 cents to 35 cents a pound. Bacon increased from 25 cents to 30 cents a pound, and brown sugar rose from 35 cents to 40 cents. Customers were told they could expect even higher prices in the near future if conditions worsened. When it did, some merchants quickly hiked up their prices by 300 or 400 percent. This prompted the *Washington Star* to write, "This charging of such exorbitant prices for the necessities of life, when no scarcity really existed, and when unwarranted by any circumstances which has transpired in the recent season of excitement, is totally unjustified, and should call down the most severe and unqualified public denunciation." The *Star*'s idea was to compile a citywide boycott list of such greedy merchants.

These overnight price increases were nothing compared to those suffered in the South, where food shortages and high prices were pervasive. Since the start of the war Southern food prices had skyrocketed to exorbitant levels. Things got so bad in 1863 that food riots erupted in Richmond and in other cities. Mobile, Alabama, sustained bread riots in 1863,[1] as did Montgomery, where weapon-wielding women ransacked shops for food reportedly while carrying banners demanding "Bread or Death."

The Richmond rioters, who were mostly women, were dismissed as being poor trash, prostitutes, petty thieves, and Northern agitators. One bystander who witnessed the food riots in Richmond knew better, recording in her diary that most of the women were simply emaciated. One young girl particularly stood out in the writer's mind. Although she was pleasantly dressed, her frail limbs resembled twigs. Rather than facing what the protesters actually were— starving—the press pilloried them as worthless hags. Instead, the women were desperately hungry and growing tired of the war. They wanted their men home and food to eat. To help quell the rioting in the Confederate capital, the protestors were provided with small amounts of rice from government stores. After that, Richmond's home guard occupied the streets with orders to impose the riot act as necessary. In the chaos of trying to feed the army while also trying to satisfy a modicum of the civilian needs, Jefferson Davis sacked his supply chief for inefficiency. Given the circumstances, the replacement, Brigadier General Alexander Lawton, worked wonders, but prices remained high. In Richmond in 1864, corn meal went for $225 a barrel, potatoes went for $3 a quart, tomatoes were $4, and apples were $1.50. Onions were $1 each, if buyers could find them; they were the one item that was said to never seem to drop in price. One Richmond newspaper identified the reason for the scarcity, reporting, "It is astounding to see what lengths gentlemen connected with the Confederate army will go for the very smallest kind of onions." A short time later, in a letter to the editor of the *Richmond Whig* submitted by "Housekeeper" and addressed to "The Vegetable People," the exasperated writer protested on behalf of many Southern consumers, saying, "How is a man of moderate means to pay his expenses, when the vegetable people ask such prices from their truck?" A few weeks later the *Whig* reported, "The markets were, as is usual on Monday, poorly supplied this morning. The beef was wretched, and vegetables and fruits scarce and inferior." By the time of this report, Richmond's fruit and vegetable vendors had learned to offer their best produce on Saturdays, selling to a select list of customers for top dollar because that was when most of their better clients were paid. In January 1864 Elizabeth Van Lew recorded in her diary something she was told by a street vender: "There is starvation panic upon the people."[2] To this she added, "I do not think it is yet as desperate as many imagine, but in all this there is great consolation."

Things were worse elsewhere. In Atlanta at about the time of Early's arrival on Washington's doorsteps, flour cost $250 a barrel, butter cost $15 a pound, and bacon was $5 a pound. In Wilmington, North Carolina, lamb quarters were going for $100, and tea was being offered for $500 a pound. One Southern belle pledged to forgo her next silk dress for just one pound of good tea. In ports like Wilmington, about the only ones who could afford such prices were criminals and those engaged in blockade-running. Elsewhere in the South, quinine was said to have cost upwards of $150 an ounce, and wool fetched $85 a yard, if they were available at all.

For many Southern civilians, flour and salt became nearly unobtainable, except through barter. The operator of a salt factory in Savannah, Georgia, offered to trade four bushels of salt for five bushels of corn and peas, or one bushel of salt for a good pair of shoes. By 1864 Confederate navy lieutenant John Wilkinson's servant frequently returned from the market in Wilmington with an empty shopping basket because she could not afford the high prices demanded for meat and produce.

For that brief period in July, Washington's shoppers were returning with empty market baskets, too. Many began to question how they were going to be able to feed their families if prices continued to rise and market stalls began to empty out.

By 11 July, Washington's markets were crowded with residents and refuges vying for whatever was available. "The city filled with strangers," wrote Edward Hill in his diary. Washington's government workers were already hard-pressed to pay for necessities, having been forced to accept paper

"Advantage of 'Famine Prices,'" a *Harper's Weekly* cartoon from 1863 relating to the shortage of quinine in the Confederacy. (Library of Congress)

Confederate navy lieutenant John Wilkinson. (Naval History and Heritage Command)

currency in their pay envelopes, money that had about half the purchasing power of gold or silver coinage. For a lowly clerk like Horatio Nelson Taft, making ends meet under normal circumstances was hard enough, but now it was nearly impossible. Fuel for his hearth and food for his table had become very expensive. Coal was $13, oak wood was $11 a cord, and a cord of pine was $8. Ham was 35 cents a pound. Taft began to question whether working for the Federal government was worth it, confiding to his diary that July, "A place in the Government Department is not worth much now with the old salaries which were fixed when gold was paid but is now paid in 'paper'...." In short order, residents took to writing family members and friends in other cities, asking what food might be available from there. One Washingtonian requested of a professional acquaintance, "Should you go to Philadelphia please send me word what hams can be bought from there with the address of the parties." By 20 July the *Alexandria Gazette* was able to report, "Produce is beginning to arrive freely in Baltimore, and prices are receding. Good news."

At least in Washington that summer it was safe to walk the streets. In Wilmington even walking during in daylight was dangerous. Many wealthy residents simply fled to the country. Those with nowhere to go kept largely to themselves, seldom venturing out. "The town was infested with rogues and desperadoes, who made a livelihood by robbery and murder," wrote John Wilkinson in his narrative of the war years. "It was unsafe to venture into the suburbs at night, and even in daylight there were frequent conflicts in the public streets." Ladies in Wilmington were rarely seen in public.

On Tuesday, 12 July, Washington's stores were closed and soldiers from the provost marshal's command filled the streets to maintain order and cordon off sections of the city deemed off limits.

Although many former slaves had little left but their rags and their personal pride and patriotism, they gladly lent a hand in strengthening Washington's defenses in July 1864. (Library of Congress)

If food was in short supply inside the city, outside of town the Confederates were eating high on the hog. Corn was a staple of the Confederate army, but while the Maryland countryside was dotted with thriving cornfields, the intruders seemed to take few sacks and barrels of ears, except for use as fodder for captured pigs. The alternatives were simply too tempting to pass up for another mouthful of corn.

That July Early's marauding Second Corps feasted on captured poultry, pork, and beef. Pig-wise, the Confederates ate everything but the oink. Poultry-wise, it was said that around Washington, the clucking and crowing of chickens wouldn't be heard for the rest of the summer with all the birds being roasted by the Rebels. Beef bones became common camp litter. Empty and broken wine and liquor bottles from many local wine cellars or cupboards also became common camp waste, the contents happily consumed by the wishful captors of the capital.

In visiting the burnt-out ruins of Montgomery Blair's home, Mary Henry and her father observed the ashes of many Rebel campfires and great piles of feathers, attesting to the banquet enjoyed during the days before.

Inside the city the sale of liquor was prohibited by military decree at any place on Seventh or 14th Streets, north of F Street. This order remained in effect until 14 July.

Outside the city, anything that households had put up for the winter was subject to plunder. Flour, salt, baking soda, and baking powder, if it could be found, was foraged for biscuits as a relished alternative to cornbread, a Confederate staple. Coffee was a prized find. Because of the Union naval blockade of the South, what passed as Confederate coffee was brewed from parched wheat, peanuts, peas, or corn.

In addition to food, whenever possible, carpets, mattresses, and whole bedroom sets were liberated from houses for use as comfortable campsite bedding. Despite General Lee's pleas to treat Northern civilians with the utmost respect and civility, many houses, once stripped of usable contents, were set on fire by individual Rebel soldiers as payback for Southern desolation.

Union officers were burning houses, too, to keep them from being used by Rebel sharpshooters. In one instance a Union officer politely asked a petrified resident for a lamp wick and some cotton cloth. Already numb

Pencil sketch of four Confederate cavalrymen captured in the Shenandoah Valley, drawn by Edwin Forbes for *Frank Leslie's Illustrated Newspaper.* Many Southern horsemen attacking Washington didn't have regulation uniforms. They also had to furnish their own mounts and much of their gear. (Library of Congress)

with fright over having invaders near her home, she obediently obliged. "What do you want to do with these things?" she timidly asked. "Burn your house Madame" was the matter-of-fact reply. The poor woman was given barely enough time to remove a few of her meager possessions before her house was put to the torch. She lost most of what little she had, according to Mary Henry in her diary.[3]

CHAPTER 10

Outside Baltimore

The house of Maryland's governor, Augustus Bradford, outside Baltimore was among those burned by elements of Bradley Johnson's force. According to a bystander, who was detained by the Rebel squad of 10 horsemen while they burned the property, they had an order from Johnson saying, in effect, "The house of Governor Bradford to be burned in retaliation for the burning of [Virginia] Governor Letcher's house by Federal troops" under the command of Major General David Hunter in June 1864. Everything was destroyed, including Bradford's books, papers, furniture, and clothes. This Rebel unit also had orders to burn railway bridges and rolling stock, cut telegraph lines, and destroy tracks. The raiding party around Baltimore reportedly consisted of about 1,500 horsemen, but such counts were always suspect. They set upon the small number of Union guards protecting the Magnolia River crossing, capturing all 20 with no difficulty. The Rebels raiders boasted that all 40,000 of them would be in Washington the following day. There weren't nearly that many Rebels under Early's command as that, but that is how the rumors of the size of Early's army got deliberately started. The Confederates wanted folks to believe they were the vanguard of a much larger and more powerful force. And the lie worked.

In seizing the Gunpowder River bridge west of Baltimore, Union Major General William B. Franklin, on medical leave, was captured by a party of about 200 Rebels while he was aboard a Harrisburg and Philadelphia train. According to an account published in the *Baltimore American* on 14 July, Major General Franklin, who was in civilian attire, was thought to have been fingered by other passengers who were apparently willing to give him up to perhaps save their own skins. He was taken prisoner and transported by carriage to Towson, Maryland, and from there to Reisterstown, a short distance away, where the party rested for the night. Franklin told his captors that he was sick and needed to rest. He faked falling asleep, waiting for his guards to do likewise. Once he was certain that they were indeed asleep, which was clear from their snoring, he escaped. He ran for more than 45 minutes in the direction of what he hoped was Baltimore. Exhausted from his mad dash, he spent the remainder of that night hiding in a grove. The next morning he kept to the woods in his trek to safety. Thirsty, hungry, and exhausted, he lucked upon a pair of farmers who gave him shelter. With the Rebels out looking for Franklin, one of the farmers, rather than allowing him to continue to Baltimore, went to alert the Federals to his whereabouts. At about midnight on 13 July, a carriage with an armed escort set out to pick up Franklin and bring him back to Baltimore. By morning he was recuperating from his ordeal at Barnum's Hotel.

There was also a rumor that Senator Charles Sumner was also on the train and was captured at the Gunpowder River, but one frustrated newspaper editor told his readers, "The report about Senator Sumner…was like a thousand other things about the late raid—a canard."

The reports that Gunpowder Bridge was largely destroyed wasn't true, either, but as far as the Federals knew, the bridges across the Bush and Back Rivers were destroyed. A typical ploy of the raiders was said to have included running any captured railway cars onto a bridge before setting everything on fire. The weight of an engine and its tender was supposed to help to collapse the spans, and any wooden cars pulled in with it only added fuel to the fire.

The War Department in Washington was in the dark regarding much of what was going on around Baltimore. Telegraph wires were said to have been cut almost everywhere, but the truth was that they were cut at Beltsville and a few other places around College Park. The Navy Department was asked to dispatch gunboats to the Gunpowder River and to Havre de Grace as precautions against further Rebel activities, but Navy Secretary Welles worried that the ships wouldn't arrive in time to make much of a difference against the fast-moving Rebel raiding parties.[1] USS *Fuchsia*, assigned to the navy's Potomac Flotilla, was among the vessels hastily dispatched to Baltimore. What *Fuchsia* lacked in firepower, it more than made up for with its shallow draft, which allowed it to get in close to any bridge or shoreline. This enabled it to provide fire support that could keep any Rebel raiders at bay.

Many houses around Baltimore were said to have been burned, including the farmhouse of Ishmael Day, who lived about 13 miles outside the city. On 11 July, Day flew an American flag from his gatepost. This act of

USS *Fuchsia,* based upon a pen-and-wash drawing by Clary Ray, done in 1896. (Naval History and Heritage Command)

patriotism may not have been the smartest move the roughly 65-year-old man ever made, as it only served to attract the Rebels. Two of Major Harry Gilmor's soldiers descended on Day's farm, and one grabbed the flag and ripped it down, calling it a "damned old rag." At this point, the crusty old farmer became defiant and rushed inside to grab his two shotguns from his second-story bedroom. While the Rebels were bunching up the flag to make off with it, Day shot at them from the upstairs window. The buckshot mortally wounded one. Shocked by the weathered old man's bravado, the other Confederate galloped off. Within minutes Day heard the sounds of more horses coming towards his house. The farmer grabbed a pepperbox pistol and a revolver and ran for it, racing to a hiding place about a quarter-mile away. Mrs. Day remained in the house and was given a few moments to grab a few meager things before the house was torched. The house and barn were burned and the livestock was taken. Mrs. Day was taken in by neighbors. Old man Day became a hero, dubbed "the Old Flag Defender." He went on to serve as a volunteer, manning the defenses of Baltimore.[2] When asked years later whether he had any regrets, the then 72-year-old admitted he wished that he'd shot the other raider and that he could have saved his $2,300 in government bonds that burned up in his house. The fervent loyalist had previously expressed himself in a letter to the editor of his local newspaper in 1862, saying, "From all sedition, privy conspiracy and rebellion, good Lord deliver us, and let all the people say amen: and cursed be he who has or may hereafter become a traitor to this once happy nation and its flag, and let all the people say amen...."[3]

Sketch by artist Edwin Forbes of a foraging party of bummers at work confiscating turkeys, waterfowl, mules, horses, and cattle to feed and support the army. While the threat to Washington was minimal, the raid, thought Gideon Welles, presented the Rebels with an excellent opportunity to steal what they really wanted—horses and livestock. The horses were desperately needed for hauling off plunder, for pulling artillery pieces, and as mounts for the men. They also were needed for Lee's army at Petersburg. About 100 mules were also taken near Beltsville, Maryland, and used for pulling wagons. (Library of Congress)

In this case, Day knew why his house was burned. In others, notes were occasionally left behind to explain the house and barn burnings. Left in one yard was a message addressed to President Lincoln, which read, "Dear Uncle Abraham—We like the way you fight—we hope you will be reelected. We have come this time to show you what we can do we will return & give you another lesson. We have inlisted [sic] for 40 years or the war. Yours, The biggest Rebel in the country for the burning of Gov. Letcher's (of Vir.) house by Gen. Hunter."[4]

Newspapers were full of reports of heavy fighting and mass destruction that didn't take place. On 13 July, the *Philadelphia Inquirer* reported that a great cavalry battle had taken place at Bel Air, Maryland, but on 15 July the weekly *Bel Air Aegis and Intelligencer* corrected this, saying the intrusion was made by a few lost Confederates who interfered with no one. The Bel Air paper noted that the *Inquirer* was "a paper remarkable for sensation reports."

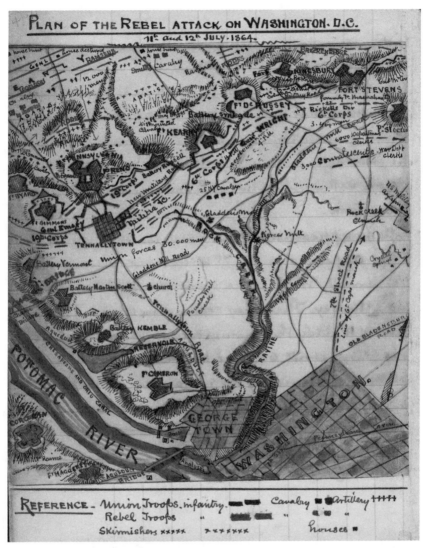

A contemporary plan of battle for 11 and 12 July 1864, showing the deployment of Confederate and Union units. The Confederate forces were estimated at 12,000. The legend at the bottom of this plan claims the Union had 20,000 men. For the Rebels, Robert Rhodes's and John Breckinridge's divisions are shown nearest the Blair family properties opposite Fort Reno on 11 July with the Rebel artillery to their right. John Bell Gordon's division is shown in front of Fort Kearney on 12 July, while Stephen Ramseur's division is shown straddling Brookville Turnpike, facing Fort Stevens. There are several errors on this map, including the placements of several of the Federal defensive works. (Library of Congress)

CHAPTER 11

11 July—Around Washington

The Rebel arrival on 11 July threw Washington into a panic. Many expected that the worst would come that very morning. For days the citizenry had been fed a steady diet of alarmist news assuring that the Rebels were charging hard towards Washington. According to reports attributed to supposedly knowledgeable military officials, these news flashes had the enemy descending upon the city in enormous numbers, and there were large blue-clad forces to oppose them. Now the Confederates were arriving, and they were expected to rush headlong at one or more elements of Washington's earthen defenses, overwhelming them in a fearful tidal wave of anger and retribution. Washingtonians held their collective breath.

Embedded war correspondent Sylvanus Cadwallader believed the Federal city was at its most vulnerable on the 11th, which was sadly true. Serving as a war correspondent with the *New York Herald,* attached to General Grant, Cadwallader had a front-row seat to observe what was truly going on both in Washington and at Grant's headquarters. "Our lines in [Early's] front could have been carried at any point, with the loss of a few hundred men," he wrote in his *Memoirs.* He was dumbfounded when Early didn't attack. "I have always wondered at Early's inaction throughout the day [11 July], and never had any sufficient explanation of his reasons," Cadwallader wrote.

Lucius Chittenden, the government's first register of the treasury, was equally stunned when nothing happened on 11 July. Chittenden believed the Confederates "would have met with no resistance except from the raw and undisciplined forces, which, in the opinion of General Grant, and it was supposed of General Lee also, would have been altogether inadequate to its defense." This was equally true. Writing after the fact, he too was perplexed regarding why Early had failed to act: "Presumptively, he could have attacked [on 11 July] when a considerable portion of his force was at Silver Spring and above Georgetown, within two miles of the defenses."

Part of the problem was that while the local newspapers were telling the citizenry one set of things, the realities Early was dealing with were very different. Had the public truly known the size and condition of the Confederate forces struggling towards Washington in the early hours of 11 July, it might not have been so afraid of an attack that Monday morning.

Some modern-day authors have faulted Early for not acting swiftly enough on 11 July. It is easy to second-guess a battlefield scenario, especially in the hindsight of 155-plus years, and say that Early was too slow in exploiting the situation that Monday or that he blinked or choked in the face of battle. He let slip a whole afternoon and evening for the decisive thrust. Was this simply a matter of Early at his weakest? Perhaps it was as simple as Early's aide, Captain William Whitehurst Old, jotted in his journal on 11 July, "Troops much broken down by excessive heat, long marches, dusty roads and exceedingly dry country through which we passed. Or maybe indeed, old Preston Blair's liquor cachet plus sylvan 'Silver Spring' were just too alluring for the tired Early and his senior commanders! At any rate, Old Jube took the true answer to his grave, if he even had an explanation."[1]

It is true that Early was a self-described procrastinator. As a lawyer he said he frequently put off preparing for a case until the very last minute and also postponed asking for fees. If this proclivity occurred on the battlefield that July day, delaying the attack on Washington when he first had the chance, even with the force he believed he then had available—"I was satisfied, when we arrived in front of the fortifications, that not more than one-third of my force could have been carried into action"—the propensity could have cost him his prize.[2] But by Early's own calculation, that meant that a midday attack would have to be carried out by only about 700 of his men. They'd be attacking an unknown number of fully dug-in defenders in well-prepared rifle pits and earthen fortifications, with fixed and field artillery from at least five positions that could concentrate fire on the open field of advance. The Federals also had erected obstacles in front of the forts that would stall the Rebel force within killing range. Despite all this, such a judgment that he suffered from a serious case of "the slows" on 11 July is unfair, given the fact that Early wasn't certain what he was facing. What is known from eyewitness accounts is that as late as 4:00 p.m. some of his men were still at Colesville, roughly 16 miles outside the capital. Clearly, his army was too spread out to attack. Besides, on Monday, 11 July, the sun set at 8:32 p.m., meaning at best he might have a few-hour window of sunlight into which to force his attack, if he was capable of pulling together his forces. That would have been tough, given that he had scouting and looting parties scattered about.

By midday, on the 11th, he had parties out reconnoitering the forts and terrain. He said that reconnaissance consumed what was left of that day and that the forts appeared to be impregnable. Additionally, eyewitnesses reported not seeing the Confederates' artillery train arriving until 2:00 p.m. on 11 July. Upon arriving, the 40 field pieces were reportedly initially parked in the orchard and fields of the Blair farm, awaiting orders. Their deployment would have taken at least another hour if Early knew where to position them effectively to support any infantry attack. Additional time would have been needed to soften up the point of attack on the Union position, but the minute any of the Confederate artillery opened fire it would be targeted by the Union's larger guns, which had greater range and lethality. At the earliest, that would mean not launching a midday attack. An attack at nearly 5:00 p.m. would be about the earliest possible. This left just enough time to affect a breakthrough, but that was if everything went off without a serious hitch, which seldom happens on an unfamiliar battlefield with a commander left to ponder many unknown variables, including where to have his artillery in position by 5:00 p.m. Without artillery support, as puny as that support was compared with the Union's, the Confederates would have had little chance of breaking through the Union fortifications in a headlong dash any earlier in the day.

While the Federal city was ringed with forts, large gun batteries, rifle pits, and abattis (lines of mature trees felled in the direction of an anticipated attacking force such that the branches, stripped of leaves and sharpened into points, created an impenetrable obstacle to any attack), the fortifications were largely undermanned. To increase the strength at Fort Stevens, the principal point of attack, invalid Union soldiers recovering from war wounds, clerks from government office buildings, civil militia, and general officers were pressed into service manning the forts and connecting trench lines around Washington until sufficient reinforcements arrived by water from Virginia. Gideon Welles recorded the dire condition in his diary on 11 July, saying, "Citizens are volunteering and the employees in the navy yard are required to man the fortifications left destitute." The Washington Navy Yard's contingent consisted of roughly 800 workers organized into its own regiment. Armed civic and fraternal groups such as the Union Leagues, German Volunteer Company, citizens of the Seventh Ward and the National Rifles also volunteered. Large numbers of freed Blacks and contrabands set about strengthening the fortifications ringing the city. For the time being, the defense of Washington depended upon this mixed bag of ranks. This was an army whose officers were said to outnumber privates. In truth there was great uncertainty over who was actually in control of all these forces, many of whose volunteers entered service on 11 July and wouldn't be mustered out until 14 July.

For both sides in the early hours of 11 July, force strengths and morale were a major concern. The few Confederates who were straggling into formations in front of Washington were largely exhausted. The few civilian recruits already standing in the fort's rifle pits were essentially terrified. The best that anyone could hope for was a stare-off.

To immediately defend the city, the army would have to scrape the bottom of the barrel. To increase the strength at Fort Stevens, invalid Union soldiers recovering from war wounds, clerks from government office buildings, and general officers were pressed into service manning the forts and connecting trench lines around Washington until sufficient reinforcements could arrive by water from Virginia. "There was no adequate force to withstand [Early]," wrote Haines Alanson in his 1883 *History of the Fifteenth Regiment New Jersey Volunteers.* "Some thousands were gathered, it is true; the odds and ends of dismounted cavalry regiments, and the scrapings from the convalescent camp, together with a thousand or two men from the Quartermaster's Department.... With no organization and without discipline, they were hardly better than an armed mob." Alanson's regiment didn't arrive at Washington until about midmorning on 12 July. Upon disembarking from its transports, Alanson observed that his regiment was "welcomed by crowds of citizens and officials, who received us as deliverers from a great peril. The arrival brought joy to Washington." Such accolades were brief, however. "Soon we heard the booming of cannon before us, and quickly, at the word, fell into ranks, and with accelerated pace hurried toward the scene of action." The 15th New Jersey was hastily ordered to Fort Stevens.

Unlike Alanson and his comrades, Edward Hill was in town on 11 July. He was recovering from wounds at a Washington hospital when he recorded in his personal diary that day, "The excitement on the increase. A proclamation hourly looked for calling upon all citizens to take up arms."[3] Gideon Welles recorded the dire condition in his diary that day, too: "Citizens are volunteering and the employees in the navy yard are required to man the fortifications left destitute."[4] By 11 July it was clear to Edward Hill that Baltimore was purely a diversion.[5]

The navy yard men were placed in rifle pits in front of Fort Lincoln and posted on guard duty at Benning's Bridge, where they remained until 15 July. A detachment of Marines was deployed elsewhere in the city.

For the navy, Lincoln's safety was its primary concern on 11 July. Unlike the apparent chaos unraveling over at the War Department, Secretary Welles's department wasn't going to be caught "asleep or dumb." During the unfolding emergency, it was preparing for the worst. It had mobilized its available manpower at the first signs of trouble ,and armed naval workers were already in the trenches around Fort Stevens. To protect Annapolis from any potential Confederate raiding party, USS *Vicksburg* deployed armed boat

View of Fort Lincoln, with artillery manned by the 3rd Massachusetts Heavy Artillery Regiment, 1865. (Library of Congress)

crews with orders to destroy any means of crossing the South River that might materialize. The navy was also prepared to whisk Lincoln to safety aboard USS *Baltimore*. Throughout the night of 11 July, Welles's assistant secretary, Gustavus Vasa Fox, was stationed at the telegraph office of the War Department to monitor the situation. At 5:00 in the morning, he sent a telegram to the president saying, "After visiting the forts last evening I saw that probabilities exist that a serious attack might be made during the night. On inspection, I did not find that any provisions had been made for your safety in case of disaster so I ordered steam up on board the '*Baltimore*' and I remained in the telegraph office during the night. All is now safe and quiet."[6] Actually, Fox was wrong on both counts. The 12th would be neither safe nor quiet. It would be the critical day. Lincoln was upset over having USS *Baltimore* under steam throughout the night. He didn't wish to give the impression that he was ready to save himself. Instead, he repeatedly went out to the forts to inspire the troops and assure the public that all were safe. He believed that having *Baltimore* on standby gave the wrong impression.

Baltimore was a captured Confederate sidewheel steamer that had been seized on the Potomac River in April 1861. Commissioned as a Union vessel that same month, it was armed with a single smoothbore 32-pound cannon. Its usual assignment was as an ordnance transport, but in May 1862 she conveyed President Lincoln and two of his Cabinet colleagues to Hampton Roads to view the carcass of the Confederate ironclad CSS *Virginia*, which had been scuttled by its own crew on 11 May 1862 to keep it from falling into Federal hands.

In July 1864, others were concerned about the safety of the navy yard. On 12 July Britton A. Hill, a visiting St. Louis lawyer, stopped by the White House at 7:30 p.m. to see the president. Lincoln was unavailable, so Hill wrote him a note on the back of his calling card that said, "Is the Navy Yard entirely secure—If the rebels could get the yard & some gun boats, it would be a bad job. I would try it if on their side."[7] Unsure whether the president saw the messages on the reverse of his card, Hill returned to the executive mansion an hour later and, upon again finding the president out, used some stationery to write Lincoln a lengthy note, which said in part, "On reflection after going out, I thought it well to state more fully my views. We are in all respects fully able now to cope with & defeat any forces the enemy has in the environs, and the only questions remaining is whether there is any current point where they can strike to our mortal injury—I could think of no other place where it may be than is no danger of any quite apart of the yard & the capture of the boats and the destruction of the magazines, but I would feel more secure if every precautions were taken." Hill need not have been so worried. Seizing gunboats and steaming down the Potomac was the furthest thing from Jubal Early's mind. Early was a soldier, not a sailor, and by then he was more concerned with bluffing the Federals into staying put behind their fortifications so he could get away with his army intact and his stolen cattle and horses in tow. That wasn't going to be by way of a water route, except by crossing the Potomac River into Virginia at the few places possible.

Not knowing what Early was thinking, insurance company executives and bankers inside the city were taking no chances. Boats were chartered to take their deposits and critical records away at the first signs of a major breakthrough.

Employees and others throughout the city also volunteered to protect various important places. The Smithsonian's secretary, Joseph Henry, was given over a dozen rifles to defend the institution, and scientists there who were more skilled with using microscopes and telescopes pledged to defend it. "Mr. Shaw has come to offer his services in case they may be needed in defence [sic] of the [institution]," wrote Mary Henry in her diary. "Dr. Hamlein & others have joined us," she added.[8] Commonly called "the Castle," the Smithsonian building is a replica medieval-style castle designed by James Renwick. Completed in 1855, the ornate red sandstone building was never intended to serve any defensive purposes, but it did have a number of advantages in that regard. Its doors were massively thick and wouldn't have been easily breached.

The Confederate attack on fortress Washington, DC, prompted Rear Admiral Goldsborough, and other naval officers to volunteer their help in defense. Secretary Welles reluctantly accepted such offers, tasking Assistant Secretary Fox with coordinating with General Halleck on how the navy brass might best contribute. Welles thought this was appropriate, even if unnecessary, reasoning in his diary on 12 July 1864, "for the Navy to hold back when all are being called out would appear bad." However, seemingly as an afterthought he penned, "It would be much better to keep them at work."[9] Goldsborough wasn't directed to lend a hand at Fort Stevens, guarding the Seventh Street Turnpike approach to the city, where the Confederates had concentrated their forces, but at Fort Lincoln overlooking the Bladensburg Turnpike, a major route to Baltimore, where Rebel skirmishing was taking place.

Southern forces roamed freely around the rural fringes of Maryland that straddled the district line, foraging and camping along Sligo and Rock Creek. The high points at what would become Takoma Park and Carole Highlands, Maryland, would have furnished ideal vantage points to many of the city's northernmost defenses. Such views would have given proof that most of the bluecoats were secure within their fortifications.

The District of Columbia's militia wasn't officially ordered to muster until 12 July while the Alexandria militia wasn't called out until 13 July. The DC mobilization order from Brigadier General Peter F. Bacon read as follows:

> In obedience to General Order No. 1, issued by Major General Thomas, calling out the militia of the District of Columbia, all officers commanding regiments in the District of Columbia are hereby required and commanded, under penalty, to call out immediately every man subject to military duty to assemble forthwith to be mustered into the service of the United States for sixty days, and when assembled to report at these Headquarters for further orders.

Edward Hill's diary entry for 12 July says, "Citizen soldiers in arms. The streets filled with [Provost] Marshall men."[10] In an earlier entry he observed, "The City filled with strange rumors of or arguments. The rebels are a coming is the Report. Troops are busy marching and counter marching." During those two days, things were clearly chaotic.

Gideon Welles blamed Halleck, Stanton, and Grant for the entire debacle. Actually, while Grant was obsessed with holding onto Lee's throat at Petersburg, he was neither dumb nor asleep when it came to the whereabouts of the Second Corps. The numbers for what men Early actually did have that summer in front of Washington are all over the charts, ranging from a high of 55,000 men to a low of 8,000, depending upon the source. Some writers have tended to place the Confederate head count at about 15,000. However, on 11 July the most critical day in the Washington campaign, Early said he only had about 2,750 infantry who might have been capable of attacking Fort Stevens, and that wasn't enough! In his *Memoirs* Early confirmed as much, saying, "The rapid marching which had broken down a number of the men who were barefooted or weakened by previous exposure, and had been left in the Valley and directed to be collected at Winchester, and the losses in killed and wounded at Harper's Ferry, Maryland Heights and Monocacy, had reduced my infantry to about 8,000."[11] The Rebel death count at Monocacy Junction was placed at 309, and according to Union medical authorities, the Rebel wounded at Monocacy who were being treated in hospitals at or around Frederick amounted to another 430 men. This would have placed his entire army strength, after he crossed the Potomac and before he marched towards Washington at approximately 8,800. Additionally, many of the soldiers that Early had on 11 July were still spread out throughout Maryland suffering from sunstroke or tending to cut feet from the little freshwater mollusk shells on the bottom of the Potomac at Boteler's Ford that acted like tiny razors for those wading across the waist-high waters barefoot. Others were off actively looting. Additionally, in his *Memoirs* Early estimated that only about one-third of the total number he had available were actually fit for action upon arriving in front of the forts at Washington. And without a ready reserve, he would have been unable to immediately exploit any possible breakthrough with follow-up force. Instead of attacking, skirmishers were deployed in front of the forts.[12] These roughly 600 pickets are what Lincoln, newspaper correspondents, and others largely saw facing Fort Stevens on 11 July. These are the Rebels that were easily seen. No one knew how many others might be out of sight.

Early doesn't seem to have been sure either. He himself contributed to the confusion. His early accounting was never very precise. As noted previously in his *Memoirs*, he placed his force at about 8,000, give or take, but then in an 1881 story about the raid published in the *National Republican* but based upon another officer's math, Early reported that his total force at Washington

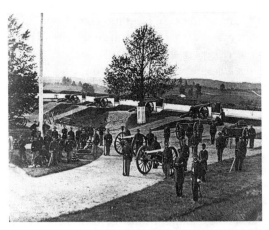

An interior view of Fort Stevens. You can see the relatively clear view the defenders had of the approaches to the fort and the clear lines of fire their elevated position provided. (Library of Congress)

was 9,570 men. In remarkable hindsight detail, this overall number was comprised of Breckinridge's division (2,104 men); Rodes's division (3,013 soldiers); Gordon's division (2,544), and Ramseur's division (1,909). This numbers did not include Early's artillery and cavalry.[13]

That sight of so few pickets caused the *National Intelligencer* to put the number capable of menacing Fort Stevens at no more than 600. The *Washington Chronicle* added to this, saying that the forces facing the fort were there merely as a diversion to tie down Federal forces while Early's main body made off with the spoils collected during the raid. The *Intelligencer* echoed this, reporting, "Only a small portion of these forces appeared in front of Washington while their comrades were collecting the booty for transportation across the Potomac." No matter what final number that was available to Early on the early afternoon of 11 July, it was highly improbable that those men could have succeeded against the well-entrenched defenders inside the nation's most fortified city, regardless of the minimal military prowess of many of its protectors. The generally accepted rule of thumb was that an attacking force should outnumber an alert defender inside prepared fortification at least 3 to 1 if the attacker expected any serious chance of success. Some experts put the ratio at 5 to 1 if the fortifications were really strong, which in Washington's case they were. At the time of the Rebels' arrival, it is estimated that the city had mobilized roughly 20,400 men, including 9,600 civilians and about 8,000 invalids of the Veteran Reserve Corps. Approximately 2,000 members of the Quartermaster Corps, plus some available sailors and Marines and veteran

Men of the 1st Connecticut Artillery at Fort Richardson at Arlington Heights, Virginia, preparing to fire a 20-pound Parrott field piece. (Library of Congress)

army units joined these men. The majority of these war fighters were deployed in the rifle trenches adjoining Fort Stevens. Based on these numbers, Early would have needed between 60,000 to 100,000 soldiers to affect a successful breakthrough. Instead, he had about 2,750 would-be attackers. On 12 July Early's numbers would be greater, but so would those of the defenders.

When Early heard the distinctive boom of heavy artillery, signifying that the vanguard of his army had reached the outskirts of the city, by about 11:30 a.m. on 11 July, he knew his army was in trouble. This meant that his men were likely within range of its fortifications and that there were at least some artillerymen who knew how to use the Union's heavy siege guns.[14]

The warning shots came from Fort Slocum, located to the right of Fort Stevens, which was manned by men of the 2nd Pennsylvania Heavy Artillery.

* * *

Until the VI and XIX Corps arrived, many of the thrown-together defenders believed the city was ripe for the taking. Others thought so too. Lieutenant Colonel Aldace Walker, an officer with the VI Corps, believed that before his Corps arrived to bolster the defenses, the city was highly vulnerable. Lincoln's young assistants, John Hay and John Nicolay, agreed, believing that Early made a serious mistake on the 11th, that he must have "looked at his own force through the wrong end of his field-glass," as Washington was not prepared to repel his forces before the VI and XIX Corps appeared.

Many Washingtonians were reading about instances of Rebel degradation in frequent special editions of the city's daily newspapers. While most articles were tales of horror, some were of remarkable valor and resourcefulness. One of the latter involved a stagecoach driver who had been robbed of his horses by Confederate forces on their way to Gettysburg the previous year. This time he was alerted to the presence of the Rebel raiding party, while he was on the Georgetown Pike. Instead of risking being robbed of his horseflesh again, he turned off onto side roads to make his way to Washington. He used his knowledge of every shortcut, pathway, and trail to avoid the Rebel patrols. Not making any stops, he arrived safely in the district several hours earlier than expected. From the stagecoach driver, and from other sources, the newspaper reported Rebels at Mount Airy, Brookville, and Damascus. It also reported, "the Rebels appear at Rockville in some force." At the same time, the *Star* published that Confederates were at Beltsville, Maryland, just North of College Park, although it said witnesses there reported that this group of Confederates appeared to be lost, because they were asking for directions. Beltsville, located on the main north-south post road between Washington and Baltimore, was the site of the Muirkirk Iron Furnace, which furnished high-grade pig iron to the Union army. The ironworks was unmolested.

The lack of accurate intelligence was no different than the day before. "Our men report the country full of Rebels," noted the *Evening Star* in its 5:00 p.m. edition on 11 July, adding, "Reports concerning the numbers and purpose of the Rebel invading force are confusingly conflicting."

On 11 July Navy Secretary Welles spoke with Secretary Stanton at the War Department regarding the Rebel intensions but received no information whatsoever. Stanton told his Cabinet colleague he knew neither the size of the enemy force nor precisely where it was. This wasn't exactly true. He had been receiving a myriad of highly detailed reports from B&O President John Garrett outlining every known Confederate movement, but the excuse enabled Stanton to dismiss Welles fairly quickly. Unsatisfied by the lack of reliable information, Welles went out to the frontlines in the early evening on 11 July to see things for himself. Also in the dark, the president did the same thing that morning, accompanied by Assistant Adjutant General Hardie and an armed escort. In Welles's case, after speaking with Generals Wright and McCook, Welles was dumbfounded by how little the army actually said it knew of the forces confronting them. When he asked specifically where

Major General Alexander M. McCook (seated in the center) and his staff at his temporary headquarters on the Seventh Street Road. McCook's field commanded ended immediately after the Confederates' withdrawal. (Library of Congress)

the main force of the enemy was, he was told they were, "over the hills" near Silver Spring. "Oh! Within a short distance, a mile or two only," he was told.[15] Owing to a lack of Federal cavalry, the officers said they had no idea how large a force the Rebels had, despite the fact that Major General Lewis "Lew" Wallace reported to the War Department that he believed he had faced about 15,000 to 20,000 Confederates at Monocacy. Welles thought the lack of adequate information was pathetic.

The 5:00 p.m. edition of the *Evening Star,* was at a loss for accurate information as well. It reported on the capture of several Confederate prisoners, noting, "They are inclined to brag, and some of them place their numbers at very high figures." At the same time the paper was saying that the Southern forces were gathering around Silver Spring in the woods of the Blair, Clark, and Brown properties and that they appeared to be about 15,000 strong.

College Park, Maryland, became the Rebel highwater mark in the attempt to liberate the prisoners at Point Lookout. This was testified to by Dr. John O. Wharton, a founding trustee of the Maryland Agricultural College who was interrogated and subsequently arrested for entertaining and aiding Johnson's forces. Wharton denied any complicity. He said he was forced into cooperating, but that didn't add up. He told his inquisitors on 14 July that he was seized by six Confederates on 12 July at 5:00 p.m. and taken to Bradley Johnson, who was then at the college. Wharton said that while there Johnson received an order at 7:30 p.m. from Early to withdraw, but Wharton said he didn't know the details of how and when that was to happen. What he did say was that the Rebel troops were still eating at his house up until 11:00 p.m. when they left by way of New Cut Road (today's Veirs Mill Road). What Wharton didn't say was that he had apparently served as Johnson's willing guide to New Cut Road. Others on campus testified that Wharton left that night with the Rebels but was back on campus the next day. Wharton was subsequently confined at the Old Capitol Prison in Washington, where he was shot for not following an instruction. Johnson's use of New Cut Road meant that his riders were to link up with Early's main body at Rockville, not Silver Spring. (Library of Congress)

CHAPTER 12

12 and 13 July

Until Early could determine the full picture of the battlefield he was facing, he'd need to hold the bulk of his men back out of the enemy's gun range, which was a good distance away. Having pushed his men so hard, this was an unwelcome realization. Restraining his men just meant there could be more looting or recuperating from their long and exhausting march.

Ordnance counts varied just as counts of troop strength and property loss did. In his *Memoirs* Early reported that he had about 40 cannons at his disposal, and Brigadier General Armistead Long's artillery were said to have been no larger than 12-pounders.[1] An eyewitness to Early's line of march towards Washington who reported seeing only about 20 cannons contradicted this, but he may not have seen all the firepower.[2] Based on what ordnance each corps of Lee's army had at Gettysburg, the 40 cannon count would have been about right. If that was indeed a correct accounting, those 40-some Second Corps cannons were 14 more guns than the five Union batteries had at the apex point of Pickett's Charge the year before. Those Union batteries at Gettysburg covered the critical 650-yard front that absorbed the brunt of the charge. The 26 Union guns at Gettysburg that helped blunt Pickett's Charge consisted of twelve 3-inch ordnance rifles, ten 12-pound Napoleons, and four 10-pound Parrott rifles. A massive Confederate artillery barrage from 150 to 170 mostly 12-pound Napoleon guns caused little Union damage preceded Pickett's Charge. Anticipating a frontal attack, the Union's artillery held its fire for about a quarter-hour before unleashing about 80 guns from various locations, including the 26 facing the anticipated point of attack. That slight lull gave the impression that the Union's guns had either been knocked out of action or were seriously low on ammunition, raising hopes of the success of the Confederate charge. But neither was the case. In that frontal attack Union canister and double-shot charges were used to deadly effect. Nearly half of the 12,500 Confederate attackers on 3 July 1863 were unable to fall back when the Rebel push faltered, because they were left lying on a gently uphill-sloping field of carnage. This was precisely the type of ground facing Early's men a year later outside of Washington, only this time the opposing cannons were far bigger and more numerous than at Gettysburg, and they were ensconced behind formidable earthworks.

While this helps to confirm that Early likely had the number of cannons he said he had, Gettysburg isn't a fair comparison because whatever artillery Armistead had at Washington was simply no match for the potential firepower inside the Union's fortifications. This meant that Early's attackers

"Pickett's Charge—a Harvest of Death," a photograph by Alexander Gardner. Jubal Early must have given some thought to the battle of Gettysburg, fought a year earlier, when 12,500 Confederates attacked 6,500 bluecoats as part of Pickett's Charge. In 1863 the attackers had to cover roughly three-quarters of a mile of open field against field artillery and concentrated rifle fire. Much of the conditions were similar outside Washington in 1864, including the oppressive heat and the gradually sloping terrain. Instead of fallen trees blocking the path, the attackers at Gettysburg faced a rail fence that held up their advance and forced some of them into channels of death. As a result, the Rebel's sustained a 50-percent casualty rate. Was Jubal Early willing to accept a similar slaughter outside Washington, especially since his men were confronted by heavier artillery concentrations and more massive firepower? Was he inclined to allow himself to go down in history as the loser who launched an ill-fated "Early's Charge" on Washington? He knew better. (Library of Congress)

and Armistead's field artillery would have come under immediate Federal bombardment long before his own guns and men were within range of doing any serious damage. Early was well aware of this. He knew what happened at Gettysburg the year before. This made him gun-shy for at least the second time that month. Early admitted as much years later in an article written for the June 1871 edition of *Southern Magazine* while living in exile in Cuba, where he recalled, "My artillery did not exceed forty pieces manned by six or seven hundred men and they would have been of no use to me in an attack, for there were so many of the enemy's guns bearing upon every position within range, and they were of so much heavier metal, that I would not have been able to put one of mine in position, and I made no attempt to do so; consequently, not a piece of my artillery was fired in front of Washington."

Major General J. G. Barnard, the officer who designed Washington's defenses, wished Early had indeed deployed his cannons. Also writing in 1871, Barnard boasted, "every important approach or depression of the ground, unseen from the forts, was swept by field guns, but also that all commanding points which the enemy would be likely to concentrate artillery to overpower that one or more of our forts or batteries were subjected not only from the fires direct and cross many points along the line, but also from heavy rifled guns from distant points unattainable by the enemy."[3]

By 12 July, Confederates seemed to be everywhere. The distribution of the Rebels prompted Gideon Welles to speculate that they weren't massed in any one particular place but instead appeared to be scattered about in small squads from Baltimore to Great Falls, on the Potomac. It seemed to Welles that the array of Confederates in front of Fort Stevens was forming a shield behind which their comrades were marauding at will, stealing horses and cattle. He raised this possibility to President Lincoln during the Cabinet's typical Tuesday noon meeting on 12 July. Only a few Cabinet members opted to attend that session. Lincoln said there was nothing essential that needed to be brought up. The few in attendance did discuss the fact that Confederate forces had somehow managed to place themselves on the Union's doorsteps. Welles wished to know where the Rebels were in any large force. Lincoln, who had just come back from visiting several of the forts with Secretary of State William Seward, told Welles that he wasn't sure where they were but that the main body of them appeared to be at Silver Spring. That evening Welles recorded his dissatisfaction over the ignorance in Washington in his diary, saying, "I am sorry there should be so little accurate knowledge of the Rebels, sorry that at such a time there is not a full Cabinet, and especially sorry that the Secretary of War is not present. In the interviews which I have had with him, I can obtain no facts, no opinions. He seems dull and stupefied. Others tell me the same."[4]

If an attack on the city was part of the Rebel plans a newspaper informed its readers that the attack would likely come at about 3:00 a.m. on 12 July, reasoning that this was "the hour of the twenty-four always selected at this season of the year for an attempt upon fortifications by sudden assault or to get in between fortifications by suddenly overpowering the defenders of works connecting fortifications." Instead, the 12th was a day principally for facing off.

That day, Gideon Welles went out to Fort Stevens to see what was going on for himself. Upon entering the fort he found the president sitting in the shade with his back against one of the parapets. In the late afternoon Union batteries opened fire on the Rebel pickets opposite the fort, and two regiments of bluecoats emerged from a small valley to attack the Confederate positions. The cannon fire scattered the pickets, who ran for cover in the nearest woods or over the closest hill, with Union soldiers in hot pursuit. Secretary Welles found the entire spectacle exhilarating. He left Fort Stevens as dark was falling. The road back to Washington was lined with numerous stragglers. From Welles's prospective, since the day had been exceedingly warm, some by the wayside were doubtlessly debilitated by the heat, while others, he thought, appeared to be drunk. "Then men on horseback, on mules, in wagons as well as on foot, batteries of artillery, caissons, an innumerable throng" passed me, he recalled. "It was exciting and wild." He wrote in his diary that evening

The original monument marker claiming to commemorate the spot where President Lincoln was shot at while at Fort Stevens on 12 July 1864. (Library of Congress)

about what he had witnessed: "In times gone by I had passed over these roads little anticipating scenes like this, and a few years hence they will scarcely be believed to have occurred."[5]

Welles was a concise and copious chronicler. His diaries are highly detailed. He had witnessed Confederate sharpshooters taking potshots at targets of opportunity. He recorded such in his diary on 12 July, writing, "Occasionally a bullet from some longrange [sic] rifle passed above our heads. One man had been shot in the fort a few minutes before we entered."[6]

One thing Welles must have missed was the often-repeated story that President Lincoln was shot at while at Fort Stevens on 12 July. There is even a bronze marker at the fort that commemorates the event. It is a fact that President Lincoln was one of those who was drawn to the battlefront. On several occasions he visited the frontlines, and according to this story, he was even shot at by Confederate sharpshooters while stupidly standing on the ramparts of Fort Stevens. As the story goes, an officer standing beside him, army assistant surgeon Cornelius V. Crawford of the 102nd Pennsylvania Infantry Regiment, was wounded by a shot intended for Lincoln.

In one version of this story, the president was ordered to "Get down, you damn fool," by Captain Oliver Wendell Holmes Jr., who later served as an associate justice of the Supreme Court. Another variation has Major

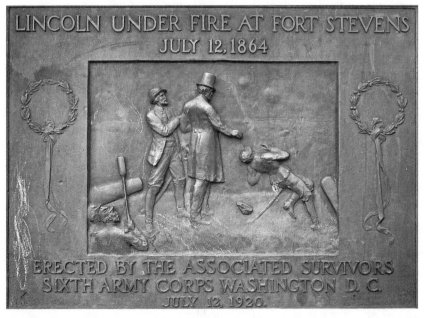

Detail of the bronze tablet in the Lincoln monument at Fort Stevens. (Library of Congress)

General Alexander M. McCook, who was the overall commanding officer of Washington's defenses, as the one who ordered Lincoln to get down. According to this version, the president curtly reminded McCook that he was the commander in chief and McCook was a mere general, but it is said that he climbed down anyway. Others said it was Major General Wright who ordered him to get down.

Lucius Chittenden claimed he was the one who advised a young artillery officer to tell the president to get off the rifle step he was on because he was creating a target of himself. According to Chittenden's telling the young office did as instructed. "He walked to where the President was looking over the parapet. 'Mr. President,' he said, 'you are standing within range of five hundred rebel rifles. Please come down to a safer place. If you do not, it will be my duty to call a file of men, and make you,'" wrote Chittenden years later.[7]

Over the years some writers claim Lincoln exposed himself on 11 July. Other say it was on 12 July. And some say he did it on both dates.

One book of Early's attack on Fort Stevens recounts the version where Holmes ordered Lincoln off the wall on 12 July. The author states that Lincoln made himself a target on both 11 July and again on 12 July, explaining that he was standing pretty much in the exact same place behind the forward parapet on both days. This author doesn't put the president on top of the wall, but at 6 feet, 4 inches tall and wearing a stovetop hat, Lincoln was a tempting target even if standing on the fort's banquettes (a firing step behind a parapet).

Lincoln did indeed visit the Fort on both dates, so the "get down" command could have come either day. According to the reminisces of a soldier who was at Fort Stevens on 11 July,

> President Lincoln visited the fort that afternoon accompanied by Senator [Zachariah Chandler] of Michigan. The enemy was firing lively from the bushes in front of the fort and it was dangerous for any person to look over the parapet. Chandler hugged close to the parapet, but the President was bound he would look over and see what was going on. Soon a sharpshooter fired at him, and he dodged, in doing so tipped over the pass box on which he was sitting and tumbled down. The ball fired at him struck one of the large guns, glanced back and went through a soldier's leg on the look-out. Lincoln gathered himself up and laughing said: 'that was quite a carom.' I was standing back of him at the time and was curious to know what a carom meant, and so I asked one of the boys versed in billiards, and he told me… Some of those standing by thought the president was given to a little too much levity and that the remark was a little too jocose for the occasion, but he did not realize what had happened until after he said it.[8]

It is hard to believe that Lincoln would have placed himself in danger twice, but being at the fort greatly exhilarated him.

Christian Hook was a witness to Lincoln's visit to Fort DeRussey on 11 July. In his pocket diary for that day, he recorded, "Old Abe was here to day [sic] about 11-o'clock and he looked through the glasses and said that they was in a house nearest of the fort. Then about two-o'clock they commenced firing on skirmishers."[9]

On the morning of 12 July, Montgomery Blair was at the executive mansion and talked with Lincoln about the Cabinet meeting coming up at midday. Lincoln said there was nothing to talk about. He said nothing about being shot at earlier in the day or the day before.

That afternoon Navy Secretary Welles rode out to Fort Stevens to see things for himself. Joining him along the way was Ohio Senator Benjamin Franklin Wade. He and Wade found the president already there. He recorded in his diary, "we found the President, who was sitting in the shade, his back against the parapet towards the enemy." Welles, whose diary was highly detailed and studiously accurate, says nothing about a sharpshooter nearly killing the president in the late afternoon of 12 July.

In 1867 Dr. George Stevens, a surgeon with the 77th New York Infantry Regiment and the author of that unit's regimental history, claims that during the afternoon of 12 July, "While the battle was in progress, President Lincoln stood upon the parapet of the fort watching, with eager interest, the scene before him. Bullets came whistling around, and one severely wounded a surgeon who stood within three feet of the President. Mrs. Lincoln entreated him to leave the fort, but he refused; he, however, accepted the advice of General Wright to descend from the parapet and watch the battle from a less exposed position."[10]

In 1896 Major General Wright confirmed to Dr. Stevens that he was the one who ordered Lincoln off the battlement, saying, "I know you are commander of the armies of the United States, but I am in command here, and as you are not safe where you are standing, and I am responsible for your personal safety, I order you to come down."[11] Wright also later fleshed out the narrative Stevens originally furnished in 1867 by advising the doctor that on 12 July,

> The President evinced remarkable coolness and disregard of danger. Meeting him as I came out from my quarters, I thoughtlessly invited him to see the fight in which we were about to engage, without for a moment supposing he would accept. A moment after I would have given much to have recalled my words, as his life was too important to the nation to be put in jeopardy by a chance shot, or the bullet of a sharpshooter. He took his position at my side on the parapet, and all my entreaties failed to move him, though in addition to the stray shots, which were constantly passing over, the spot was a favorite mark for the sharpshooters. When the surgeon to whom you allude was shot, and after I had cleared the parapet of every one [sic] else, he still maintained

his ground, till I told him I should have to remove him forcibly. The absurdity of the idea of sending off the President under guard seemed to amuse him; but, in consideration of my earnestness in the matter, he agreed to compromise by sitting behind the parapet instead of standing upon it. He could not be made to understand why, if I continued exposed, he should not; and my representations that an accident to me was of little importance, while to him it could not be measured, and that it was, moreover, my duty, failed to make any impression on him. I could not help thinking that in leaving the parapet he did so rather in deference to my earnestly expressed wishes than from any considerations of personal safety, though the danger had been so unmistakably proved by the wounding of the officer alluded to. After he left the parapet he would persist in standing up from time to time, thus exposing nearly one-half his tall form to the bullets.

This version was backed up by General Frank Wheaton, who commanded a brigade under Wright. Wheaton claimed in 1901 that Lincoln persisted in standing on top of the parapet and that made Wright extremely anxious, causing him to insist that the president get down and stand behind it instead.

John Hay recorded that the event took place on 11 July, not the following day, as the commemorative bronze marker at Fort Stevens states. Writing in his diary for 11 July he noted, "At three o'clock P.M. the President came in bringing the news that the enemy's advance was at Ft Stevens on the 7th Street road. He was in the Fort when it was attacked, standing upon the parapet. A soldier roughly ordered him to get down or he would have his head knocked off."[12] Secretary Welles also visited Fort Stevens on 11 July, finding Major Generals McCook and Wright already there, but he heard nothing about any such shouting or shooting incident involving the president.

In a letter to J. E. Boos, a Lincoln memorabilia collector, written in 1922, Associate Justice Holmes confirmed that he saw his commander, Major General Wright, walking on the earthworks, but he told Boos, "But for a certainty, the 6-foot-4 inch Lincoln, in frock coat and top hat, stood peering through field glasses from behind a parapet at the onrushing rebels, bullets whizzing past his head...."

Holmes doesn't claim to have been the one who demanded the president "Get down, you damn fool," as in duck for cover. "Some say it was an enlisted man who shouted at Lincoln; others suggest it was General Wright who brusquely ordered Lincoln to safety," noted Holmes, who said he witnessed all of this as he was entering the fort with the VI Army Corps on 11 July, not on the following day. Clearly "ducking down" behind a parapet isn't the same as "getting down" off of one, but over the years the story may have been modified in the telling to assume the latter was what actually happened. Remarkably, this version directly contradicts what Associate Justice Felix Frankfurter said Holmes told him, which was that it was indeed he who ordered Lincoln to "get down." But, again, this version said

Oliver Wendell Holmes. (Library of Congress)

nothing about Lincoln standing on top of the ramparts to see better. In Frankfurter's telling, vouched for by biographer Harold Laski and published in 1938, the president was amused at Holmes's assertiveness toward the commander in chief and said, "Colonel Holmes, I am glad to see you know how to talk to a civilian."

Why Holmes changed his story is unclear. What is clear is that while Holmes and his men were marching from the wharfs to the fort, Washingtonians turned out to cheer the troops and furnish them with buckets of ice water and snacks. The VI Corps arrived around Fort Stevens in the early afternoon of 11 July. When this fact is matched up with the recollections of one of the president's security detail, it supports the claim that Lincoln was standing behind the battlements, not on top of them, on 11 July. According to Sergeant Smith Stimmel, a member of the president's bodyguard from 1863 to 1865, The 11th of July was an anxious day for the President, and for all who knew the situation. In the 1920s Stimmel stated, "During the afternoon of that day the President drove out along the line of some of the forts on the north to investigate the condition of things for himself. I was with the escort that accompanied him on his rounds that day, and it looked to me as though the chances for a scrap were mighty good. I did not see why the Confederates did not make an attack then." The president, he said earlier, "made a bee line for Fort Stevens, about as fast as the old coach horses could take him, and arrived before the whole of the Sixth Corps got there. On arriving at the Fort, the President left his carriage and took his position behind the earthworks of the Fort, which left us at liberty for the time being to put in the time as we saw fit."[13]

If John Hay's account of what the president said happened on 11 July is accurate, and if Major General Wright's statement to Dr. Stevens is correct about what happened on 12 July, then Lincoln indeed made a tempting target of himself on at least two occasions. In the scheme of things, whether Lincoln mounted the battlements on 11 and/or 12 July may not matter as much as the fact that he was willing to risk his life to be with those who were defending Washington at the battle front. His presence inspired the citizenry and the army.

And yet, conveniently, the stories of Confederate riflemen attempting to kill President Lincoln remarkably muted any pretext of outrage by the South over the disgraceful act purported to have been contemplated by Ulric Dahlgren in the suspect document found, or planted, on his body alleging that the North had planned to kill Jefferson Davis during its unsuccessful raid on Richmond months earlier. Now, during the payback raid on Washington, the South could no longer claim offense after it allegedly tried to do the exact same thing in attempting to kill Lincoln at Fort Stevens... if it ever did. Just the stories behind the assassination attempt, true or not, suitably eliminated any Southern affront by equaling out the indignation.

While this was happening, the Confederate cavalry under the command of Brigadier General Bradley T. Johnson was supposed to be heading from the outskirts of Baltimore to Point Lookout at the tip of St. Mary's County, Maryland. Johnson's orders, outlined in a communiqué from General Lee to Jubal Early on 3 July, was that his 800-strong Confederate cavalry was to be at Point Lookout by 12 July. That arrival was timed to coincide with an effort that would be made to release the prisoners using a naval force, but how far did Johnson's cavalry actually get before calling off that part of his mission? Early hadn't calculated the time it would take to harass the enemy, burn bridges, cut telegraph lines, and pull up tracks. It took longer than expected. During the late afternoon of 12 July, Johnson's Rebel cavalry was nowhere near Point Lookout. It was paying a visit to the campus of Maryland's Agricultural College, now the University of Maryland at College Park, northeast of Washington. Reportedly the Confederates arrived on campus between 5:00 and 6:00 p.m.

Johnson and his men received a hero's welcome at College Park. Because many of the students and teachers there at that time were from Maryland's eastern shore, an exceedingly pro-Southern part of the state, those members of the faculty and the student body welcomed the Rebels with open arms. Johnson temporarily used the Rossborough Inn, at the time faculty housing, as his headquarters.

Johnson's arrival at College Park coincided with Early's preparations to begin his withdrawal from Washington. This is precisely when the Union attacked his skirmishers in force and rushed forward to threaten his skirmish

Rossborough Inn at College Park, Maryland, served a faculty residence hall for the Maryland Agricultural College during the Civil War. The college became the University of Maryland in 1920. (University of Maryland Archives)

line. This threat was beaten back with little setback to Early's planned withdrawal. In his *Memoirs*, Early recounted, "About dark we commenced retiring and did so without molestation." By then Johnson's riders were still at College Park, Maryland, where they stopped for nearly 5 hours because some of the students and staff were throwing a party for their Southern brothers. From all accounts, Johnson's cavalry left the campus by about 11:00 that night.

By then there was no rush to reach Point Lookout. Johnson's position on the evening on 12 July, with his Maryland cavalry, plus a battery of horse artillery, was far from ideal for any planned dash to Point Lookout prison, at least 80 miles away. Some scholars believe that Johnson's men got as far as Upper Marlboro, Maryland, before being recalled, but that is highly unlikely. Time-wise they couldn't have gone the extra 22 miles from College Park to Upper Marlboro and still made it back to link up with the tail end of the main body of Early's retreat by about midnight. Needing a rest, Johnson's men formed the rearguard of Early's withdrawing army. Johnson must have received the wave-off on the prison raid on 12 July, if he didn't already know it was really only a ruse.

This didn't stop Southerners from wishful thinking. The *Camden (South Carolina) Daily Journal* published in the *Richmond Sentinel* on 20 July that quoted a lady who arrived at New Market, Maryland, as saying, "our prisoners at Point Lookout have been released." The *Daily Journal's* banner announcing this news was cautious regarding its veracity, warning, "Glorious News If True."

Of course, it wasn't true! That same edition of the newspaper also wishfully reported that General Grant had been mortally wounded.

General Grant always thought that Early's force was nothing more than a small raiding party. He believed that sending the 8,000 men from the VI Corps would be more than enough to deal with the threat to Washington. If he had come to the aid of Washington himself, he might have confirmed his belief, and instead of being frozen in fear by the inflated counts being bantered about, he might have acted accordingly. Early then might have found himself squeezed between Hunter coming at him from the north, albeit probably kicking and screaming; Wallace, drawn out from his protective shell at Baltimore again and approaching from the east; and Wright rushing forward out of Washington from the south. But even if all this had happened by Grant's orders, all it would have done was force Early to flee across the Potomac, which he did anyway. This was likely what Grant was expecting would play out, in Early's mind at least.

With the Union attack on Early's force in front of Fort Stevens on the evening of 12 July, which likely occurred sometime between 5:00 and 7:00 p.m., the Confederate commander might well have needed Johnson's horsemen at Silver Spring if the bluecoats created a serious threat to his defensive positions and planned withdrawal. As it was, Early's men were said to have been pushed back about a mile and a half.

Even if Johnson's horsemen weren't needed to repel Federal forces, Early's entire army was about to start its retreat. College Park was only a short 6-mile ride away from Silver Spring. This was a far shorter distance than to Upper Marlboro or Point Lookout. Besides, a horse can typically walk at a rate of 4 miles per hour. It can trot at a pace of 8 to 10, but a full gallop for a long distance, as to Point Lookout, was out of the question. Covering the 80 miles through southern Maryland to Point Lookout at night could not have been done at a gallop. It would have been slower going. That 80-mile journey would have taken roughly 10 to 12 hours to complete, if all went well.

It is more likely that Johnson never intended to attempt the trip. Instead, having his force at College Park during those critical hours around dusk was essential in protecting the left flank of Early's army as it began its withdrawal north. From there Johnson could monitor any Federal troop movements on the Bladensburg Turnpike coming north or on the Baltimore and Washington Turnpike heading south. He could also keep an eye on any railway movements along the tracks running past College Park, and he could ensure that the telegraph lines that paralleled the tracks remained down until after Early's force began leaving the District of Columbia. Johnson's force moved out from College Park late on 12 July. Reportedly, one of the school's professors willingly served as a guide for Johnson's regiments. The faculty member was said to have been back on campus the next day, indicating that he didn't go

Samuel Phillips Lee was Robert E. Lee's first cousin. He remained loyal to the Union, serving as a senior naval officer. Gideon Welles never really trusted S. P. Lee because he was always running to his father-in-law for help in twisting Lincoln's and Welles's arms to get what he wanted. His two brothers-in-law—Postmaster General Montgomery Blair and Navy Assistant Secretary Gustavus Vasa Fox—weren't particularly fond of him either; in fact neither shared anything more than idle pleasantries with him, and then only when it was necessary to maintain the appearance of respectable courtesy. (Library of Congress)

very far. Logically, he likely served as the guide for the Confederates in their rendezvous with Early's army around, not for any mad dash to Point Lookout. Time-wise, Johnson's men couldn't have gone in any other direction and still ended up when and where they did. From this, it seems abundantly clear that Johnson's raiding party never got any closer to Point Lookout than roughly College Park, Maryland.

The chaos during July 1864 had curious personal consequences for at least one of the city's grand families. Acting Rear Admiral Samuel Phillips Lee was married to Elizabeth Blair, Montgomery Blair's sister and the daughter of Francis Preston Blair, the influential editor of the *Congressional Globe*. Seeing all the upset and alarm in his wife's letters during the first two weeks of July 1864, Lee, on his own initiative, without orders, pulled an ironclad and four warships off the blockade line at Hampton Roads, Virginia, on 12 July and ordered them to Washington.

The following day Lee learned that all communications with Washington had been cut. Fearing the worst for his family, and for the Federal city's safety, he ordered his flagship, USS *Malvern*, to proceed to the Washington under a full head of steam. When Lee's boss, Gideon Welles, learned of his disobedience and dereliction of duty, he dispatched a scorching cable telling

Lee to turn back immediately. Unfortunately, Lee failed to receive the recall notice until he reached Washington. By then Secretary Welles was livid. He ordered *Malvern* not to drop anchor but immediately turn about and head back to Hampton Roads. He also insisted that Lee be severely disciplined.[14] The writing of that reprimand fell to Gustavus Fox, Lee's brother-in-law. Lee and Fox weren't close; in fact they hadn't spoken pleasantly in years. In writing the admonishment, Fox appears to have gone overboard in making it as personally offensive as possible.

In dealing with Lee, Welles would do what he pretty much always did: balance the wishes of the Blair family with the needs of the navy. Because of Lee's family connections, Gideon Welles was always making exceptions for him. As the son-in-law of Francis P. Blair Sr., Lee relied on his father-in-law's pull with the president for plum postings and special treatment. The elder Blair was constantly lobbying the president and/or Welles for key assignments for Lee, but nothing too far away from the main family's summer residence at Silver Spring, Maryland, or from its adjoining townhouses almost directly across the street from the executive mansion, a location which made it easy for Blair to simply drop in on the president or navy secretary whenever it was opportune. (Blair's and Lee's houses were so conveniently situated to the

Totally armored and armed with at least two 11-inch Dahlgren guns, ironclads such as this *Monitor*-class warship were the Union navy's most lethal weapon platforms. The arrival of a monitor at Washington appears to have led to a Civil War-era urban legend that persists to this day. The lore is that the ship was there to take Lincoln away from Washington if the city's defenses faltered. Actually, the navy was prepared to use USS *Baltimore* for that purpose. (Naval History and Heritage Command)

northwest side of the White House that the now-combined Blair-Lee House serves as the official state residence for foreign dignitaries and VIPs visiting the president.)

Washingtonians assumed that the Blair's were a close-knit clan, but there were serious tears in the family's fabric when it came to Lee that weren't so obvious to outsiders. He could not count on receiving any kind words of support from Montgomery Blair, Lincoln's first postmaster general; the two were not on speaking terms and hadn't been for years. Elizabeth Blair Lee and Mary Elizabeth "Minna" Blair, Montgomery's wife, weren't close either. Lee might have had another potential alley in Blair's brother-in-law, Gustavus Vasa Fox, who was married to Minna Blair's sister and was Welles's principal assistant, but there was bad blood there too. Welles alluded to this fracture in his diary entry of 7 October 1864, writing "of the narrow animosity of Lee towards Fox."[15] This most recent ill will he attributed to Lee's reprimand for bringing a portion of his fleet to Washington without orders in July 1864. Elizabeth Blair Lee was certain that Welles would never have written such nasty things and saw Fox's hand behind the censure note. If Elizabeth was Lee's most ardent champion, she was also the worst nightmare of her husband's detractors, even if the detractor was a family member. When she became convinced that the nasty note from Welles was indeed written by Gustavus Vasa Fox, she personally washed her hands with "Fatty," as she called him. An old hand at masking her distain for those on her enemies list, Elizabeth told her husband, "Last night I met Fatty; it cost me a struggle to be civil but I

Watercolor painting of USS *Malvern*, Acting Rear Admiral S. P. Lee's flagship, by R.G. Skerrett, done in 1900. *Malvern* was formerly the Confederate blockade-runner *Ella and Annie*, which was captured in November 1863 off New Inlet, North Carolina. (Naval History and Heritage Command)

was." Such were the dynamics within Fox's extended family. Fox's professional family was far more civil.[16]

The great irony in all of this is that the ironclad and the four warships ordered to Washington by Acting Rear Admiral Lee on 12 July would have reached the mouth of the Potomac at Point Lookout shortly after the two Confederate relief ships planned to free the Rebel prisoners at Point Lookout were expected to arrive had their mission not been called off. This coincidence would have ensured that neither Confederate ship could have escaped, and their mission would have been foiled.

CHAPTER 13

14 July

"Reconnaissance made last night and this morning make it plain that the rebels have disappeared from the front of the fortifications of Washington."

WASHINGTON *EVENING STAR*

14 JULY 1864

On 14 July the *Bedford (Pennsylvania) Inquirer* published a wire dispatch from A. L. Russell advising, "The rebels retiring across the Potomac and skedaddling. The siege of Washington may be considered raised and the National Capital out of danger. No excitement now in Washington." On the contrary, the District of Columbia was full of ferment, but just not the type that had occurred a few days before. When it became clear that the Rebels had retreated, the recriminations began, and there was plenty of finger-pointing and anger to go around. The magnitude of some of the failings were small, others great. At this point damage assessments dominated local and national thinking. For the refugees, it was time to go home and do their assessments. And for many of those who had been harmed by the raids, it was time to begin thinking about settling scores with secessionist neighbors.

Feelings were raw and confused. No one was certain what to believe. The weekly *Bel Air Aegis and Intelligencer* expressed, "Probably no event of the war has been so well shrouded from the popular gaze as this raid."

During the first week following the raid, army-related publications and the *Washington Chronicler* proclaimed that Washington had witnessed a great deliverance. Other publications, such as the *National Intelligencer,* deemed it a "ridiculous subject," and considered the army's performance a national humiliation. Along those same lines, the *Daily Pittsburgh Gazette* informed its readers, "The absurd and ridiculous and yet disgraceful siege of Washington is over." The *Philadelphia Evening Telegraph* straddled the fence, saying, "It is too early yet for us to make up our mind whether we ought to laugh over the denouncement of an affair more farcical than tragical [sic], or whether we should feel a devout thankfulness for a great deliverance. There is enough that is droll to justify the former, were it not checked by the reflection of how much there is mortifying and humiliating in the circumstances of this Rebel raid." Clearly, no one was certain what to think.

One of the universal questions was why no one in authority seemed to know how many Rebels there really had been in the capital. After the fighting, General John G. Barnard wanted an answer, perhaps hoping for a response that would showcase just how effective his fortifications had been in defending Washington. To provide him with what he wanted, his aide, Lieutenant General Oberteuffer, accompanied by an officer of the Office of Coast Survey, examined the ground immediately after Early's retreat. They examined the locations and extent of the bivouacs sites and tracked down tidbits of information gathered from local residents as to the time enemy troops occupied specific spots. Inhabitants were also grilled about any conversations and statements made by the Rebels. Not surprisingly, given Barnard's probable desire for a highest numbers possible, the counts were likely colored to show off how well his defensive works had withstood the mighty scourge. The finding by the Coast Survey in 1864 was that between Silver Spring and Boteler's Ford there were more than 10,000 camp sites and that "The estimate based thereon assigned more than 20,000 men in the force." When this finding was reported in 1871, the analysis also concluded, "The intended assault on 'Tuesday morning' mentioned in Early's narrative [as published in *Southern Magazine* in 1871] was gathered by some of the residents from the conversations of the soldiers. In the foregoing there is a mass of circumstantial evidence that Early's force was much greater that he states it."[1]

The numbers being touted around Washington in 1864 were 15,000 or 20,000, even as many as 55,000. But if any of these had been true, where had those Rebels been? They certainly weren't in front of Fort Stevens. Refugees didn't report seeing such masses. They typically reported seeing only small bands. And nowhere near those numbers descended on Frederick or Rockville. If there had actually been such numbers at Monocacy Junction, General Wallace's small force would have been mauled within minutes. Even the Richmond newspapers made fun of the counting quandary. The *Richmond Dispatch* playfully asked, "Who are these rebels? Where did they come from? Did they spring up out of the earth, or drop down from the clouds? — Are they a large army of regulars or a small squad of raiders? We do not know, the *Washington Chronicle* does not know, Lincoln does not know, Grant does not know, the *New York Herald* does not know." The lack of accurate information was no laughing matter. It was a serious failing, and it went all the way to the top of the army food chain. The fact that the Rebels appeared in so many different places prompted Gideon Welles to doubt Henry Halleck when Halleck assured him the enemy force was a large one. Welles said he didn't believe that was so. From what Welles could gather, the enemy had about 5,000 men. His assistant, Gustavus Vasa Fox, thought that count was still way too high. Fox believed it was closer to 3,000 or 4,000. Halleck sternly told Welles he was greatly mistaken and said he was certain the navy secretary did not get such a faulty impression from any military man. Welles retorted that during the past few days he hadn't gotten *any* useful information from anyone dressed in an army uniform, and that was at the heart of the problem. All he had heard was fear-inspired nonsense.

About Halleck and the army, Welles recorded in his diary on 13 July, "They were defiant and insolent, our men were resolute and brave, but the…generals were alarmed and ignorant, and have made themselves and the Administration appear contemptible."[2] On 13 July General Halleck telegraphed General Grant

Henry W. Halleck's nickname was "Old Brains." It was a title he was given because of his supposed military scholarship, but it soon took on derogatory overtones. Gideon Welles had a low overall opinion of him. "Our army operations have been a succession of disappointments," he wrote in his diary. Welles believed, "General Halleck has accomplished nothing, and has not the public confidence…." As a postscript to this diary entry for 29 December 1862, he added, "With General Halleck there seems neither military capacity nor decision." Welles was convinced that Halleck was the reason why Washington was so ill prepared to confront the Confederate threat in July 1864. (Library of Congress)

to advise, "The enemy fell back during the night.... From the most reliable estimates we can get of the enemy force, it numbered 23,000 to 25,000, exclusive of cavalry. They state that a part of [A. P.] Hill's Corps is coming to reinforce them, and without them they would have captured Washington if the Sixth Corps had not arrived."[3]

To Welles's way of thinking, it was only the army's pride that forced it into claiming it had fended off such large numbers, especially given the fact that the Rebels had gotten off scot-free with so much booty. Lincoln didn't know what to think either. At a Cabinet meeting on 15 July, Lincoln said he wanted to believe there had been a large enemy force, but the evidence before his eyes during visits to Fort Stevens indicated the opposite. That same day the *Pittsburgh Gazette* said it had evidence that proved the Rebel numbers were small. "A critical inspection of their camping ground will convince any one [sic] at all accustomed to such matters that they never had more than eight hundred or, at the very outside, a thousand men on the Seventh Street Road besieging the City."

Within days, other Washingtonians began to wise up to what had actually just happened. Despite efforts by some newspapers intent on making it appear as though the Rebel force was enormous and that the city had been delivered from great danger by the army, Welles's view was, "It is evident there was never any force sufficient to have interrupted [communications], had there been ordinary ability and sagacity on the part of the military." Newspapers tried to figure out just how many men Early truly had. The 15 July edition of the *Daily National Republican* reported, "The statements of our morning contemporaries in regard to the number of the Rebel invaders exhibit a remarkable discrepancy. One puts them down at 500, and the other puts them up at 50,000 to 55,000." At the same time, the *Philadelphia Evening Telegraph* didn't give a number, because it did know, but it did say that in its opinion the mischief in Maryland had been caused by a "small force." From Early's accounting, it is also unclear whether this number included the small force with him under Bradley Johnson that was to attempt to liberate the Confederate prisoners at Point Lookout or the other small forces threatening Baltimore and marauding in Maryland. Additionally, as Gideon Welles suspected, Early's remaining force during his short-lived Washington campaign on 11 and 12 July was spread out. At various times he briefly had troops at College Park, Bladensburg, Beltsville, Laurel, and Colesville in Maryland, while other small bands were roving in Pennsylvania and West Virginia. None of these bands appeared to be very large.

The small number of Rebels at Laurel were advised by Southern sympathizers not to attempt to burn the bridge at Laurel, which was guarded by a unit of Union Veteran Reserve Corps because it would take at least 500 or 600 to dislodge them, and the raiders were nowhere near that strength. The commander of the invalid troops told his wife, "they could not spare that number and it would take too long to whipe [sic] us out for them to stop."[4] This showed the value of the Invalid Corps. Its men were mocked by some of their able-bodied colleagues as belonging to the "Crippled Brigade" or the "Condemned Yanks," because they couldn't march great distances and charge an enemy, but what they could do was stand and fight as a dedicated defensive guard force.[5] They also were used to enforce military discipline and ensure martial law as an arm of the provost marshal, including tracking down people suspected of being disloyal. In their own headquarters, many good-naturedly called themselves members of the "Infidel Corps." Regardless of the characterization, as a result of them doing their duty, the bridge at Laurel, Maryland, was untouched. They also proved to be good at rooting out and jailing Southern sympathizers in the tiny hamlet north of Beltsville.

Such odd incidents reinforced Welles's suspicions that on 12 July Early's main force around Silver Spring probably amounted to about 5,000, not counting cavalry. Others agreed. The *New York World* published a letter, which it editorially supported, which said that if even 12,000 were among the Rebel host, "the expedition would not have consisted of a series of plundering operations and destructive raids, but would have aimed at the taking of Baltimore or Washington, two cities which have been, during the last four days, exposed to the greatest danger, and might have been easily surprised." The newspaper's opinion was that the fact that Early's men didn't mount a serious attempt to take either city clearly showed that neither was an underlying aim. This was backed up by a letter covered in the *National Intelligencer* from one of Early's officers to his family in the area saying that the Rebel force consisted of only about 8,000 men, and their primary purpose was to obtain cattle, horses, and other supplies for Lee's starving army. According to the letter only a small portion of that force appeared in front of Washington, while comrades of those men collected the booty and got it moving across the Potomac.

Another commonly heard complaint was: How could the Rebels had gotten so close to the city without being hotly molested, and why were they so easily able to simply slip away? Someone must have been guilty of something to let that happen! "Somebody was to blame—first, for the advance of the enemy into Maryland, and again for allowing a great inferior force to threaten the very gates of the capital," wrote the *Philadelphia Evening Telegraph*. The paper demanded to know "Who was the man?" saying, "There is no leather medal large enough which with to reward him for his military ability." Lincoln's friend and journalist Noah Brooks's opinion was, "while a great force of effective men was kept at bay within the defenses of Washington, the bulk of Early's army was busy sweeping up all available plunder and sending it southward across the Potomac." Benjamin Brown

Leading the herd, part of "life studies of the great army," by Edwin Forbes. (Library of Congress)

French, who served as the chief marshal of Lincoln's inaugural parade in March 1861 and would oversee his funeral arrangements in 1865, penned in his diary, "The first thing I heard Wednesday was that the invaders were retreating with all their booty, and now we know that they are gone—all got away safe & with whatsoever they captured. It is humiliating enough, and it seems to me as if it ought not to have been permitted. My friend Abraham has got to do something to retrieve this awful blunder or he is 'a goner!'" Secretary Stanton blamed the debacle on Generals Halleck and Grant, one for doing nothing, the other for ordering nothing. The secretary had his assistant, Charles Dana, write to Grant: "advice or suggestions from you will not be sufficient. General Halleck will not give orders except as he receives them; the President will give none, and until you direct positively and explicitly what is to be done, everything will go on in the deplorable and fatal way in which it has gone on for the last week."

The *New York Times* laid some of the blame on the people of Maryland and Pennsylvania for not offering greater resistance to the invaders. It believed that many small Maryland communities should have been barricaded, turning them into mini fortresses. This was also the position taken by the *Malone (New York) Palladium*, which told its readers, "The citizens of Maryland seem to have no idea of anything but escape—there is no organization among them to protect themselves or their property, and these raiders have everything their own way—roaming about in squads of ten or twenty—within half a dozen miles of Baltimore, plundering and burning houses as they list [sic]." The *Charles City (Iowa) Intelligencer* thought the same. In its opinion, "Enough able-bodied men ran away from Western Maryland and Southern Pennsylvania to have captured and caged every rebel who had crossed the Potomac." The paper specifically faulted Marylanders, reporting that while their state had at least 100,000 able-bodied men of military age, it had furnished less than 10,000 to the Union army, and it offered up only 1,000 militia at the Battle at Monocacy Junction. In a slap at the state's pride, the paper suggested, "We trust that her metropolis will erect another monument to Maryland valor after the war is over; but the deeds of heroism that are to glorify it are yet in the future."

The weekly *Palladium*'s position was somewhat self-serving. As a New York newspaper, it was concerned with the fact that so many men from New York had been sent to protect Maryland, while Marylanders did little to protect themselves. New York regiments lost 18 men protecting Fort Stevens, more than any of the other five states with infantry units stationed there. The *New York Tribune* took a different approach, saying this was a time for showing the world that the North was committed to total war, asking its readers, "Is the North at length prepared for war in earnest?"

Other papers questioned the army's leadership. Under a banner story labeled "Being Prepared," the *New York Sun* questioned how such an invasion could have happened. "The fact that any large body of Rebels could penetrate into the loyal States far enough to inflict serious damage upon the inhabitants is an event that calls for investigation," it told its readers. According to the *Sun*, part of the problem was the large number of political generals in the Union army. These were leaders who were there because of their connections but who knew little or nothing of military tactics and training. They were, the paper stressed, generally considered poor leaders of men.

Additionally, some in Washington wondered why, if the city was in such great peril, did it take until 12 July for the government to mobilize all its available manpower. Somebody must have been remiss.

Some Washingtonians were deeply embarrassed that their city had been allowed to come under such an attack. They were also angered that for a time their city, the nation's capital, had to be defended by an untrained, ragtag collection of clerks, laborers and mechanics, and questionable sorts who tended to step forward once the Rebels were gone, while to the South, Lee's entire army was defending Richmond with everything it had. This was a terrible reflection on Lincoln, Stanton, and the army.

Some of Washington's more unsavory types did indeed volunteer once the threat was past. Solomon Brown, a free Black and the Smithsonian's caretaker, described this rabble to the institution's assistant secretary, Spencer Baird, in a 15 July letter: "to see the great number [of] Brave fighting men that came out from their hiding Places and Paraded through streets in serch [sic] of arms to meet the Rebels, but they was mustered out to return to they several dens, i.e., the drinking saloons, gambling halls and other low places, to fight among them selves [sic], for it was Imposable [sic] for decently disposed persons to pass cirtain [sic] localities with out [sic] be[ing] interfered with by this brave men who wanted to fight when the Rebel had gone."

Others bemoaned the fact that shadows and specters had been allowed to rule Washington's thinking. The *Bel Air Aegis and Intelligencer*'s opinion was, "during the last few days, we have seen the administration startling at spectres [sic], uttering panic cries of alarm, and with its hands palsied by imaginary terrors, simply because it had neglected to take the most ordinary precautions for properly watching and occluding the Shenandoah valley." This, said the paper, was the fault of the nation's military men, men like Lew Wallace, who it said had an "alacrity for blundering" and a history of improper dealings, presumably on behalf of the interests of the B&O Railroad. And there was plenty of other "military imbecility" to go around. The newspaper also laid blame for such a great national humiliation at the doorstep of the executive mansion, saying that the president must either take immediate corrective action or be voted out of office.

Maryland farmers were miffed because the military wouldn't permit them to drive their livestock into Washington for protection when the enemy

Smithsonian caretaker Solomon G. Brown in 1891. (Smithsonian Institution)

approached. They were turned away at army checkpoints and forced to herd their animals back home, where most were promptly stolen by Early's riders. After the raid was over, farmers also had no horses to harvest their grain and transport their harvests because they had been taken, too. Entire crops were lost. The full extent of the cattle rustling shocked many. "Long trains of cattle & other booty [had] been sent before them," wrote Mary Henry in her diary, describing the retreating Rebels.[6] The *Washington Evening Star* reported that one band of Confederates had 950 head of cattle in tow, plus about 200 horses. The *Pittsburgh Daily Gazette* reported that 2,000 head of cattle stolen outside Baltimore had crossed the Potomac. Another herd's-worth of horses and cattle was reportedly stolen around Bladensburg, Maryland. All told, the Confederates reportedly fled with 10,000 head of cattle and horses, besides droves of sheep and hogs during their Maryland rampage, according to a *New York Tribune* estimate. The *Tribune* adjusted the count downward to 7,000 within a few days, while at the same time adding mules to the overall mix. Clearly, no one knew for certain what the real number was. That still was a lot of livestock. Prewar Western cattle drives seldom included more than 3,000 or 4,000 head of cattle. Drives of 2,000 head were more common. While 12 drovers could usually lead 2,000 cattle, it took far more than that to round up such livestock from the countryside. Hundreds of Early's men would have had to be detached from their units to form the necessary pillaging parties to gather such numbers.

Horse-wise, the ultimate motherlode would have been the capture of the Giesboro Point Cavalry Depot, which is now the site of the Joint Base Bolling–Anacostia military complex, across the Anacostia River from Washington. This was the largest such cavalry depot in the world, including 32 stables and a 15-acre corral capable of holding roughly thousands of horses. The complex employed more than 100 blacksmiths. Over the course of the war the Union used Giesboro Point to acquire, train, and hold over 170,000 horses. At any given time it was ready to hold roughly 30,000 horses. As part of the defensive plan for Washington, it was defended by Forts Carroll and Greble.[7] Both forts, and their accompanying batteries, were latter-day additions to the city's defensive perimeter. They were specifically constructed to protect the horse depot. Because of their relative isolation with respect to the other fortifications surrounding Washington, and to their relatively small numbers of guns, either of these forts might have been easier to attack than Fort Stevens. But if successful, such attacks would have still left the Rebels on the wrong side of the Anacostia River, leaving the Federal city beyond their reach.

Regarding the looted livestock, the Confederates' problem was lack of excess fodder for the numbers Early ultimately was driving back to Virginia. Most of this treasure trove had to be immediately slaughtered and consumed upon arrival. As it was, Early was relying on Northern farms for forage to

Compared to many of the other forts that surrounded Washington, Fort Carroll, a late addition to Washington's defensive scheme, was relatively under-armed. As seen here, it mounted a few 32-pound seacoast guns and howitzers. Because it was lightly defended, it might have proved an easy prize for an attack by Jubal Early's forces, yielding an even greater prize a few hundred yards beyond it—the thousands of horses in the Union's newly created cavalry depot. (Library of Congress)

The Giesboro Cavalry Depot, located on the Potomac River below the Anacostia River, was established in July 1863, a year before Early's raid on Washington. Its existence doesn't seem to have figured into the Rebel plans to attack Washington. Because of its recent construction, Early may not have been aware of its existence as a significant military target. Some of the horses at the depot in July 1864 would be used to put an end to Early's military career a short time later, when they were assigned to Philip Sheridan's cavalry in the Shenandoah Valley. (Library of Congress)

sustain his own animals, and he needed a lot of it. The average horse or mule consumed roughly 14 pounds of hay and 12 pounds of grain a day, and carting away such commodities required a great deal of wagon space. For Lee's famished army, the feasts from Early's raid on Maryland lasted a mere matter of weeks.

Early's retreating column was said to include roughly 400 wagons, twice what he arrived with. Some of these would have been ambulances. Each regiment typically had its own wagons, and more could easily have been confiscated from local farms if the need arose. A Confederate wagon was usually pulled by four mules. Any remaining wagons might have been used to haul off food, fodder, and plunder. The average military wagon could move 12 to 24 miles a day. This meant that the trek from Silver Spring to White's Ferry—roughly 38 miles—would have taken at least 15 hours. This meant that Early likely had to send the captured livestock and wagons heading for White's Ferry well before he withdrew his army from around Washington. Time-wise, the last of the men involved in the operation to round up wagons and livestock likely left for Virginia no later than 7:00 p.m. on 12 July, arriving at White's Ferry at about 10:00 a.m. The bulk of Early's army bugged out in front of Washington at dusk, and his rear guard, comprising about 2,000 horsemen, passed Forest Glen, Maryland, at 5:00 a.m. on 13 July.

Because Early's food haul was consumed so quickly, another Rebel food raid was carried out in September 1864 by Major General Wade Hampton and roughly 3,000 riders outside Petersburg. This time the rustling—dubbed the "Beefsteak Raid"—netted roughly 2,500 head of cattle meant for Federal forks. The cattle stolen in September 1864 near Coggin's Point on the James River was so poorly protected that Hampton's force had no difficulty overpowering the Federal sentries. President Lincoln was apparently impressed by the Rebel's audacity, reportedly saying the raid was a clever bit of cattle stealing. Hampton's force had gone completely around Grant's army, hastily repairing a key bridge destroyed by the bluecoats, using it to get to the cattle and herd it successfully back to Confederate lines. Once again, because of a lack of fodder, the captured cattle had to be quickly consumed.

* * *

Two months earlier, in July 1864, farmers around Baltimore drove their cattle into the city for protection. They herded as many as possible until the government ordered roads closed. The road closures signaled something else for some city dwellers who panicked when the roads were closed, fearing they'd be trapped inside Baltimore. They rushed to the docks for the first available boats to Philadelphia, New York, or anyplace less likely to be attacked. In their mad dash, many left their baggage behind on the wharfs. Upon their

War artist Alfred Rudolph Waud wrote an accompanying note to his sketch of the September "Confederate Cattle Raid," saying, "The rebel soldiers were much inclined to joke with the pickets on the loss of their meat rations; the Union men, on the other hand, thanked them heartily for removing the tough remnants of herds that had been driven behind the army all summer and which were at once replaced by a fresh stock much fitter for the table." Whether these were dregs or not, the stolen beef was deeply appreciated by the Rebels. For the last half of 1864, Lee's army went from feast to famine, living off Northern livestock stolen by Early in July and Wade Hampton in September, or forced to rely on slim pickings. (Library of Congress)

Major General Wade Hampton. (Library of Congress)

return there was great upset over not being able to find their abandoned luggage at the docks.

For those not acquainted with the looks of war, the extent of the damage so close to Washington and Baltimore was truly shocking. "Everything looks warlike here," wrote Captain Edward Hill on 13 July, "including the desolation of war." Others in the North didn't know what to think, because other than what their local newspapers were saying, there wasn't any reliable news. This fact prompted Union-loving but Lincoln-hating New Yorker Charles Willoughby Dayton to note in his diary for 13 July, "the news from the war is meager as far as truth is concerned for communication is stopped between here and Washington. It is reported that the Rebels are making good progress and that Washington is being shelled but that I deem an impossibility [to] believe they could get near enough to it. We have one thing to be thankful for at this very dark hour in the history of the nation for it is past one year ago to day [sic] since the Great Riots in our City broke out. There is no disturbance at all though a few fire-eaters talked about it. We must cheer at for I do wish the Restoration of the Union as it was."

Damage-wise, the burning of Montgomery's Blair summer home, Falkland, in the early hours of 13 July was considered to be among the raid's great losses. Jubal Early disavowed any role in it. "I had nothing to do with it and do not yet know how the burning occurred," wrote Early in his *Memoirs*. He openly admitted that he firmly believed that such retaliation was fully justified, but said he wouldn't have ordered it because it might have signaled his intentions to withdraw to his enemy.[8] This was a terribly weak rationale given what destruction was wrought throughout Maryland and Pennsylvania, and the wholesale threats to burn entire towns, including Frederick early in July and Chambersburg later in the month.

The first few weeks after the raid was also a time for getting even with secessionist neighbors, including those who had already gone South. The *Chronicle* claimed that the marauding Rebels were away scrounging for supplies and that they were acting like latter-day Robin Hoods. According to the paper, in Montgomery County, Maryland, the Confederates appeared to have taken more from wealthy farmers than they did from poor, simple dirt farmers. The newspaper said, "the rebels did not make an indiscriminate sweep of horses and cattle, but that in many cases they levied upon property somewhat in respect to the means of the possessors to contribute." Colonel Charles F. Johnson commanding an Invalid Corps unit guarding a bridge in neighboring Prince George's County, Maryland, found the exact opposite to be true. In writing to his wife with details of the Rebel raid, he told her, "all the rich are sechesh [a new slang word for secessionists] and all the poor are staunch union."[9] In either case that may not have exactly been what was happening but there appeared to be a degree of favoritism.

The weekly *Gallipolis [Ohio] Journal* thought that the depredations in Maryland probably did more harm than good when it came to curbing anti-Unionist sentiments. The newspaper believed that in its rush to steal livestock it made Union sentiments stronger, saying, "They seemed to pay less respect to the property of sympathizers, than Union men. The losses sustained by the former were much greater, because they relied on their friendship for the rebels, but in which they were much mistaken." Either way, the general belief was that the Rebels didn't take much, if anything at all, from the families of Southern sympathizers. The general consensus was that they stole only from Unionists. This perception was at the heart of a Maryland act, proposed by the delegate from Frederick and passed by the state's legislature overwhelmingly in late July 1864. The act demanded that the president levy damages for "losses and spoliations" endured during the raid by loyal residents of the state and caused by those with secessionist sentiments. Some citizens were appalled by this idea, including Mary Henry, the daughter of the Smithsonian's first secretary, who confided in her diary, "The Loyal Citizens of Maryland have presented a petition to the Pres, asking that the recent losses be assessed upon the sympathizers with the south—It is sincerely to be hoped the pres. will not yield to so unjust a demand."[10]

Newspapers began announcing the sales of confiscated secessionist property, animals, furnishings, and even seized corporate stocks, all taken by the Federal government. These were sold to the highest bidders. Loyal citizens in Maryland and Pennsylvania were also encouraged to file claims for compensation for damages incurred during the raids.

Arrests of known or suspected secessionists in the Maryland suburbs of Washington and elsewhere began on 13 July.

A shake-up within the region's temporary command-and-control structure quickly followed the Confederate retreat. General McCook, was relieved of his field duties in Washington and General Lew Wallace was relieved of overall command of Baltimore's regional defenses. Wallace was replaced by Erastus B. Tyler, who had been in charge of Baltimore's immediate defenses and who had distinguished himself in leading two regiments of 100-day men at the Battle at Monocacy Junction. President Lincoln believed that Tyler leadership was one reason why the defense of Washington wasn't a total disaster. "The country is more indebted to General Tyler than to any other man for the salvation of Washington," he reportedly said. And Lieutenant Colonel Joseph A. Haskins was promoted to brigadier general to head up the artillery department of Washington as a reward for his outstanding service in protecting the city.

By 20 July, talk of the Washington raid briefly faded as the nation's attention moved to news in Georgia and Sherman's march, but the respite was short.

Office Provost Marshal,

FREDERICK, MD., July 22, 1864.

The following Order has been received at this Post:

HEAD-QUARTERS DEPARTMENT W. VA.,
HARPER'S FERRY, W. VA., July 18, 1864.

Major JOHN J. YELLOTT,
1st Maryland P. H. B. Infantry, Commanding Officer, Frederick, Md.

Major,—Your communication of this date relating to persons in Frederick City, Md., having "pointed out to the Rebels during their late raid the property of Union citizens, and otherwise manifesting their sympathy with the enemy," has been submitted to the Major General Commanding the Department.

In reply, he directs that you arrest at once all persons who are known by Union citizens to have given such information, and to send them with their families to this place under suitable Guard, that the males may be sent to the Military Prison at Wheeling, West Va., and their families beyond our lines South. You will seize their Houses to be used for Hospitals, Government Offices and Store Houses, and for Government purposes generally. Their Furniture you will have sold at Public Auction for the benefit of Union citizens of the Town, who are known to have suffered loss of property from information given by these persons.

The Maj. General Commanding further directs that all male Secessionists in Frederick, with their families, must be sent here at once. You will make the same disposition of their Houses and Furniture, as has been directed already in this letter for the Houses and Furniture of those who gave information as to the property of Union men.

I am Major, Very Respectfully, your obedient Serv't.,

P. G. BIER, A. A. G.

To prevent infliction of such punishment as is specified in the above order, it is hereby ordered That, every male citizen of this Town and that portion of Frederick County lying within the limits of the Department of West Va., shall appear at this Office between the hours of 8 o'clock, A. M., and 5 o'clock, P. M., beginning on the 25th day of July, 1864, and ending on the 30th day of July, 1864, and subscribe to an Oath of Allegiance to the Government of the U. S. In default of thus appearing and swearing Allegiance to the National Government, all persons thus failing will be regarded as Secessionists, and treated as directed in the above order. By order of

Maj. Gen. HUNTER,
Commanding Department West Va.

JOHN J. YELLOTT,
Major Commanding Post and Provost Marshal.

Printed by Schley, Keefer & Co., Examiner Power and Rotary Presses, Fred'k.

July 1864 provost marshal's notice to secessionists and those who aided Jubal Early's raiders in Frederick, Maryland, to turn themselves in or be rooted out by their neighbors.[11] By 14 July the process was already underway. The *Philadelphia Evening Telegraph* said that on 14 July, "Many Secessionists have skedaddled, but they will be held accountable on returning; others freely reported themselves." Regardless of who might step forward, all males in the town had to submit to taking the oath of allegiance to the United States. The property of those who wouldn't was to be seized for the benefit of loyal citizens in Frederick who had suffered during the recent raid. (Maryland Broadside Collection, David M. Rubenstein Rare Book & Manuscript Library, Duke University)

This tintype of an unidentified Confederate soldier was purchased at an estate sale decades ago at Abingdon, Virginia. (Library of Congress)

CHAPTER 14

Back Again

"The Rebel Raid is a fizzle...."

CHARLES WILLOUGHBY DAYTON, OHIO
14 JULY 1864

After withdrawing from Washington, President Lincoln wanted to know where Early had gone. At 10:00 a.m. on 27 July, Major General David Hunter wired the president from the safety of Harpers Ferry, saying,

> Early's force is still we believe near Winchester. We can hear nothing of the enemy east of the Blue ridge [sic]. If you have any information of the enemy in that direction please inform me. I have sent out in several directions for information and will keep you posted. I have left [William W.] Averill to protect the upper fords of the Potomac but he needs infantry. Can it not be sent from Penna? In the present state of affairs I believe it much more important to make Wash & Balto perfectly secure than to attempt to interrupt the rebels from gathering their crops in the valley.[1]

The ever-cautious Hunter, who had done so little to protect Washington and Baltimore before, was wrong about all the Rebels.

Three days later a Confederate force burned Chambersburg, Pennsylvania. It was left to Union colonel William W. Averill's men to avenge the burning, which his little mounted force did at Moorefield, West Virginia, in an early morning raid on the Rebel camp.

Fed up with Hunter's timidity and Selig's propensity for hiding atop Maryland Heights, Lieutenant General Grant finally sacked both of them. Hunter was replaced by Philip Sheridan, who would earn a reputation for

The northwest corner of Chambersburg's public square after Rebel forces under Brigadier General John McCausland set fire to the town on 30 July 1864. The Rebels also demanded extortion money from Hancock and Cumberland, Maryland. (Library of Congress)

Colonel William W. Averill with his 3rd Pennsylvania Cavalry staff at Westover Landing, Virginia, August 1862. (Library of Congress)

being a far worse arsonist than Hunter ever was. Grant's order to Sheridan was, "nothing should be left to invite the enemy to return. Take all provisions, forage, and stock wanted for the use of your command. Such as cannot be consumed, destroy." Because the Shenandoah Valley had repeatedly served as the avenue for so many Confederate incursions into the North and it was the Rebel's breadbasket, Grant directed Sheridan's men to act like a giant scythe. "Do all the damage to railroads and crops you can," he told Sheridan. Grant wanted the valley to be transformed into a wasteland.

As dutifully directed, Major General Sheridan became the Angel of Death in the Shenandoah Valley. The destruction started in late September 1864. Within 13 days, much of the valley was unlivable. Sheridan's 1st Cavalry Division alone burned more than 1,100 barns filled with wheat and flour. The men destroyed three factories and six distilleries. They slaughtered, drove off, or confiscated more than 5,500 head of cattle and more than 1,100 hogs; torched 49 mills; ruined crops still in the fields; took every bit of beacon, butter, and bread in farmhouses; axed orchards; smashed farm implements and machines; and seized horses and mules. Nothing useful for future farming was intentionally left intact. Many of the more that 5,800 sheep captured were put to death simply to further starve the South's soon-to-be-famished soldiers and farm families. Additionally, the 1st Cavalry Division made off with, contaminated, or set fire to more than 30,000 tons of hay, more than 39,000 bushels of wheat, nearly 8,000 bushels of corn, and roughly 2,000 bushels of oats. Nothing that could fill even the youngest valley mouth was intentionally left behind by the 1st Division's horsemen.

Sheridan's 2nd Cavalry Division had a better track record than the 1st when it came to destroying Southern railroad property.

As ordered, much of the valley became inhospitable. "The whole country from the Blue Ridge to the North Mountain has been made untenable," Sheridan boasted. It was said that anyone could track his army by following the smoke that rose into the sky from burning farm buildings and crops. This vision greatly pleased General Grant. It also pleased Lincoln, who sent Sheridan his personal regards on 22 October for his "splendid work."

Sheridan had upwards of 50,000 men in October 1864, and he had nearly two weeks to accomplish his mission of laying waste to the Shenandoah Valley. By comparison, Jubal Early had far fewer men and only a fraction of that time in Maryland. But his aim was not to destroy the region. He wanted to leave it capable of blossoming again in case further food raids were required.

What no one in the Southern command seems to have counted on was how much Early's raid irked Grant. He was miffed over how it might adversely impact the outcome of the 1864 presidential election and what it did to his plans for another push at Petersburg. No one apparently factored in the extent of Grant's anger over such annoyances.

As a result, what Early had done during the previous July had severe unintended consequences. Grant demanded that Early's force be utterly crushed and the Shenandoah Valley be rendered totally useless as Lee's breadbasket. He also wanted to place a permanent stopper in the valley's ability to serve as the great Confederate causeway into the North. That could only be accomplished if the valley was no longer capable of supporting an army on the move with friendly forage. Grant wanted to put an end to all these pesky problems once and for all—and Sheridan did just that!

For both sides, turning to the torch unleashed a demon. Chambersburg burned, as did the Shenandoah Valley and Atlanta and many other places.

After slipping back into Virginia in mid-July in the aftermath of what Charles Willoughby Dayton dubbed "a fizzle," Early was again in Pennsylvania and Maryland at the end of the month in search of more supplies and ransom money. Again, his demand was pay up or burn up. He also said the time was right to show one or more Northern towns what tit-for-tat truly felt like: "I came to the conclusion it was time to open the eyes of the people of the North to this enormity, by an example in the way of retaliation."[2] In a statement published in the *Richmond State* in 1887, he said his acts of retaliation were intended to try to put a stop to "this mode of warfare." Yet, in this same statement to the newspaper, he negated the best intensions behind this explanation, saying that the burnings at Chambersburg "was in strict accordance with the laws of war and was a just retaliation." He added, "It afforded me no pleasure to subject non-combatants to the rigors of war, but I felt I had a duty to perform to the people for whose homes I was fighting and I endeavored to perform it, however disagreeable it might be."

In the case of Chambersburg, Pennsylvania, on 30 July, Early set the ransom price high, demanding $100,000 as a suitable payoff, believing that equaled the cost of replacing several of the important homes David Hunter had destroyed in the Shenandoah Valley. He demanded that amount in gold, or in the equivalent amount of greenbacks, which he said was $500,000. It is likely that he didn't expect to be paid, because this time the raiders also took eight hostages to force the townsfolk to pay. But they didn't. The locals believed deep down that the Rebel chief was bluffing. They saw him as a paper tiger because he hadn't burned any other Northern towns yet, despite repeated threats, and they were certain that a Union relief force was at hand. But Early wasn't bluffing. Brigadier General "Tiger John" McCausland dutifully carried out his orders.

At Chambersburg, many of McCausland's men were so drunk by the time he ordered that the fires be set that they had difficulty remaining in their saddles. Despite their intoxicated condition McCausland deployed them in squads around town to randomly wreak destruction. The burning began at about 8:00 a.m. By 10:00, much of the town was ablaze. At least 300 buildings were destroyed. The fires left an estimated 2,500 homeless. All the dispossessed were destitute. The damage claims amounted to more than $1.6 million, and 155-plus years later, more than half of the claims remained outstanding.

The courthouse at Chambersburg destroyed by Confederate cavalry on 30 July 1864.
(Library of Congress)

Significant looting and some robberies also occurred. By noon the Rebels
fled fearing the approach of a large Federal force.

There were a few acts of Confederate kindness at Chambersburg.
McCausland wouldn't allow the house of Union Colonel William H. Boyd
Sr. to be burned. Boyd was the commander of the 21st Pennsylvania Cavalry.
The two men were mutually respected adversaries, and Boyd was known
for having spared many a Southern home in the Shenandoah Valley from
being burned. Additionally, only one church in town was burned, and one
company of Rebels was so ashamed of what their brothers had done that they
assisted the townspeople in combating the blazes. These actions did little to
persuade the townsfolk that the Confederates weren't anything but simple
Southern brigands. While Chambersburg was the only Northern city put to
the torch in this way during the war, it set a tremendous example that other
communities wanted to avoid.

Next, McConnellsburg, Pennsylvania, was plundered. The Confederate
bivouac at McConnellsburg on 31 July 1864 was the last Confederate camp
site north of the Mason-Dixon Line. This was followed by a raid on Hancock,
Maryland, where McCausland demanded a contribution of $30,000 for not
burning the town. This was one demand too many. Many of the Rebels
were Marylanders, and they wanted nothing to do with this latest cash grab.
Fistfights broke out among the raiders. Instead of pushing the demand,
McCausland ordered his men to move on to Cumberland, where another

Public buildings at Chambersburg were burned along with private homes. The county courthouse was doused with two barrels of oil and packed with straw before being set on fire. A guard standing watch over a group of hostages held in the courthouse walked away from his post while the building was being prepared to be torched, allowing the hostages to flee. Confederate soldiers turned rags into firebombs, soaking them in turpentine, balling them up, and tossing them to accelerate the fires. This is what remained of the Bank of Chambersburg building. (Library of Congress)

ransom payment was demanded. Around Cumberland, Union troops attacked the invaders and ran them off after fierce fighting.

* * *

Early could have forbidden his men from burning noncombatant properties, which would likely have put a stop to it, but he didn't. Instead, he did nothing to indicate his disapproval of such conduct on any particular occasion. He justified this in his *Memoirs*, stressing, "Not content with taking provisions, cattle, horses, sheep and other things which they might use, [the bluecoats] often took what was of no earthly use to them as soldiers, and destroyed what they could not carry away. I have seen where they had torn up the clothes of the women and children, hacked to pieces furniture, pianos and other articles, destroyed valuable papers and books, burned besides houses, plows, carts and a variety of such things. This I have seen in not a few instances, but I have seen whole communities rendered destitute in this way."[3] This destruction was what Early had witnessed firsthand at Locust Grove, Virginia, carried out by George G. Meade's men during the Mine Run campaign in late 1863. To Early's way of thinking, if Benjamin Butler, David Hunter, and William

Adelphi Mill in Prince George's County, Maryland, before its restoration. It is now used as a community recreation center. (Library of Congress)

Sherman were applauded in the North for allowing these sorts of things to happen, he certainly should have earned some degree of acclaim in the South for extracting paybacks. The only problem with what Early's men did was that they were second- or third-rate despoilers by comparison. Rather than burning anything and everything in their path, Early's men were relatively restrained. Maryland's gristmills, for example, were left pretty much unmolested, and the skyline from Frederick, Maryland, to Silver Spring wasn't filled with smoke rising from homes and barns. Early wasn't hell-bent on burning farms and gristmills. He knew the South might need to revisit them again for additional food drives in the years to come.

Southern forces roamed freely around the rural fringes of the district line, foraging and camping at sites along Sligo Creek, such as at the location of the old Sligo Mill, which, although abandoned by 1864, still had a refreshing mill pond. The mill was served by Sligo Mill Road, essentially present-day New Hampshire Avenue. Excavations of a suspected Rebel campsite on the eastern bluff overlooking the Sligo Mill site in the 1960s uncovered a single-shot pocket pistol and a bent military-style rifle trigger guard assembly, as well as an array of liquor bottles and cow and chicken bones.

Other potential mill targets a short distance from Sligo Mill included Freeman's Mill, Kemp's Mill, and Powder Mill. Freeman's Mill was built in 1796 on the northwest branch of the Anacostia River. Now known as Adelphi Mill, it was the oldest and largest gristmill in the region.

Kemp's Mill, also located on the northwest branch of the Anacostia, was a grist and lumber mill. Powder Mill, located on Paint Branch, initially

This view is of the Owing's flour and meal mill outside Baltimore, circa 1910. Most mills operated as sawmills during the winter months. (Library of Congress)

The Hager's Mill in Hagerstown, Maryland. (Library of Congress)

produced gunpowder for the army, but by the Civil War it was producing wool blankets and lumber. The annual output of Kemp's Mill would reach 700 barrels of flour, 7 barrels of rye, 167 tons of meal, 28 tons of feed, and 4 tons of buckwheat.

There were at several hundred major mills between Frederick and Silver Spring, including many outside Baltimore and in Montgomery County, such as Black Rock Mill, Liberty Mill, DuFief's Mill, and Clopper's Mill. DuFief's was capable of grinding as many as 12,000 barrels of flour a year. Any pillaged flour from such mills was valuable to the South. Weight was an issue. A barrel of flour weighed nearly 200 pounds. Regrettably for Early there wasn't much time or manpower to locate and visit all flour mills. That was unfortunate for the South, because each was a worthwhile possible target for the food-obsessed marauders. In preserving the mills, Early may have simply been following General Lee's orders to leave civilian property alone, or maybe he was listening to public sentiments in the South, which was that such destruction was uncivil and un-Southern. It was something that only the Northern barbarians did. Southern gentlemen within the Confederacy were said to be Christian soldiers, men of honor who did not make war on defenseless women and children and noncombative civilian populations. Or maybe he was looking to the need for subsequent food raids, where such mills would need to remain intact.

Even if Early had been vengeful, the loss of a few mills in Maryland would not have been catastrophic to flour prices in the North. Boston at the time had a surplus of 350,000 barrels of flour and was receiving 35,000 barrels a week. As there was little in the way of foreign demand, this was all intended for domestic consumption.

Regardless of the reason for not destroying gristmills, crops still in the fields don't appear to have been of major interest, either, perhaps because Early admitted that he didn't have the time to harvest them. Nor did he have time to locate, harness, and commandeer the necessary farm wagons needed to move any unmilled hauls. The average farm wagon could haul 10 barrels of flour, but those had to come from the farms that were scattered around the mill sites and these were widely spread out.

Northern farms were like a food pantry for the South. Compared to filling wagons with barrels of flour, livestock took little time to collect. A few men could get a herd of cattle moving in a matter of minutes, and there were certainly plenty animals available for the taking. During the Civil War, Montgomery County, Maryland, had approximately 5,700 cattle and 4,000 milking cows. Prince George's County had about 4,800 head of cattle and 3,400 dairy cows. Baltimore County had more than 6,000 cattle and nearly 10,000 milk cows. There were more than 10,200 head of cattle in Frederick County and nearly 11,200 dairy cows. And Howard and Anne Arundel Counties combined had more than 5,700 cattle and more than 6,000 milkers. And the six counties noted here had more than 106,000 hogs plump for the taking.

As for arson, most fires were confined to areas around Washington and Baltimore. Gideon Welles had witnessed the destruction of one of the houses in front of Fort Stevens, but there were many others beyond his view. Just north of Washington the ruins of burned-out buildings became common sights. The house of Postmaster General Montgomery Blair, was among those consigned to the flames, although who actually burned it became a subject of speculation.

Welles, a good friend of Blair's, was disgusted with the whole chain of events. He and his sons visited what remained of his friend Blair's home on Sunday, 17 July. Welles sadly wrote, "we turned down the lane which leads to [Falkland] and went to the walls of Montgomery Blair's house, situated pleasantly on a little wooded eminence. But all was silent. Waste and war."[4]

Regardless of who set the fire or why, Blair blamed the army for needlessly destroying Virginia Governor John Letcher's house and provoking retaliation. The army also did not provide sufficient protection for his own property, Blair believed, or for the nation's capital, calling the leadership "cowards and poltroons."

Part of Blair's upset was due to the fact that he had relied upon the army for intelligence regarding Early's movements leaving town earlier in the month. According to the army, Early was holed up around Harpers Ferry and expected to stay there. July and August heat and humidity in Washington

First page of General Halleck's letter to Secretary Stanton regarding Montgomery Blair's affront to the army. (Library of Congress)

can be beastly, causing many to flee the city for cooler climes. The Blair men had done just that, going off to the mountains of Pennsylvania on a hunting and fishing excursion, while the women and girls of the family had gone off to Cape May to escape the heat at the New Jersey shore. This left none of the family at either Montgomery's or Francis Preston Blair's homes when the Confederates came. Montgomery Blair's accusation of military negligence set off a firestorm within Lincoln's Cabinet. Some members, such as Welles, agreed with Blair, saying, "on our part there is neglect, ignorance, folly, imbecility, in the last degree."[5] Blair's characterization outraged many in the War Department.

General Halleck was livid, realizing that Blair's charge was mostly aimed at him. Stanton also was furious. Welles already suspected that Stanton disliked

Montgomery Blair's reply to President Lincoln's request for his resignation. (Library of Congress)

Blair, and that only made matters worse. While there were calls for Blair to be removed from the Cabinet for such outrageous insults, other forces were at work to orchestrate his ousting. Lincoln wouldn't use Halleck's petty upset to remove Blair. He responded to Stanton on 14 July: "I do not consider what may have been hastily said in a moment of vexation at so severe a loss, is sufficient grounds for so grave a step." Blair would go, but not for this.[6]

Welles thought that Stanton, or Salmon Chase, or Thurlow Weed, or even Illinois Congressman Elihu B. Washburne might well have had hands in instigating Blair's downfall, but his real money was on William Seward. In the end, Lincoln had to accept Blair's resignation, which Blair had offered to Lincoln long before. Lincoln explained this to Blair on 23 September 1864, saying, "You have generously said to me, more than once, that whenever your resignation could be a relief to me, it was at my disposal. The time has come."[7]

That same day, the disheartened Blair intercepted Welles while he was walking with Attorney General Edward Bates near the White House to explain, "I suppose you are both aware that my head is decapitated,—that I am no longer a member of the Cabinet."[8] Although he was no longer a part of Lincoln's government, Blair remained a powerful force within the Republican Party and in Washington social, political and religious life.

CHAPTER 15

Point Lookout

At first glance the plan to free Confederate prisoners from Point Lookout was borne out of desperation. It would be undertaken for want of fighting men to prolong the war. General Lee summarized the outcome of the mission in one sentence: "Great benefit might be drawn from the release of our prisoners at Point Lookout if it can be accomplished." And Early acknowledged that he'd give it his best effort. But there was more to it than that. Early's entire mission was predicated on drawing as many Federal forces away from Petersburg as possible and finding food to feed the Rebel army. Regarding both, the ploy succeeded.

Gideon Welles wrote in his diary that he had heard there was a great deal of upset at the War Department in July 1864 between Grant and Stanton. Grant had ordered "[Brigadier] General [Edward W.] Hinks to Point Lookout and Stanton countermanded the order for General [James S.] Barnes."[1] Hinks had been the commander at Point Lookout from March to May 1864 before being put in charge of the 3rd Division of the XVIII Corps at Petersburg. Now he had been ordered back to Maryland, only to have that instruction overruled. Lee had almost gotten part of his first wish. Federal troops were almost peeled away from Petersburg.

From the start, Lee said he expected Maryland men to affect the escape at Point Lookout. To his way of thinking, this was to be an "all Maryland operation." In outlining the plan to Jefferson Davis on 26 June 1864, Lee noted, "I can devote to this purpose the whole of the Marylanders on this army, which would afford a sufficient number of men of excellent material and much experience." Finding the best leader was tough. Lee realized that it should be a Marylander, but who? Lee considered Colonel Bradley T.

Johnson the best choice for the assignment, calling him "bold and intelligent, ardent and true," but he doubted he possessed the other qualities needed for such a command. "Everything in an expedition of the kind would depend upon the leader," Lee told Davis. The first scheme was to ferry Johnson's 1st Maryland Cavalry across the Potomac opposite Point Lookout, but that was soon dropped.

A better approach was needed. Lee wanted a greater naval role and he believed the naval portion of the operation would also need to be commanded by a Marylander. For this reason, Lee recommended John Taylor Wood.

The initial plan, concocted in early June 1864, called for sending Captain Wood with 800 "Marine volunteers" to Point Lookout by water and landing them on the beach in a surprise attack against the Union garrison there. Lee believed, "By throwing them suddenly on the beach with some concert of action among the prisoners, I think the guard(s) might be overpowered, the prisoners liberated and organized, and marched immediately on the route to Washington." As first proposed, the plan called for the Confederate navy to secretly ferry the raiding force across the Potomac opposite Point Lookout. The river at that point is exceptionally wide, and Lee wasn't certain the Navy had the capability to carry out that part of the plan because there weren't that many small boats available to ferry those numbers across the river and building boats wouldn't go unnoticed.

Robert E. Lee's next plan called for the use of multiple small gunboats to land the raiding party and evacuate the prisoners in relays to Virginia.

John Taylor Wood held the rank of captain in the Confederate navy and colonel in the Confederate cavalry. He was a renowned risk-taker who commanded numerous naval operations on the Chesapeake Bay and its tributaries, and at one point even considered steaming into New York Harbor in an attempt to attack the Brooklyn Navy Yard. He was precisely the kind of officer Union planners would have expected the South to select to lead a naval raid on Point Lookout. His association alone gave credence to the plan. (Naval History and Heritage Command)

A third version of the operation was to use two steamers of light draft that were to be loaded with weapons and ammunition and were to carry, in addition to their crews, an infantry force under the command of General Custis Lee that would be landed at Point Lookout and capture the prison.

A fourth version was subsequently outlined in a directive from army major and navy captain John Tyler Wood to Major Sterling Price on 9 July. According to Wood, "The plan is that [Jubal Early] shall seize Baltimore and hold it with his infantry while his cavalry proceeds to Point Lookout to liberate our prisoners there concentrated to the extent of nearly 30,000. In the meantime Captain (John Taylor) Wood, of the Navy, proceeds from Wilmington with five gunboats and 20,000 stand of arms for the same point by water." If successful in thus liberating and arming our imprisoned soldiers, Johnson was to march them to Bladensburg where they would join forces with Early in attacking Washington. Together this combined force would assault the city and no doubt carry it. "This I regard as decidedly the most brilliant idea of the war," thought Price.

A fifth, hybrid, plan was actually put in motion. This involved the use of two steamers from Wilmington, North Carolina, not multiple gunboats. As they proceeded on water, Maryland cavalry under the command of Bradley Johnson would travel overland through Maryland.

Johnson was first informed of Lee's scheme on 8 July. Based upon Lee's instruction, he'd leave for Point Lookout the following morning. For Johnson and his 1st Maryland Cavalry Regiment, the assignment meant riding roughly 250-plus miles in 96 hours. Johnson believed that this couldn't be done, that his horses couldn't be pushed like that.

After 48 hours, Johnson's unit was still far from southern Maryland. After rampaging around Baltimore, his troopers were only at Reisterstown, where most of his men fell out from sleep deprivation. That left more than 125 miles to go, and the clock was ticking away. Alternating between trotting and walking, Johnson's men might have covered that remaining distance in roughly 25 hours, assuming they stopped for nothing. Arrangements were made to exchange horses south of Bladensburg. This could have put them at Point Lookout with a little time to spare, but by then they'd be alone, with no navy support. There'd also be no rifles. President Davis learned that the required 20,000 rifles simply weren't available.

Unfortunately, as with many such "bright ideas," it didn't remain a secret for long. Uncle Sam uncovered the plans for Point Lookout during the first week of July from a deserter. Benjamin Butler was informed on 7 July and notified the Navy on 8 July. By the morning of 8 July, Union naval and army forces were on full alert. Cavalry units were immediately ordered to patrol all roads in the vicinity of Upper Marlboro and Port Tobacco that led towards Point Lookout and to report back as soon as they spotted any enemy cavalry heading that way.

In his narrative, John Wilkinson recounted how the mission was betrayed: "It failed, however, owing to the fact that secretly as all the preparations had been made, information of it was speedily conveyed to the authorities at Washington, and prompt measures taken to prevent its success." How the Federal government learned of the raid will, perhaps, remain a mystery, but there was a belief in the Confederacy that an individual near the president was a traitor. Someone in Elizabeth Van Lew's network?

Washington appears to have learned about the planned breakout at Point Lookout about as soon as Early did. It seems that Early was informed of Bradley Johnson's assignment to his command on 3 July, in a special letter from Lee. Lee told Early that he didn't have all the particulars of the prison break worked out, but that Johnson's brigade of Maryland cavalry and a battery of horse artillery was to attempt to gain the release of the prisoners at Point Lookout on 12 July. Early wasn't told how this was to happen or what he might expect if the effort was a success. He knew only that Johnson's efforts were contingent upon his own force reaching Washington. Before risking a raid on Point Lookout, Johnson's men were to wreak havoc on the railroads operating between Baltimore and Washington via Harrisburg and Philadelphia.

Jefferson Davis was alarmed by how many people seemed to know about the planned prison break and about the possibility that word of the breakout had already reached Washington. He was so concerned that the plan had been thoroughly compromised that on 10 July, he called it off, justifying his decision by noting, "The object and destination of the expedition have somehow become so generally known that I fear your operation will meet unexpected obstacles." The wave-off came at the last minute, with Wilkinson noting, "The steamers had dropped down the Cape Fear River, and were on the very point of putting to sea when countermanding orders were telegraphed from Richmond; for the Confederate Government, through their secret sources of information, had been promptly notified of the fact that the plot had been betrayed to the United States authorities."

In all likelihood Elizabeth Van Lew's spy network pulled the alarm on the prison break in early July. This seems to be the case because the Union reacted so swiftly to it its possibility. As example, as early as 5 July Major General C. C. Auger ordered Union scouts posted at Upper Marlboro and Port Tobacco to patrol the upper and lower routes to Point Lookout. These were "to report daily, if there is anything like small bodies of cavalry (rebels) going down that way."

Additionally, everything about the naval portion of the plan was ill thought out.

If Captain Wood started for Point Lookout under cover of darkness before midnight on 10 July, and if he steamed at 17 knots all the way, that would give him about 30 hours to arrive off Point Lookout. At 17 knots, the cruise alone would consume roughly 18 hours. While this would indeed have put him off the prison in advance of the morning of 12 July, such a timetable was unrealistic. It assumed a straight cruise up the coast, at full speed, with no apparent headwinds, no strong currents, no adverse weather conditions, and no time for maneuvers to evade or fight off any enemy vessels, if sighted. If Captain Wood encountered any of the 50 or so Union warships engaged in the Wilmington blockade force along the way, running sea battles would surely have ensued, dogging the Rebel ships. This would have consumed many additional hours of maneuvering and/or fighting. Further, as likely as not, the Rebel dash north would have resulted in a Union naval pile-on with attacks from many Federal vessels, a massive feeding frenzy of hungry sharks off the North Carolina coast or at the mouth of the Chesapeake Bay just hoping to get a piece of the prize money from the capture of the Confederate ships.

Regardless of President Davis's rationale for pulling the plug, stories began to circulate mocking the idea of the raid. One version was that two armed transports had been fitted out at Wilmington, North Carolina, with arms and ammunition that were to provision the freed prisoners. That was a true reporting of the plan, but the 22 July issue of the *Washington Daily National Republican* called this version "a pretty story," saying, "There is nothing like 13,000 prisoners at Point Lookout, and the idea of armed transports from Wilmington passing the gunboat fleet at Fort Monroe on such an expedition is absurd." The newspaper was wrong on both counts. There were indeed more than 13,000 prisoners at Point Lookout; estimates range from 15,000 to 19,000. Then there were the Union warships at Norfolk. But these weren't the only nautical obstacles facing Captain Wood. The Federal navy's blockading squadron outside Wilmington was a far bigger problem. And then there were the really big guns of USS *Roanoke*, anchored off Point Lookout, and the smaller yet more numerous warships of the Potomac Flotilla at the mouth of the Potomac. Any planned waterborne Confederate landing on the Point Lookout peninsula would certainly be hotly opposed by alerted Union naval forces.

Statistically, getting out of Wilmington probably wasn't going to be a serious problem. Wilmington was a major gateway to the Confederacy, and it was a sieve for Southern supplies. The majority of the South's blockade-runners enjoyed a roughly 75-percent success rate coming and going from the port. At the start of the war, only 1 in 10 blockade-runners were successfully stopped. As the war progressed, the Union blockade became more impervious, with three crisscrossing layers of blockaders patrolling offshore. The first line in this zone-like defense consisted of about 30 slower Federal ships or picket

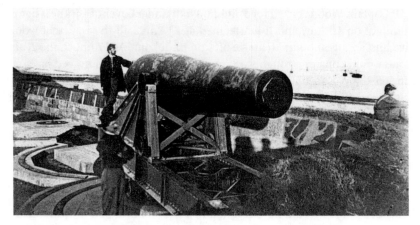

One of the 15-inch Rodman guns at Fort Monroe. A gun of this size could hurl a 500-pound solid shot over 3 miles using a 50-pound powder charge at an elevation of 25 degrees. Guns such as this weighed more than 49,000 pounds.[2] (Library of Congress)

boats stationed close to the coast. These were arrayed in a 10-mile arc just beyond the range of Confederate shore batteries. The ships in this zone would signal other larger and faster ships farther out when they spotted a runner. The second blockade line was posted about 12 miles out, and the third line cruised back and forth beyond that. The value of the zones was that any could be downsized or eliminated if ships had to temporarily be pulled away. They also enabled the blockaders to swarm towards a runner. By the war's end, the number of captures increased to 5 in 10. The rate of capture was low because there were two ways in and out of port, which kept the blockading fleet on alert. In all, about 1,500 vessels failed to elude the blockade.

Many of the successful blockade-runners and Confederate commerce raiders were converted or purpose-built vessels. They were sleek and fast, capable of operating at speeds of 10 to 17 knots. They were built principally for speed.

The blockade-runners typically made their runs on moonless nights and were painted flat white or dull grey to help conceal their low silhouettes. Many had collapsible masts and folding funnels to lower their profiles further, and most burned smokeless coal, making them harder to spot in the dark. However, these weren't the type of ships John Tyler Wood was describing when he used the word "gunboats" in describing the specific version of the escape plan he was addressing. During the Civil War, a "gunboat" was typically a converted tugboat, about 120-feet long. These were armed with a single bow or stern gun. A small crew typically manned each of these small boats.

If this version of the Point Lookout breakout plan, had indeed been used, the five gunboats would likely have never made it much past Fort Fischer at the mouth of the Wilmington inlet. As secondhand commercial vessels, they made speeds of 5 to 7 knots, a tugboat's typical operating speed. At 7 knots (about 8 miles per hour), the gunboats would certainly never have gotten safely past the Federal blockaders outside Wilmington, and if they could somehow have done so, the trip to Point Lookout would have consumed every bit of 48 hours under ideal steaming conditions. The problem with the gunboat scenario is that Captain Wood is said to have left Richmond with about 800 marine "volunteers" on the night of 7 and 8 July. This was way too many men for five tiny tugboats. It would have been impossible to accommodate 160 men on each, plus the crews.

The use of the word "volunteers" is a misnomer, because they certainly couldn't have been actual marines. For the longest time people have taken Wood's use of "volunteer" to mean literally "marines who volunteered," but that wasn't the case. He meant that they were volunteers who would act like marines in that they'd be attacking from the water. They weren't actually Confederate marines. Here are the reasons why that is logically so.

First, the 800 marines that Wood had, according to contemporary reports, exceeded the total number of mustered marines in Confederate service at that time. When it was establishment on 16 March 1861, and as organized on 20 May 1861, the Confederate Marine Corps was never expected to be a large force. It was initially to consist of 1 colonel, 1 lieutenant colonel, 1 major, 1 quartermaster major, 1 quartermaster sergeant, 10 captains, 10 first lieutenants, 20 second lieutenants, 40 sergeants, 40 corporals, and 840 privates. The corps was also originally envisioned to have 10 drummers and 10 fifers, plus 2 musicians. This was a total of 1,067 marines. Nineteen of the Confederate marine officers were US Marines who had resigned from Federal service to serve the South at the start of the war. In September 1862 the Confederate Marine Corps was expanded by the authorized addition of 20 sergeants, 20 corporals, 20 drummers, 20 fifers, and 2 principal musicians. These were organized into six understrength companies, plus a 6-to-8-member headquarters staff.

Second, Colonel Lloyd James Beall, the commandant of the Confederate Marine Corps, reported on 30 October 1864 that the aggregated strength of his corps was only 539 men and that these were scattered around at sites such as Mobile, Savannah, Charleston, Wilmington, and Drewry's Bluff overlooking the James River, as well as some at sea serving as "sea soldiers" aboard warships, such as CSS *Virginia, Tallahassee, Savannah, Sumter, McRae, Atlanta,* and *Chickamauga,* and 27 other vessels overtime. Shipboard postings accounted for most of the marines, and assignments to key Confederate ports consumed most of the rest of the marine manpower. As of September 1863, as example, Mobile had 100 marines. Confederate warships typically had a complement of 21 marine guards, many of whom were foreign-born. While commanding CSS *Sumter,* Raphael Semmes expressed his great frustrations with the difficulties he was having shaping up his marine guards, noting, "the Marines, being most foreigners—Germans—are the most difficult set of men I have on the ship. It is difficult to lick them into shape." Desertions were common.

Third, the reality is that it was impossible for 800 "marines" to have been quickly mobilized at Richmond in July 1864 to assist Captain Wood. The largest force close to hand was at Camp Beall, near Fort Darling, at Drewry's Bluff, but a muster roll of marines at Camp Beall in August 1864 lists only 106 men. Clearly, to take any of those away from that location would have significantly weakened the camp's defensive capabilities. As it was, the Confederate Navy Department had already withdrawn its sailors from the defensive works at Drewry's Bluff on 30 April 1864 so they could be assigned to ships. This left this strategic position on the James River vulnerable to attack, which is precisely what happened. Fort Darling came under Union attack in May 1864 by a sizeable Federal force, but this attack was repulsed by mid-month. With Drewry's Bluff largely defended only by marines, it seems unlikely that they could so easily have been siphoned away for a risky amphibious operation in southern Maryland. Marine Commandant Colonel Lloyd J. Beall didn't attempt to consolidate his corps at Richmond until February and March 1865, when he called for all his available men to gather to defend the Drewry's Bluff river approach to the Confederate capital. His consolidated marine force joined General Lee's army in its retreat from Petersburg in April 1865.

Fourth, where the supposed 800 "volunteers" accompanying Captain Wood were to come from, and how many men were actually available, remains unclear. But they weren't really Confederate marines. This was affirmed by a publication from the former Museum of the Confederacy that confirms that there never were more than 600 Southern marines at any given time, despite the numbers authorized. Clearly, the "marines" chosen for this mission were truly "volunteers," deputized for this particular duty. The misleading use of the word "marines" was likely invoked to evoke a certain "scare factor."

If the "volunteer marines," weren't the real deal, Captain John Taylor Wood certainly was. He had a well-earned reputation for doing daring things. Jefferson Davis described him as "an officer of extraordinary ability and enterprise." Because of his ability to serve in a saddle as well as on a deck, Wood had been given both army and navy ranks. This was just the kind of person that Union military leaders would have expected the South to tap to lead such a risky enterprise. His selection added credibility to a possibly bogus undertaking. Wood indeed appeared eager to go. He reported that he was ready to run the blockade on the night of 9 July under a half-moon.

Everything appeared to be part of a legitimate plan, but the adopted plan called for the use of a pair of blockade-runners, namely *Florie* and *Let Her B,* rather than of five small gunboats. These were two of the 588 blockade-runners built by English shipyards to carry desperately needed cargoes of saltpeter, arms, lead, iron, and medical supplies into Southern ports. British cannons were another highly prized cargo.

This latter scenario had the South willingly sacrificing two of its best blockade-runners. These would be a tempting prize to any Northern naval officer. Any skipper in his right mind would have jumped at the opportunity to capture either or both of these vessels simply to share in the prize money that would come from their sure sale to Uncle Sam. Gideon Welles clearly would have loved to convert them into Union warships.

Both *Florie* and *Let Her B* were exceptional ships. Considered by the *Illustrated London News* to be one of the South's fastest and most beautiful blockade-runners, *Florie* was a Clyde-built, iron-hulled, three-funneled side-wheeler built in 1863 for a private import and export company based in Georgia. *Florie* showed up in an official Union navy report to Navy Secretary Gideon Welles from Commander George Preble, the commander of USS *St. Louis,* when it took on coal at Funchal Roads, Madeira, in late January 1864. Funchal Roads had two rival coal merchants who were eager to supply Confederate blockade-runners. *Florie* cleared that port on 4 January bound for Nassau and the blockade-defying trade.

Likewise, *Let Her B* was at Madeira on 17 April 1864 bound for Nassau. The ship was a sleek Liverpool-built, iron-hulled paddle-wheeler made especially for blockade-running for the Chicora Exporting Company. In sea trials it could make up to 19 knots, but her normal operating speed was 14. Built in 1864 by William C. Miller and Sons, *Let Her B* was armed with a pair of 12-pound cannons, an oddity for a blockade-runner. The ship was painted dull grey and had collapsible funnels to help hide its silhouette. It had two mast poles that mounted crow's nests instead of yard arms. It burned smokeless coal and its steam pipes were vented underwater to help conceal her location. Like all blockade-runners, *Let Her B* did not allow live roosters aboard as food for the crew, because their crowing might alert enemy sailors to her whereabouts. The ship's odd initial name was derived from the fact that during construction, the hull had a large letter "B" marking on it, which caused workers and others to refer to the ship as "the Letter B." It was also known as *Let Her Be,* and later in the war, her name was changed to *Chicora.*

After reaching Point Lookout, it was envisioned that the two ships would be burned. That was because coal would be their Achilles' heel. Once on the run, coal would be impossible to come by, and all blockade-runners burned huge amounts of coal. For example, *Banshee 1,* a steel-hulled blockade runner, typically consumed 31 tons of coal a day to make her normal cruising speed of 10 knots during her eight trips into Wilmington, North Carolina. In one particular close call with Union blockaders, *Banshee 1* burned so much coal in a 15-hour struggle to outrun pursuers that the crew had to burn the mainmast, bulwarks, and some cargo to reach the Bahamas safely. This would almost assuredly be *Florie*'s and *Let Her B*'s problem, too if they were pursued coming out of port. According to an 1864 naval report on 9 July 1864, 179 tons of superior imported Welsh coal were placed aboard *Let Her B*. This was enough to make her ready for a run to Point Lookout, but it was not originally clear where she'd go after that.

At the same time, the Mallet and Browne Coal Company furnished *Florie* with 85 tons of inferior coal from the firm's Egypt Coal Mine in Fayetteville. At *Florie*'s top speed, that amounted to about eight or maybe nine days' worth of fuel. Because the ship had no rigging to speak of, it couldn't rely on sails to augment its speed once the coal was gone. At that point it would be a sitting duck.

Once out of the Cape Fear River, they'd both have to be under full steam heading north for the Chesapeake Bay and Point Lookout, instead of attempt to disappear into the vastness of the Atlantic Ocean. An immediate chase from the Union's North Atlantic Blockading Squadron was almost certain to ensue. Such a mad dash meant trying to squeeze every ounce of speed out of the boilers.

In such cases where a Union pursuit was highly likely, captains would take on more coal than the ship's coal bunkers could handle, storing great quantities on the deck in bags and baskets.

Without re-coaling there was likely no coming back. Sufficient opportunities to re-coal anywhere in the North was out of the question. As a Marylander, Captain Wood knew there were no major coal piles on the Potomac except at Baltimore and Annapolis, Maryland; Alexandria, Virginia; and the Washington Navy Yard. He also knew that getting to the latter two sites would require a knowledgeable pilot who knew how to navigate the Potomac River, especially the area around Kettle Bottom Shoals. He'd also need an abundance of good luck. As though the river weren't full of natural obstacles enough, there also were numerous Union gun emplacements all along it. The biggest of these was Fort Washington, a brick fortification across from Mount Vernon that had been built after the War of 1812 and mounted a large number of seacoast guns. Then there was Fort Foote, a fortification named in memory of Admiral Andrew Hull Foote during the Civil War, located on a bluff about 3 miles above Fort Washington. Fort Foote mounted 15-inch smoothbore Rodman guns. With a 50-pound powder charge, these large cast-iron guns could hurl a 500-pound shot roughly 3 miles. These were truly impressive guns. President Lincoln and a number of other dignitaries visited in 1863 to witness the firing of the Rodman guns. The concussion was so severe that the guests were advised to open their mouths and curl their toes when the guns were fired. At the invitation of John Barnard, the planner of Washington's defensive forts, Navy Secretary Gideon Welles also visited the fort, on 22 October 1863. Welles was deeply impressed, calling it a "strong position," but he realized it would likely never be used because no enemy in its right mind would wish to engage with it. Following the visit, Welles noted in his diary, "No hostile fleet will ever ascend the Potomac."[3] Wood certainly wasn't going to be giving it a try.

Additionally, Wood knew that coaling up was a time-consuming process. In his diary entry for 6 March 1863, Union sailor Aaron S. Oberly wrote, "[USS] *Kineo* steamed alongside a coal vessel." This was followed by an entry for 7 March that said, "Coaled the vessel all day—Had some amusement during the day with a tame raccoon on the coal vessel." *Kineo*'s coaling wasn't completed until 9 March. *Kineo* was one of 23 *Unadilla*-class ships built to interdict blockade-runners. These ships were dubbed "90-day gunboats" because of their abbreviated construction times. They weren't overly fast, with maximum speeds for ships averaging about 9 knots, but despite that limitation, they captured or destroyed more than 140 blockade-runners during the war. *Kineo* was 158-feet long, with a 28-foot beam. By comparison, *Florie* (also spelled *Florrie* in the *Official Records of the Union and Confederate Navies in the War, Volumes 1–9*) was 222 feet long with a 23.5-foot beam. At any rate, *Kineo* is an apt example because if either *Florie* or *Let Her B* attempted to take on a large load of coal anywhere in Northern waters, they'd be sitting ducks.

Captain Wood knew enough to reject thoughts of attempting to reach any of these coaling spots. Trying to get to the coal at the Washington Navy Yard was the worst of all options available. It not only meant passing Forts Washington and Foote, but also passing the guns of the national arsenal at the confluence of the Anacostia and Potomac Rivers and then steaming directly into the gunnery range of the navy yard's experimental test battery. This was the site of the navy's first ballistic gunnery range, a test battery that had zeroed in on every navigable point approaching the yard. Additionally, the yard was testing 11- and 15-inch Dahlgren guns at the time.

With the Washington Navy Yard's complement of guns and its Marine contingent, mooring there wouldn't have been a likely alternative. In fact, given all the obstacles and risks, opting to search for coal anywhere along the Potomac clearly wasn't wise.

Alternatively, while Baltimore was a hotbed of secessionist sentiments, getting to any of its coal required passing Fort McHenry, which had held off a much larger British fleet 50 years earlier and now mounted large-caliber Rodman Guns. In any case, the hours spent taking on even a partial load of coal in any of these hostile settings would have been suicidal.

From the moment *Florie* and *Let Her B* began their voyage to Point Lookout, Captain Wood knew that his coal heavers would be steadily at work feeding the ship's boiler boxes and he'd either have to replenish the dwindling coal if his ships were to survive or scuttle them after completing his immediate mission.

Another portion of the naval plan that made little sense was the idea of sending ships into an unfriendly estuary dominated by Union naval forces. Once *Florie* and *Let Her B* entered the Chesapeake Bay, they'd likely have no way out other than to fight their way to the open sea. And given the number of Union ships that would almost assuredly be immediately dispatched to catch them, they would fail.

Tides and locations to tie up were other issues. Captain Wood likely expected to land his troops at Pont Lookout's wharf, located on the Potomac side of the neck of land.

Before the war Point Lookout had been a popular summer resort, and Wood likely was acquainted with its wharf. Now, with the summer patrons prohibited, the wharf fronted closer to a military hospital than to the prison camp, but with all the advance notice of the raid, the wharf was likely to be barricaded and covered by cannons.

An amphibious landing at Point Lookout was highly risky. High tide on 12 July occurred at 1:36 a.m. During the Civil War, beach landings weren't done in the dark. Too much could go wrong.

Additionally, shallows surrounded most of the shoreline at Point Lookout, the entrance point of the Potomac River. These extended about 1 mile southward from the tip of Point Lookout and could easily have grounded *Florie* and *Let Her B*. Cornfield Harbor, on the Potomac side of Point Lookout, experienced 1.5-foot tidal swings, but depths for some distance from the shoreline averaged only about 3-feet or less. The silting was gradual, except off Cornfield Point at the southernmost part of Cornfield Harbor and at the south end of the shallows that extended southward from tip of Point Lookout. The water was also shallow for a good distance out on the bay side of the point.

And then there was the impractical notion of launching a Confederate amphibious assault on Point Lookout from two large Confederate ships. The drafts of *Florie* and *Let Her B* were far deeper than all but a few spots at Point Lookout, causing any Confederate landing party to have to come ashore by either small boats or by wading great distances, making them easy targets. Getting men into small boats would take forever. Even getting them over the side and into the water to wade to shore could have taken great time. To make matters worse, the water's depth for several yards closest to the shoreline was only about a foot deep at all but the highest tides, meaning the attackers would likely have been splashing ashore in sandy shallows for some distance without any cover, all the while hotly opposed by Union soldiers protected inside the earthworks of Fort Lincoln or behind barricades.

The exact strategy to be used in quickly off-loading 800 assaulting Confederates from *Let Her B* and *Florie* by wharf, small boats, or wading ashore was never clear.

The Rebels had little practical experience in coordinated shore landings from ocean-going vessels and likely had little serious intelligence regarding the lay of the land or water around the point. As a result, such a landing party from blue-water ships onto a brown-water shore would probably have resembled little more than a seat-of-the-pants, hit-and-run, Viking-like raid, rather than a seriously well-planned and well-coordinated military operation.

John Taylor Wood had expertise in landing a raiding party in the dark using small ships and barges. He had done it before using 12 small boats and 3 large barges manned by 300 men when he attacked the Federal fortifications at New Bern, North Carolina, in an attempt to recapture the city, which had been seized by Federal forces in March 1862. Part of Wood's action at New Bern included the seizure of USS *Underwriter* on 3–4 February 1864 on the Neuse River. This surprise raid was halfway successful. *Underwriter* was burned, but Wood's Confederate forces were repelled.[4]

The Rebel raiding party at Point Lookout in southern Maryland in July 1864 would come as no surprise. The camp's guard force would be ready. Brigadier General James Barnes had ordered the expansion of the earthworks around the prison compound and deployed artillery to cover any potential landing areas. He received five navy gunboats, along with USS *Minnesota*, to contest the arrival of any Confederate naval force.

In January 1864 the South lost a number of its finest blockade-runners, including *Dare, Laura, Mayflower, Rosita, Ranger, Vesta, Ceres,* and *Bendigo.* The following month *Nutfield* and *Fanny and Jenny* was destroyed off Florida, while transporting critical shipments of munitions. Twenty-eight additional steamers were lost between February and July 1864, and the South needed every blockade-runner it could get.[5] Additionally, all these were fast steamers. These numbers don't include sailing ships—slower and smaller schooners, sloops, brings, and barks, which were lost in even greater numbers.

Given such losses, it made little sense to consider deliberately forfeiting *Let Her B* and *Florie* five months later. They were far too valuable as assets to the Confederacy to risk throwing them away on an ill-conceived fool's errand, but that is precisely what the South said it planned to do.

If coaling was out of the question, and a fight on the Chesapeake Bay was all but a certainty, only one option was left. According to John Wilkinson's recounting of the plan, "In the event of success, the steamers were to be burned." Wilkinson justified this sacrifice by saying, "These futile projects for the release of prisoners, serve to show the desperate straits to which the Confederacy was reduced, for want of soldiers."

By 1864 every blockade-runner lost meant less outside aid to sustain the South's crumbling war effort. This is the Confederate blockade-runner *Advance*, in a pen-and-wash illustration by R. G. Skerrett done in 1899. *Advance* was captured when it was overtaken in 1864 because her speed was greatly reduced by the use of low-grade coal. Purchased from a prize court by the Union navy, it was converted into USS *Advance*. (Naval History and Heritage Command)

Realizing that the hastily prepared naval portion of the plan had slim chances of success after the word got out, Captain John T. Wood, instead of being ordered to capture Point Lookout, was hastily reassigned to command CSS *Tallahassee*. An 1864 naval report from Confederate Navy Secretary Stephen Mallory confirmed that the unused portion of the coal "after the expedition upon which these vessels were destined had been abandoned," was to be transferred from *Florie* and *Let Her B* to *Tallahassee*.

Tallahassee steamed out of Wilmington in August 1864 under Wood's command.

Wood and *Tallahassee* proved to be a particular thorn in a series of raids along the Northeastern coast from New Jersey to New England. After a 19-day rampage during August 1864, Navy Secretary Welles called out a fleet of *Tallahassee*-hunters. The search parties included three vessels from the Brooklyn Navy Yard, several warships from Hampton Roads, a number of ships from Boston, and three vessels from the Philadelphia Navy Yard. All commanders were instructed to run *Tallahassee* down. Welles reported at the time, "Every vessel available has been ordered to search for [the] pirate."[6] This time *Tallahassee* eluded her hunters, thanks in part to a failure by Rear Admiral Hiram Paulding, commanding the Brooklyn Navy Yard. Intelligence indicated that *Tallahassee* was at Halifax, Canada, taking on coal.

USS *San Jacinto* was freshly arrived at the Brooklyn Yard, and on 14 August 1864, Welles ordered that it be immediately dispatched to Halifax to catch *Tallahassee* while it was vulnerable. Paulding immediately responded that *San Jacinto* was underway. In reality *San Jacinto* wasn't in any condition to leave port.[7] It was in Northern waters to escape from the dreaded yellow fever, and many of her crew was still sick. Moving ships into colder waters was one of the ways the navy dealt with "yellow jack." Naval doctors at the time weren't sure why this worked, but it did. In the case of *San Jacinto*, this was its second bout with the fever. It had had a previous outbreak aboard ship in August 1862. But on 18 August 1864, Welles was advised by the executive officer at the Brooklyn Navy Yard that the ship had not yet actually left port in search of *Tallahassee*, but was coaling. An exasperated Welles was told that *San Jacinto* would be ready to go out later that morning. "I know not when I have been more disappointed and astonished, and have just written for an explanation," recorded Welles in his diary.[8] "It cannot have been otherwise then there was inattention and neglect, for there could have been no purpose or design to defeat my orders."[9]

Greatly disappointed, Welles hoped that perhaps one or more of the other search ships in the area would discover *Tallahassee*'s whereabouts. USS *Pontoosuc* and USS *Merrimack* might have been capable of catching *Tallahassee* at Halifax. *Pontoosuc* was off the coast of Massachusetts and could likely be reached by a dispatch ship sent out from the Boston Navy Yard, but Welles needed to act fast. Once informed, *Pontoosuc* did indeed make it to Halifax, but four hours too late. The Rebel cruiser had already put to sea. *Tallahassee* had slipped away, departing only about two-thirds fueled, a fact that raised suspicions in Welles's mind regarding the wisdom of sending the urgent orders for *Ponoosuc* via Boston by unencrypted telegram. Welles knew he would be blamed, saying, "the sin—which is great, and almost inexcusable—of this neglect will fall on me, and not the guilty parties." Livid over the massive set of mistakes, Welles uncharacteristically sent Paulding a stern rebuke on 19 August, blaming him for botching the entire effort. *Tallahassee* had put on just enough coal to return to Wilmington.

During its rampage as a commerce raider, *Tallahassee* burned or sank 26 merchant vessels, bonded 5, and released 2 others. It slipped back into the Cape Fear River, heading for Wilmington, all the while fighting a running gun battle with Union blockaders. Once past Fort Fisher it was safely home. There it was renamed CSS *Olustee*. Leaving Wilmington again at the end of October 1864, *Olustee* captured another 6 ships, 5 of them on 3 November 1864. In December 1864, it was converted into a blockade-runner and renamed CSS *Chameleon*. It survived the war and was ultimately seized by British authorities upon arrival in England on 9 April 1865. It was turned over to the United States a year later.

Compounding any Confederate efforts to send ships to Point Lookout was the unplanned arrival of CSS *Florida* off the Maryland coast less than 35 miles from the state's eastern shore on 10 July. In quick succession *Florida* captured and burned the bark *General Berry* and captured the Federal mail steamer *Electric Spark*. These acts prompted the Union navy to dispatch USS *Mount Vernon* and USS *Monticello* to search for and engage *Florida*, assuming they could find her. Having *Mount Vernon* and *Monticello* start a search pattern from almost precisely the point where Wood's ships were planning to be about 12 July was really unfortunate timing. Besides, CSS *Florida* could offer no support even if her commander knew Wood was coming. By 12 July *Florida* was well out in the Atlantic, eluding any Union search party. By 6 August *Tallahassee* was at sea too. She had slipped out of Wilmington, eluding several blockaders, and began a rampage that included the capture or destruction of over 30 Northern ships in just two weeks.

Wilmington would have been the ideal starting point for Captain Wood's proposed attack on Point Lookout. To protect the entrance to Wilmington, the South constructed its largest coastal fortification—Fort Fisher. For the Union navy, the capture of Wilmington was the final great squeeze along the Atlantic seaboard according to the Anaconda Plan, the Union's strategy for winning the war by constricting the South's waterways. "The importance of closing Wilmington and cutting off Rebel supplies and communication is paramount to all other questions—more important, practical, than the capture of Richmond," wrote Gideon Welles in September 1864.[10]

The port of Wilmington—the terminus of vital Confederate rail links to much of the South, including the Petersburg and Weldon Railroad, which by late 1864 was Robert E. Lee's principal lifeline at Petersburg—had been in the Union navy's crosshairs since the winter of 1862.

Taking Wilmington would not be easy. The heavily blockaded shoals at the mouth of the Cape Fear River wouldn't permit a navy-run, Mobile Bay–type operation. Instead, Wilmington's capture would have to wait until sufficient troops were available to assail its fortifications, which included Fort Fisher, a casemated earthwork of sand and two- and four-gun batteries en barbette. By the autumn of 1864, a joint army-navy attack on the defenses of the Cape Fear River was possible.

Despite Welles's constant personal misgivings of David Dixon Porter, Porter was a suitable pick to lead the navy's expedition and play out this final act in the Anaconda Plan. He was a great gunnery officer, and thanks to Welles, he had a formidable attack force available to him. Welles had pulled out all the stops, depleting every other squadron to make this expedition a success.

Outside Washington in July 1864, the timing of Early's raid couldn't have been better either. Because of the 1864 presidential race, such rampaging Rebels and the fall of the nation's capital might have become just one more thing that could have cost Lincoln the election. Some in Washington believed that was indeed going to be the case. "Mr. Welling thinks the Presidents hope of a realection [sic] is entirely destroyed," wrote Mary Henry in her diary on 18 July.[11] A few days later she recorded a meeting between her father and Chief Justice Roger B. Taney. Of that visit she wrote, "He think [sic] Pres. Lincoln will be reellected [sic] & that there will be revolution afterward."[12] Neither of those predictions came true. As for John C. Welling, clerk of the United States Court of Claims, he resigned in protest with President Lincoln's reelection. Regarding the chief justice after his death on 12 October 1864, New York lawyer George Templeton Strong summed up the national sentiment by writing in his diary, "The Hon. old Roger B. Taney has earned the gratitude of the country by dying at last. Better late than never." Despite the naysayers like Welling and Taney, the news of the Early raid didn't cause much concern in other parts of the North. It was largely dismissed. In Boston, for example, it was characterized by the *Daily Advertiser* as "The annual invasion of Maryland, which next to the weather, supplies the 'sensation' of this week, does not excite any very disturbing apprehensions for the safety of Baltimore and Washington." What struck a sour note with most Northern newspapers was that the Rebels were allowed to send their marauders into Maryland and Pennsylvania yet again. Without calling Secretary of War Stanton out by name, the *Daily Advertiser* placed the blame on him, saying, "For the occurrence of this mortifying state of affairs we must certainly hold the military administration in some degree responsible." The *Philadelphia Evening Bulletin* agreed, telling its readers, "All this is humiliating enough. It shows that there is folly or incompetence somewhere in our military administration, and the President ought to be able to find where." The *Chicago Tribune* dismissed it for what it was—a food raid and a horse grab. It told its readers, "Lee's army will taste beef and pork once more, his cavalry will get new horses, and Richmondites will have a new lease of life for two months more. Over that we grieve."

If these newspapers didn't find great fault with the Rebel raid, at least one Southern newspaper was at fault for completely dashing the hopes of the raid on Point Lookout. Unfortunately, or perhaps by plan, the *Richmond Times-Dispatch* published details of the planned breakout at Point Lookout well in advance. By spilling the beans, it seemingly made the raid a possible trap for the would-be liberators. This was tempting bait for General Grant to perhaps pull troops away from Petersburg to trap such raiders.

The plan may well have been a half-baked scheme that was nothing more than a Confederate ruse concocted to help smoke out "Babcock" and her spy network. Jefferson Davis realized he had a serious security problem when Ulric Dahlgren's body went missing, if he didn't realize it before that point. The deception might also manage to draw more Federal troops away from Virginia. My rationale for this is based on the fact that the plan was simply too poorly thought out and hastily devised to be taken seriously, and even Lee admitted to Early when it was sprung on him that he didn't know all the details.[13] That is because it was a seat-of-the-pants plan. Think of the location of Point Lookout if you believe the gambit had a chance. It is on a finger of land bounded by the Potomac and the Patuxent Rivers. If Johnson's raiding party had actually made it that far, the Union soldiers holed up in Fort Lincoln, the earthen fort guarding the point, could have fired upon the prison compound, and Union naval vessels off shore in the Potomac and Chesapeake could have reduced the prison campground and the point's causeway to craters before many could have fled. For the South, without the proposed naval component to the plan, any freed prisoners would have had to walk at least 90 miles north to Washington to join Early's force. The time when Bradley Johnson's raid was called off is also in question. One scholar believes it was given the wave-off on 11 July, but communication with a roving raiding party wasn't easy and could have taken days, even if Jubal Early had established telegraph communications with General Lee at New Market, Virginia.[14] For under-nourished prisoners, that trek would have consumed at least a week. In the meantime, Federal troops at Annapolis, Washington, Alexandria, and Baltimore could have bottle up southern Maryland at Piscataway and Brandywine, Maryland, and begun sweeping south, capturing or killing the escapees along the way.

With Washington proving impossible to capture, and fearing that Federal forces were closing in from multiple directions, Jubal Early said he reluctantly recalled Johnson, writing in his Memoir, "I sent an order for him to return."[15] Early said that in recalling Johnson, he was now deeply concerned that Federal forces had somehow learned about the attempt to liberate the prisoners at Point Lookout. In his Memoirs, he included the words "of which I was informed by General Lee" in describing the prison-break plans, seemingly as a way of clarifying that the breakout wasn't his idea and that he had nothing to do with its planning.

In retrospect, Johnson's force wasn't likely to have succeeded anyway. As Early knew, Federal authorities were apparently well aware of what Johnson was up to, and with USS *Roanoke* standing by offshore, they likely had sufficient capabilities in place to thwart his attempt had he continued. In effect, Johnson's band of Marylanders could have been riding into a trap. Topography was on the Union's side. Point Lookout prison was pretty much on an island, connected only by a narrow land bridge, an earthen causeway that could easily have been blockaded.

In addition to *Roanoke*, the Union could have called on the navy's Potomac Flotilla for fire support and the rapid transport of troops. The idea of the flotilla was like something from the Vietnam era. The idea was to create a

USS *Roanoke*'s three armored gun turrets contained devastating firepower, including a pair of 15-inch Dahlgren guns, two 11-inch Dahlgren guns, and a pair of 150-pound Parrott rifles. These could have easily destroyed *Florie* and *Let Her B*. (Library of Congress)

swift, agile, shallow-water riverine force that could be used in interdicting enemy supply lines, conducting reconnaissance of enemy troop movements, threatening enemy strongpoints, convoying supplies and merchant ships, conveying military dispatches, engaging with small troop concentrations or light shore batteries, and inserting landing shore parties for limited search-and-destroy missions. Of course this came nearly 100 years before its Vietnam brown-water counterpart. This swift boat force was the brainchild of James Harmon Ward. His little force would ultimately consist largely of a rag-tag collection of hastily armed tugboats, converted passenger ferry boats, schooners and small sloops-of-war, and vessels that could get in close to shorelines and maneuver up its shallow, backwater creeks and anywhere a determined enemy might hide.

Just as in Vietnam a century later, many of the initial ships in this hodgepodge, brown-water flotilla weren't expected to carry a great deal of firepower. None was expected to act alone in slugging it out with a major enemy force. Instead, these early, tiny unarmored vessels were meant to hit and run. If confronted by a superior force, they were to retire, gather additional forces, and return in strength to fight on more equal terms. This would be the strategy used in the deltas and rivers of Vietnam a century later. After 1863, the Potomac River, and the greater part of the Chesapeake Bay, became largely Union-dominated waterways, especially during the day, with blockade-running violations largely eliminated, except for the occasional interdiction of a skiff, oyster boat, or canoe with limited contraband.

At the beginning of August, the Union navy also stationed four gunboats in the waters off the prison. And in another post-raid clampdown, newspapers were prohibited from the prison camp.

Between late June and early July, the plan for the raid was hastily incubated, quickly hatched and constantly tinkered with as the Confederacy's real capabilities were assessed and a plan of action materialized. Unfortunately, the details, and the realistic possibilities of the scheme, were doubtful from the start. Too much was up in the air. Portions of the plan were jettisoned, and new scenarios were added in quick succession. Further, the breakout attempt by a relatively small force became overly complex once it was firmly incorporated into Jubal Early's seemingly ambitious mission. In the end, the prison break was based upon too many pie-in-the-sky expectations. It was predicated upon being accomplished under a tight timeline. It required covering several hundred miles through potentially contested enemy territory. And it required secrecy. Regrettably, the final plan had too many potential points of failure, especially when it was tied in with the questionable nature of Jubal Early's overall mission. The raid on Point Lookout should have been its own operation.

The breakout attempt at Point Lookout wasn't the first such scheme concocted by the Confederates or their sympathizers. In February 1864 Colonel Lafayette C. Baker, the head of Lincoln's detective forces, alerted Navy Secretary Gideon Welles to a mass prison break to free Confederate prisoner at Johnson's Island on Lake Erie, near Sandusky, Ohio. The plot involved hijacking a Great Lakes steamer for use in ferrying the escapees to Canada. This scenario would be resurrected several more times before finally being abandoned with the end of the war. The prison on Johnson's Island closed in September 1865.

Despite all the stumbling blocks, freedom for the prisoners at Point Lookout would have been a blessing. The prison there was a dreadful place. It was designated as a "depot prison," which meant that its captives were supposed to be there temporarily, awaiting reassignment to one of the other roughly 150 Northern prisoner-of-war facilities as permanent places of incarceration. Because of the transient status, the prisoners were housed in tents holding 16 or more captives each. The tents were saunas in summer and icehouses in winter. One prisoner described how five Rebels froze to death one night while sleeping on the ground, because the occupants received only a few twigs every other day for firewood. The tents were generally arranged in nine orderly rows. Each row was expected to hold about 1,100 prisoners. The tent city was supported by seven cookhouses for sectional mess service and one commissary building.

A Lafayette V. Newell Photograph Gallery carte de visite of a Confederate prisoner from Point Lookout, Maryland, dressed in tatters. The photo was intended to be mailed home to his family. Although Newell's gallery was in Portsmouth, New Hampshire, he made many photographs of prisoners and guards at Point Lookout during the war. Unfortunately, most of his glass plates from this period were destroyed. Among the Rebel prisoners at Point Lookout was future American poet Sidney Lanier. Lanier, who was captured in 1864 and served four months at Point Lookout, contracted tuberculosis there. He died from complications of the affliction in 1881. Before the war he was a post office clerk at Macon, Georgia. (Library of Congress)

The Point Lookout holding facility was located on a barren finger of land at the confluence of the Potomac River with the Chesapeake Bay. One section of the camp was designated for officers and the other for enlisted ranks. The prison compound was surrounded by a 15-foot stockade that included an exterior palisade enabling guards to walk the perimeter. A shallow ditch 15 feet from the fence line was the demarcation for the no-man's-land, known as the "dead line," that surrounded the inside of the camp. Any prisoner crossing the dead line was subject to being shot immediately by the trigger-happy guards. Union officers were said to have encouraged the sentries to be quick on the trigger by unofficially offering bounties for each Rebel killed within this zone. The going rate was reportedly $10 to $15 per kill. The guards also received praise for their diligence and marksmanship.

Escape was nearly impossible. In the camp's 22-month history, only 50 successful escapes are known to have occurred. Swimming was pretty much out of the question. Few Civil War soldiers on either side knew how to swim and none were likely Olympians, which they needed to be to swim from Maryland to Virginia; the distance from Point Lookout, Maryland, to Smith Point on the Virginia side of the Potomac River was 11 miles. Confederate prisoner Simon Seward knew how to swim and he used his rare aquatic skills to be among the first to make a break for it, while the camp was still being constructed. Under cover of darkness he swam up the Chesapeake Bay towards Baltimore. He came ashore a few miles above the prison and made his way over to the Potomac side of the cape, moving mostly at night. He recounted his daring escape at the Confederate encampment at Fort A. P. Hill at Petersburg on 5 September 1889. With the help of several sympathetic Marylanders and an old log canoe, he was ultimately able to reach the Virginia side of the Potomac and make it home, despite being hunted much of the way. A few other escapees floated away on debris that drifted by the camp's bathing beach. And a few tunneled to freedom, although the soil was almost entirely sand, which could collapse on any would-be diggers. Groundwater was another problem. Being located only a few feet above the bay on a sandy peninsula, the water table was very shallow. This made it easy to dig wells, but the water furnished by them was brackish. The shallowness of the wells wasn't lost on the prisoners, who realized that any tunneling would be quickly flooded out. They did have the option to swallow their pride and take the oath of allegiance to the United States or enlist in the Federal army by accepting to serve out West. Those that did this were dubbed "Galvanized Yankees." A few prisoners apparently simply walked away from the prison compound unnoticed on an offshore sandbar.

Prisoners were allowed to bathe and wash clothes on the beach and to crab and fish from a small pier to supplement their meager food rations and to use for barter. The camp's main barter currency was tobacco and crackers, the latter of which were also the typical betting medium for the principal prisoner pastime of gambling. The crackers were hardtack, otherwise known to soldiers as "worm castles," "sheet-iron crackers," or "molar breakers" because they were so hard and worm-infested.[16] A shave, for example, typically cost one cracker. A haircut was two. Hardtack boxes were also highly sought-after. They were prized for use in constructing tiny shelters inside the prison compound. These became valuable real estate.

In addition to bartering with crackers, prisoners could purchase luxuries such as molasses candy sticks, pies, fruits, vegetables, and lemonade from camp vendors.

Hardtack was at least recognizably edible. Prison camp food, which was served twice a day, was wretched. Breakfast could consist of a half a loaf of bread and a slice of beef or pork. Dinner could be a cup of soup, typically a cup of greasy water with beans or potatoes or something questionable in it. To supplement or replace such rations, rat and squirrel banquets were often conducted within prison compounds. Rats became a common part of the prisoners' unofficial diets. Rat-catching became a major diversion from camp boredom.

Hunger was so pervasive that grown prisoners often cried themselves to sleep.[17]

Besides baiting rats, prisoners constantly had to contend with flies, mosquitoes, fleas, and lice. Boiling was the best way to rid fabrics of the latter pesky hitchhikers. Along with such vermin came a wide array of illnesses. Diarrhea and dysentery were also extremely common, as were malaria and typhoid. Medical care was minimal. Approximately 3,000 prisoners died.

The military prison at Point Lookout was established in August 1863 to house captives from the battle of Gettysburg. It was meant to accommodate 10,000 prisoners, but by the time of Early's raid on Washington, it housed approximately 14,000, becoming one of the Union's largest prison sites. Approximately 300 of these were pro-Southern civilians from the local area, many of whom had been awaiting trial for more than 14 months.

Then there were the latrines. For daytime use, the latrine was a walkway out over the water. At nighttime, buckets and tubs were used.

The Rebel officers previously imprisoned at Camp Hoffman, Point Lookout prison's official name, began being relocated to other Federal prison facilities in June 1864. That month, a large number of all ranks were transferred to Fort Delaware.

By 9 July 1864 the *Alexandria Gazette* was reporting that even more prisoners were being sent to the new prison camp opened that month at

Fort Delaware, located on Pea Patch Island in the Delaware River, was a terrible prison. Freezing in the winter and always unsanitary, in part stemming from its poor drainage, this prison had a well-earned reputation for being the Union's counterpart to the infamous Confederate prisoner of war camp at Andersonville, Georgia. (Library of Congress)

Other Federal prison-of-war camps, such as the one at Elmira, New York, shown here, accepted the overflow from Point Lookout. The camp was dubbed "Hellmira." (Library of Congress)

Elmira, New York. They were being transferred there in batches of 200 or 300 at a time. The 20-acre camp at Elmira was designed to hold 5,000 prisoners, but it soon had far more than that living just in tents. The relocation of the prisoners was cited by Josiah Gorgas in his diary entry for 13 July as one of the reasons for calling off the raid on Point Lookout. The movement of the prisoners greatly disrupted the flow of POW-related mail, which usually included many prisoner necessities, such as parcels from home containing coats, pants, socks, writing paper and envelopes, and especially tobacco.

The prisoners inside the camp at Point Lookout were well aware of what was going on. On 13 July 1864 Confederate Bartlett Yancey Malone, a sergeant with the 6th North Carolina who was captured in November 1863 and became a prisoner at Point Lookout, wrote in his diary, "it was reposed the General Ewel was a fiting at Washington And that our cavalry was in 4 miles of this plaice the Yanks was hurried up sent in all Detailes at two o'clock in the evening and run thir Artilry out in frunt of the Block house and plaised it in position." (Not all the information in Malone's diary was correct, but the quote demonstrates the extent to which the prisoners had an inkling what was going on. They clearly were well aware that the camp's defenders were prepared for the raid.)

If Bradley Johnson's raiding party had been ferried across the Potomac, as originally envisioned, the prisoners could have been ferried back to Virginia in the same boats. This would have taken time, given the number of prisoners held in the camp, and their questionable condition. And it would have been impossible to hide such boats from the Union's Potomac Flotilla. Additionally, even if the ferry boats could somehow be concealed, the Union navy would have to be slow to respond and not interrupt the rescue effort, which wasn't going to be the case.

USS *Roanoke* blocked the water route down the Chesapeake Bay. *Roanoke* was the Union's largest turreted warship, with three armored gun turrets mounted on the cut-down hull of a converted steam frigate. Envisioned as an oceangoing vessel, this top-heavy ship was prone to rolling precariously when all three turrets were fired or when operating in heavy seas. Critics at the time considered *Roanoke* a failure, criticizing it for "only making six knots per hour; and our only safeguard against invasion, and our only means of aggression in case of a foreign war...." In terms of lethality, however, *Roanoke* was considered the Union's most powerful monitor, but in reality it was anything but. As a monitor, it never really worked. Its hull, which had been given 4.5 inches of armor plating, was too weak to support the trio of 23-foot-diameter gun turrets plus the massive array of ordnance, which included two 15-inch Dahlgren guns, two 11-inch Dahlgren guns, and a pair of 150-pound Parrott rifles. The gun turrets alone weighed 125 tons each. With all of this weight, the ship was also simply too top-heavy to function as a seaworthy gun platform. Instead, it ended up serving as a security ship at ports and key tributaries, such as the confluence of the Chesapeake and Potomac off Point Lookout.

The model of massive 15-inch-shell guns on *Roanoke* was naval ordnance genius John Dahlgren's largest practical cannon. First produced in June 1862, Dahlgren never liked his 15-inch creation, believing it to be a serious untested threat to gun crews. Dahlgren claimed that he was forced into hastily creating the monster gun at the direction of the Department of the Navy, but never got the chance to fully test it. He also believed that the navy's biggest gun should not exceed 13 inches. The new 15-incher, which could penetrate 4.5 inches of steel, was intended to crush the Confederate defensive forts at Charleston. John Ericsson believed that even that wasn't good enough. He wanted a 20-inch gun mounted in his monitor turrets, arguing that his ships were impregnable and the immense caliber of the guns would be irresistible. Unfortunately, the muzzle of the 15-inch gun was so wide it couldn't pass through the gunports of the *Passaic*-class monitors it was designed for. As a result, to handle the smoke resulting from discharging the gun inside the turret, John Ericsson devised a "smoke box" inside the turret that directed the gun smoke out of the vessel. In test firings, the muzzle blast was so powerful that it demolished the smoke box. In response, Dahlgren insisted on having the gunports suitably enlarged. But Ericsson claimed that would seriously weaken the structural integrity of the turret. Secretary Welles backed Dahlgren's view, writing in his diary on

1 November 1862, "Ericsson makes a proposition to fire the fifteen-inch gun through the orifice [of *Passaic*] instead of protruding the piece. I have no faith in it." Ericsson's solution was to build a stronger smoke box. Dahlgren and Welles relented. The first 15-inch gun was delivered to the Washington Navy Yard for testing in October 1862. The gun was a beast, weighing in at 42,000 pounds and firing a 350-pound shell. President Lincoln and Secretary Welles visited the navy yard to observe some of the test firing of this gun. Despite limited, yet successful testing, Dahlgren declined to accept responsibility for the cannons of that size.

In terms of stopping any Confederate attempt to get to Point Lookout, *Roanoke* was ideal. Considering the ordnance aboard *Roanoke*, Johnson's force would have come under constant heavy bombardment miles before ever reaching the prison camp.

This also meant that Johnson and his freed prisoners would have to walk to freedom under a constant hail of cannon fire from *Roanoke* for many miles of their odyssey. Confederate troops typically moved at a speed of roughly 2 to 3 miles an hour under good circumstances, but because most of the prisoners had been starved and many were sick, it would have been slower going. The pace of their 90-mile trek back to Washington, in 80-degree-plus temperatures, with little food and water, would have been glacially slow. The rate of fire from *Roanoke*'s guns could have decimated much of the procession well before it managed to escape gun range. After that, there still were at least 80 more miles to go before crossing the Potomac River into the safety of Virginia. Such a trek to freedom would have taken those from Point Lookout days. At best, Early realized he might have two days before his entire force could possibly become trapped in Maryland. If that happened, he and his men risked becoming reluctant residents at Point Lookout, too.

Given the lack of serious planning that seemingly surrounded the Point Lookout expedition, General Lee may never have realistically contemplated saving the prisoners. Instead, in making good their great escape, Lee may have hoped that the breakout threat would draw thousands more Federal troops away from Virginia to try to thwart the attempt or to track down and recapture fleeing prisoners. It is clear that the Confederates were spreading misinformation regarding their numbers, inflating the size of their invading force to spread alarm and confusion. With this apparent deception, it is not far-fetched to consider that all of the chatter over the raid was a deliberate attempt to trick the Federals into shifting even more troops from Virginia to guard the prison or to be available to search for the prison runaways if they got out.

* * *

Because the prison guards had predominantly been from the 24th and 36th Infantry Regiments, US Colored Troops, General Lee reckoned that they weren't the most proficient for their job. "I should suppose," Lee told President Davis in June 1864, "that the commander of such troops would be poor and feeble. A stubborn resistance, therefore, may not reasonably be expected." This fact might have prompted General Grant to send others to deal with any prison uprising or breakout. And there should be a degree of urgency in doing this. This is precisely what happened, but it occurred much earlier than Lee had expected, and without any particular prompting from him. On 21 June Point Lookout was added to the army's Department of Washington. This included all the area between the Patuxent River, the Chesapeake Bay, and the Potomac. Additionally, on 6 July Brigadier General James Barnes replaced Colonel A. G. Draper, commanding the 36th Infantry Regiment, US Colored Troops, at Point Lookout, with three regiments of militia. Grant moved the 36th regiment to Petersburg. All of this was detailed in the Northern newspapers, which always seemed to promptly turn up in Confederate hands. In reading such news, and learning of other moves made by the North, Point Lookout should have begun looking to Lee like a less and less appealing target for a prison break. At the same time, Grant's staff began thinking about who Lee might have tapped to command the break. The consensus of opinion was Bradley Johnson and his 1st Maryland Cavalry. Johnson's unit, unofficially called the "Maryland Line," was somewhat of an independent organization. It was a unit that had faithfully proved itself in the past by serving as Lee's rearguard in tight situations.

James Barnes was a veteran of the battle of Gettysburg, where he was wounded. He was posted to Point Lookout following his recovery and he remained there for the rest of the war. If the Rebels did somehow manage to escape in masse, Barnes would have needed help rounding up his runaways. The longer the Federal government delayed in mounting such a concerted search, the more scattered the Rebels could become, but that didn't seem likely to happen. And as famished as the Point Lookout prisoners were, even if a breakout did happen, they would certainly have become human locust, consuming every morsel of food they could find throughout southern Maryland. General Lee expected that the freed prisoners would indeed live off the land. "Provision, etc., would have to be collected in the country through which they pass," Lee explained to President Davis on 26 June in outlining his initial idea. This could have turned some of the sympathetic southern Marylanders against their Confederate comrades, but it is just as likely that, because this area was so highly pro-Southern, many of the escapees would have been willingly taken in and sheltered by locals, making rooting them out even more painfully slow and manpower-intensive for the bluecoats.

Manpower was the biggest factor behind this harebrained scheme in the first place. General Lee seemed to hope that he'd gain numerous regiments worth of Point Lookout's fighters for his front at Petersburg if Early, Johnson, and the naval contingent he planned to employ could pull it off.

On 27 June Colonel Johnson and his battalion of Maryland cavalry were ordered to join the cavalry forces of Major General Robert Ransom Jr. in the Shenandoah Valley. In receiving this order, Johnson wasn't told about the planned raid on Point Lookout.

Early submitted his general plan of action to General Lee on 29 June. This plan conformed to all the instructions Lee had previously given him, with one great exception: Lee said nothing about Point Lookout. The delay was in part due to the fact that there still was the question in Lee's mind of whom to tap to lead the Point Lookout raid and how it would be carried out.

Command of the naval portion of the enterprise was equally unclear. In his *Narrative of a Blockade-Runner,* published in 1877, navy Lieutenant John Wilkinson summarized his short leadership of the mission: "I was summoned by telegram to Richmond. The Confederate authorities were then projecting an attempt to release the Point Lookout prisoners. There appeared to be no insuperable obstacle in the way; and it was believed that the prisoners, if released, and furnished with arms, would be able to join the forces under the command of General Early, then in the vicinity." Wilkinson, an exceptionally daring blockade-runner and skilled leader, was almost immediately relieved of overall naval command by John Taylor Wood. Wilkinson was miffed by the change of command, writing, "After all the details of the expedition had been arranged in Richmond, the naval portion of it was ordered to Wilmington under my command. There were sufficient reasons why I took no subsequent part in the expedition, the naval portion of it being placed under the command of Captain J. T. Wood, of the Confederate States Navy and also one of the President's aids." Wood was also Jefferson Davis's nephew.

While Wood and his Confederates were making their way to Wilmington, Jubal Early was being briefed on the planned breakout attempt by Robert Lee, General Lee's son. The plans Lee was explaining were still very much in flux.

CHAPTER 16

Fort Stevens

"Fort Stevens, the theatre of our shame.
Oh heavens! The whole area around increases a hundredfold the criminality of our commanders."

ADAM GUROWSKI'S DIARY ENTRY, 14 JULY 1864

For many Washingtonians Fort Stevens was the best theater in town during the third week of July 1864. Playing out was a comedy, a farce, and a tragedy. Some, like the feisty Polish Count Adam Gurowski, who came to the United States in 1849 and worked for the US State Department as a translator, suspected this was why the Union's response to the Rebel presence was so feeble, noting in his diary, "Now I understand why Halleck did not fire on the Rebels, who quietly at from five hundred to fifty yards deployed before Fort Stevens. The first scare over, Fort Stevens became the object of fashionable promenade. Our highest men, our Secretaries, and ladies pilgrimed [sic] to the fort to gape at the Rebels. Halleck was too polite to fight seriously, having such a public for spectators."[1] This diary entry assumed Halleck didn't want to risk a repeat of what happened during the battle of Bull Run, when prominent picnickers from Washington witnessed the Union army getting mauled in July 1861. Others were also publicly outraged by the showing in 1864. Ohio Senator Benjamin Wade protested for what he was said to consider "the crowd of d—f—s who presided over those unsoldierlike exhibitions."

Gideon Welles brushed off anything Gurowski had to say. "Poor Gurowski," he wrote on 8 August 1864, "Of course, no cause of offense having been given, there is no way of appeasing this Polish bear."[2]

Some slept through the acts being played out; others were too scared. The Rebel army settled in for the night. The veterans of the Second Corps ate and slept well. Early rested well too. While the Union veterans slept, the armed civilians did so with great difficulty, if they closed an eye at all. The occasional rifle or cannon shot at night paralyzed the uninitiated.

By the morning of 12 July it was clear that the chances for Southern success were slim. During the night many of the civilian-clad defenders seen in the works the day before had been replaced by Union veterans dressed in uniforms that showed they were no strangers to the rigors and cruelty of battle. An attack now was going to be no pushover. During the night, the fortifications also appeared to have been greatly strengthened thanks to the help of large numbers of freed Blacks and self-emancipated contrabands. Blacks also took up arms to defend the city.

Faced with limited prospects of success, Early elected to demonstrate before Washington on 12 July and withdraw that night by the shortest route possible. According to Rebel General Alexander, "It is scarcely credible that [Early] would have made more than a demonstration, for any real attack would have been but a bloody farce."[3] At the time Early's men arrived, Alexander estimated that the city's defenders number 20,000. "These troops alone, without aid, could have defended the city indefinitely and forced Early to undertake a siege."[4]

During the day, those opposite Fort Stevens made the most of the stalemate with what the local houses had to offer. The house of Dr. S. Heath, about a mile from the fort, was ransacked. Threadbare Confederates took whatever

Part of a set of 19th-century depictions that showcased the roles self-emancipated Blacks played in taking up arms and the winning of the Civil War. (The Metropolitan Museum of Art/Library of Congress)

clothing from the doctor's wardrobe that fit. Union artillerymen were active too. The doctor's house was hit at least eight times by Union artillery fire. All of the shot apparently passed completely through the house, but the impacts dislodged doors, shutters, and sideboards. The doctor's yard contained 11 Confederate graves, and the cornfield across the road contained 15 more.

Unfortunately, as sometimes happens, the southern demonstrations on 12 July at one point became so sharp that Union forces responded in the late afternoon with an attack of their own on the Rebel skirmish lines. This response threatened to spiral out of control, evolving into a full-fledged battle that could have forced the Confederates to commit a significant portion of their forces to holding their position. The Union sweep of the Rebel skirmishers came at a time when Early was focused on beginning to retire from the field. Luckily for him, the Union push did not have sufficient strength or intent to escalate into a major conflict.

As friends, Gideon Welles and Montgomery Blair had much in common. However, their views on how to treat the conquered Rebels were exactly opposite. Welles wanted them all severely punished. Blair, like Lincoln, wanted them to be allowed to go home. Welles personally took a hard stance towards the rebellion's leaders, one not shared by Blair and their boss. Welles believed that they were all traitors and as such should be hung. His view was, "Death is the proper penalty and atonement, and will be enduringly beneficent in its influence."[5] He hoped there would be consequences that would give pause to what in his mind was the aristocratic class that had perpetrated the war, one which had been at the very heart of the rebellion. "Were a few of the leaders to be stripped of their possessions, and their property confiscated, their families impoverished, the result would be salutary in the future," he thought.[6] But Welles was a realist. He knew Lincoln's sentiments, saying, "But I apprehend there will be very gentle measures in closing up the Rebellion. The authors of the enormous evils that have been inflicted will go unpunished, or will be not slightly punished."[7] Lincoln was indeed intent on being lenient. "Let them surrender and go home," Sherman recalled the president saying during a conference on the *River Queen* with Grant, Sherman, and David Dixon Porter in March 1865. "They will not take up arms again. Let them all go, officers and all, let them have their horses to plow with, and if you like, their guns to shoot crows with."[8] Deep down Welles remained vengeful. After Lincoln's death, he toured portions of the Southern coast. In visiting Charleston he reflected upon the calamities the Rebellion had wrought. "The results of their theory and the fruits of their labors are to be seen in this ruined city and this distressed people," he wrote. "Luxury, refinement, happiness have fled from Charleston; poverty is enthroned there. Having sown error, she has reaped sorrow." Welles had gotten his wish. The South had been punished. "I rejoice that it is so," he recorded in his diary.[9] Blair thought the opposite. In later years he showed great compassion for the South, especially for the fallen members of the Second Corps who were left in shallow graves on many of the farms around Silver Spring.

When Early withdrew in 1864, many of the dead had not yet been properly buried. The Confederates had interred their fallen comrades in shallow graves lined with straw. The foot of one of the hastily buried Rebel projected above its earthen canopy. These soldiers were laid to rest in poorly marked sites spread out in many places. In 1874 seventeen of these fallen Rebels were reinterred in consecrated ground thanks to the efforts of the priest of Grace Episcopal Church. The congregation—formed in 1855 thanks in part to the efforts of the Blair family, particularly Montgomery Blair's sister, Elizabeth Blair Lee—was said to be in the process of completing the sanctuary when Early's troops passed on their way to Washington. Jubal Early was an Episcopalian, and he was said to have given the congregation $100 to complete the church's roof in exchange for a pledge to care for his Southern fallen, although this has never been proven. What is known is that the roof had already been completed by July 1864. The church's priest in 1874, Father James Avirett, had served as a chaplain with the Confederate 7th Virginia Cavalry. He was sadly aware of how unkempt these scattered Rebel graves had become. He launched an effort to give his former comrades a proper burial in Grace Church's graveyard. According to the church's submission for historic preservation standing, the soldiers' bodies were exhumed and consolidated into six coffins for relocation to the churchyard. At the time of exhumation, it was discovered that the majority were mere teenagers. Three were officers. The others were privates. Only one—James B. Bland of Highland County, Virginia—could be positively identified. Bland was a private with the 62nd Virginia Mounted Infantry Regiment. With the approval of the church's vestry, which included Montgomery Blair, on 11 December 1874, the remains of the unknown Southern soldiers were reinterred between the primary entrance of Grace Episcopal Church and the turnpike, in a plot paid for by Montgomery Blair. In the possible likelihood that Bland's family might step forward and come looking for his remains, his body was placed in the northernmost portion of the plot. A monument maker was placed over the graves in 1896. The plot and marker were subsequently moved because of streetcar and road work, essentially moving them closer to the current church. The 1896 monument to the men was toppled over in 2020. The unidentified group that pushed over the monument also spray painted it with the words "here lies 17 dead white supremacists who died fighting to keep black people enslaved."

Rodes's division was the vanguard of the Rebel army. As soon as his troops were within sight of the Federal fortifications, he was ordered to deploy skirmishers and advance into the works as quickly as possible. Before that order could be carried out, Federal forces occupied positions opposite his force.

Union skirmishers were immediately deployed, and Federal artillery from a number of positions gave the Rebels an ominous welcome to Washington. Johnny Young, with Early's army in West Virginia, wrote a letter home on 18 July that described the Union gunfire: "from their Forts they threw shell at us as large as a nail keg." If that signified Washington's welcome, the torch symbolized the Southerners' response. Young, a native from Charlotte, told his family, "the houses of some of the prominent Lincolnites were gutted and burnt in retaliation for their depredations in Virginia." This sentiment reflected the thinking of many within the Confederate Second Corps that July despite Jubal Early's calls for restraint.

Because of the immediate response to the appearance of the Rebels, Early recounted in his *Memoirs,* "This defeated our hopes of getting possession of the works by surprise, and it became necessary to reconnoitre [sic]."[10]

The Federal line of fortifications appeared formidable. "On the left, as far as the eye could reach, the works appeared to be of the same impregnable character," wrote Early. "The position was naturally strong for defence [sic], and the examination showed, what might have been expected, that every appliance of science and unlimited means had been used to render the fortifications around Washington as strong as possible."[11] The positions on the right were just as strong, including Rock Creek, a stream running through a deep ravine that had been filled with felled trees that made any approach impossible.

Union engineers had indeed thought of everything. The forts were well spaced. They were placed on high points with clear lines of interlocking fire. They were connected by rifle pits and trenches. They were supported by smaller battery positions. And, unbeknownst to Early, they were connected by telegraph lines so that communications could be maintained with the War Department headquarters in real time. The communication lines were installed under the direction of Thomas Eckert, the chief of the War Department's Telegraph Office. Clearly visible to Early, a signal tower also stood on the heights of the Soldiers' Home, which could be seen on both sides of the forts facing Maryland, so that the enemy's movements could be observed and communicated by signal flags to commanders in the field, enabling Union forces to be shifted to meet any evolving threats. Known as "Scott Tower," the signal tower at the Soldiers' Home was erected on Washington's third-highest point. "Under the circumstances, without understanding the state of things, would have been worse than folly," wrote Early after the war.[12]

Jubal Early was also greatly disappointed that no Southern supporters emerged from the city to tell him what was going on inside town. Early had sent word to Colonel John Singleton Mosby, the Confederate guerrilla chief known as "the Gray Ghost," who operated in central and northern Virginia, to cross into Maryland and cut telegraph lines, wreck railroad tracks, and

SIGNAL TOWER
FORT RENO
D.C.

Drawing of the signal tower constructed at Fort Reno at Tenleytown between 1863 and 1865. (In 1864 the little hamlet was spelled "Tenallytown.") This signal tower was erected on the highest point in the District of Columbia, 417 feet above sea level. From this vantage point, Union observers first spotted the advancing Rebel raiding party in July 1864, and they observed Southern troop movements over the next few days. Each of the forts had its own smaller platforms for commutating with signal flags. (Library of Congress)

scout out information on the city's defensive capabilities. But Mosby failed to act on that request.[13] His band of partisan raiders operated with relative impunity through much of the war because of its ability to blend in with the local populations during the day and become "Mosby's Rangers" at night. One of the group's more notable feats was the capture of bluecoat Brigadier General Edwin Stoughton at Fairfax Courthouse in March 1863. Stoughton was caught sleeping. Awakened from a deep slumber by a slap on the butt, he was asked if knew Mosby. Confused as to why he was being asked such a question so late at night, he blurted out, "Have you got the rascal?" "No," came the reply, "He's got you." That night, Mosby's raiders also captured a herd of mules. When Lincoln was advised of the loss, he was livid over the capture of the animals. He said he could make a brigadier general any time he wished, but he couldn't make mules. They were tougher to come by and more valuable to him than any two-star officer.

The lack of local intelligence greatly frustrated Early. Inside the city, the eyes and ears of his cavalry were utterly useless, and sympathetic townsfolk weren't talking. "If we had any friends in Washington," he said, "none of them came out to give us information, and this satisfied me that the place was not undefended."[14] Early could only rely on what he could see around

The Treasury Department Building, circa 1860, was one of the city's largest buildings at the time, rivaled perhaps only by the Capitol. Since 1861 the Treasury Department building was to be the fallback position for housing the heads of government and their families, including the president, if the city's outer defenses were overwhelmed. Additionally, four large burglar-proof vaults were added to the building in 1864. (Library of Congress)

him. And even if he had been more aggressive because of what he saw and possibly broken through the Union's fortifications in the late afternoon of the 11th, his prospects for success were never all that good. If his meager force had somehow been able to breach the Federal defenses on the 11th, it faced the possibility of a protracted urban war that might take days just to reach the White House and Federal Treasury building. Early was well aware of the pitfalls associated with street fighting, but not on the scale of what his men might face inside the Federal city.

The war's first urban fight had occurred at Fredericksburg, Virginia, in December 1862. It was a costly street-to-street and house-to-house battle for both sides. In Fredericksburg the Confederates fired from houses on opposite sides of the streets. Intersections became major Union killing zones, with fire coming from all directions. Clearing houses became a costly Union lesson. For the defenders holed up in those houses and fighting from behind fences and outbuildings, Federal artillery across the Rappahannock River destroyed many of their hiding places, killing or burying men under the rubble of urban warfare. One soldier at Fredericksburg described the hell of hunkering down inside the houses: "Tons of iron were hurled against this place, the deafening roar of cannon and bursting shells, falling walls and chimneys, bricks and timbers flying through the air, houses set on fire, the smoke adding to the already heavy fog, the bursting flames through the housetops, made a scene which has no parallel in history."[15] None of the men in his Mississippi brigade expected to survive. More than 150 heavy cannons were pummeling the city from across the river, leaving almost every building riddled with holes and many in flames. Spencer Bonsall, a hospital steward with the 81st Pennsylvania Infantry, was an eyewitness to the carnage. Not only was the town wrecked, but it was sacked, too. "I cannot describe the destruction that has taken place and is still going on; almost every building has been ransacked—fireproofs [safes] broken open, drawers rummaged, immense quantities of books and furniture thrown about," he wrote in his journal on 13 December 1863. "The men have supplied themselves with tobacco, pipes, and cigars in abundance. Liquor stores have been broken open and the men are carrying wine, brandy, and whisky along the streets in everything that will hold it; watering pots, buckets, coffee pots, stone jars,—utensils, etc. etc."[16] Bonsall was appalled by what he saw. Ornate and antique furniture was broken and scattered about. Fine clothing was in torn into tatters and left as litter in the streets. Larders and coops were raided. Any chickens were roasted and all eggs were eaten. If stealing food from civilians seems heartless, it is important to consider the alternatives for the soldiers subsisting on military diets of questionable quality. One soldier from Indiana spoke for many when he complained of "Rotten meat, mouldy [sic] bread and parched beans for coffee are common occurrences now." Meat in any form came in a variety of unpalatable colors, indicating that it was unfit to eat. One Union soldier described the beef that he was served as shoe-polish black on the outside and yellow on the inside from putrefaction. Another from New Jersey was disgusted by having to scrape off maggots before cooking. This Garden State soldier became numb to the fact that "The salt junk as we called our pork was sometimes alive with worms." Eating anything else, anything that appeared to be fresh, was preferred no matter where it came from.

In Fredericksburg, personal chinaware borrowed from any vacant house was used and then smashed or left for the homeowners to wash. Some Union soldiers took to wearing ornate bonnets and other female finery while dining. "This is the first sacked town that I have yet seen, and I trust sincerely that I may never see one of our Northern towns in the same condition." If Washington had fallen in 1864, the damage would have been far worse. Luckily for Washingtonians, the odds of Early's success were limited on 12 July.

The tables would have been reversed in Washington. Early had been at Fredericksburg. As a brigadier general, he commanded Ewell's division of the Army of Northern Virginia, and although none of his brigades had been engaged in the street fighting, and he doesn't write about the street fighting in Virginia in his *Memoirs,* he had heard about it and seen the results in Fredericksburg. He had also been at Gettysburg and seen the fighting in the town. Fredericksburg and Gettysburg were tiny compared to the District of Columbia. It wasn't easy to get lost inside either of those hamlets, but it would have been very easy for an unfamiliar invader to do so inside Washington. Besides, the elements of the Union army that were on hand in Washington

Washington wasn't Fredericksburg or Gettysburg. This is a wartime view of the District of Columbia taken from Capitol Hill looking to the northwest, the direction Jubal Early's men would have come from if the defenders at Fort Stevens had failed to keep them out. House-to-house combat and contested street fighting in a city like this would have become a disaster for Early's small army. Urban warfare on a scale such as this back then was unimaginable. Early knew it. Additionally, judging from the amount of looting that had already taken place in the countryside the prospects of urban plunder may have simply been too enticing for Early's army to pass up. (Library of Congress)

in July 1864 had thousands of armed civilians who were likely to use their personal weapons or government-issued rifles and ammunition to protect their homes, businesses, and neighborhoods. Some civilian street fighting and sniping was inevitable.

Additionally, Federal heavy artillery from the ring of forts and batteries surrounding the capital could have been redirected into the city to zero in on any Rebel breakthroughs or Confederate troop concentrations. In this way each fort could have become a strong redoubt that focused on and slowed any lanes of advance.

As was done in Washington in 1861, and had been done at Fredericksburg in 1862, urban barricades could have been erected at strategic points. During the first month of the war, for example, strong points were created around the district's main post office building and the Patent Office along Ninth Street, as well as around the White House and Treasury Department building. The field artillery from the array of smaller Union batteries ringing the city

This is the intersection of Seventh and D Streets, Northwest, in 1863. Artillery hastily placed in the middle of this intersection could have swept any advancing Rebels in all four directions with relative ease. House-to-house fighting here could have lasted for days and cost hundreds of lives. (Library of Congress)

could also easily have been repositioned behind hastily erected barricades at intersections to sweep the lengths of streets in any direction.

Spencer Bonsall wrote about the effectiveness of Confederate field pieces at Fredericksburg: "the enemy's batteries were placed so as to sweep the cross streets, and there was no part of the town that was free from danger." If the Federals did the same thing inside Washington, Early's little band would have been diluted, forced into narrow corridors, and swallowed up piecemeal in an urban killing contest. Washington could have become a Confederate Stalingrad. And even if Early had been remotely capable of conquering the city, he couldn't expect to hold it without risking becoming a prisoner of his own folly. Additionally, his force had no prospects of fleeing by water down the Federally controlled Potomac, and it could just as easily have been bottled up inside the walls of Washington. Early pondered all of these factors in retrospect, recalling in his *Memoirs*, "A glance at the map, when it is recollected that the Potomac is a wide river, and navigable to Washington with the largest vessels, will cause the intelligent reader to wonder, not why I failed to take Washington, but why I had the audacity to approach it as I did, with the small force under my command." In effect, Early realized that if the Rebel mouse had caught the Union cat, it would have had to quickly figure out what to do with it before the prize clawed its captor to death.

Early assumed that at least one Union force—Hunter's—was possibly descending upon one of his proposed escape routes into Virginia. He considered that other Union divisions might be heading towards Washington as well. If all these attacks were well coordinated, Early's little army could be assaulted and swallowed up from all sides.

The reality was there was no well-coordinated defensive effort and Hunter's force remained at Cumberland until 14 July. Hunter would have been no help at all in catching Early.

Early said that he uncharacteristically debated the situation of attacking Washington on 12 July with his unit commanders on the evening of the 11th at Francis Preston Blair's house over what remained in Blair's wine cellar. There was no clear consensus on what should be done. In the end Early had to decide. Having come this far and facing a chance to succeed, albeit a relatively slim one, at breaking into Washington, Early elected to attack at dawn on 12 July, with the caveat that the final go-ahead would be determined in the morning, when it might be clearer in his mind that an all-out assault was practical.

One of the great finds of 11 July was a detailed map of Maryland discovered among the things in Blair's house. The map was taken to the house of Thomas Gettings, located at the third tollgate on the Washington and Rockville Turnpike, where the Rebel's had established a mobile aid station. There a number of Confederate engineers made duplicate copies for distribution among the Rebel units. Having identical maps made the task of coordinating troop movements much easier for Early.

Some of Francis Blair's personal papers were taken then, too. Blair would later ask Jefferson Davis to personally intercede on his behalf to facilitate their return. The senior Blair's request was written on "Headquarters, Armies of the United States" stationery: "The loss of some papers of mine which I suppose may have been taken when Gen'l Early's army was in possession of my place induces me to ask the privilege of searching Richmond & beg the favor of you to facilitate my inquiring in regard to them." Blair was going to be in Richmond on a peace mission and had a safe-conduct pass signed by President Lincoln.

The likelihood of any successful attack on 11 July was in doubt from the start, thought Brigadier General Edward Porter Alexander. Writing after the war in his book *Military Memoirs of a Confederate*, the chief of artillery for Longstreet's First Corps, believed that the hodge-podge Federal forces assembled at Fort Stevens and elsewhere that morning alone, securely positioned behind well prepared forts, ditches, palisades, and obstacles, could have defended the city indefinitely, forcing Early to initiate a siege.

Allow the bearer, F. P. Blair, Senr. to pass our lines, go South and return

Dec. 28. 1864   A. Lincoln

Francis P. Blair's safe-conduct pass, signed by President Lincoln. (Library of Congress)

That would have been tactical suicide, recalled Alexander. And with the arrival of additional Union forces in the city by noon and their massing at Fort Stevens by 4:00 p.m., the window of opportunity for a frontal attack that day was securely shut.

As refugees in the vicinity were fleeing into the city, others were making their way to the fort for a front-row seat to watch what was unfolding. Military authorities had established a ban against sightseeing civilians entering the area. Visitors were required to have permits signed by Secretary of War Stanton or the district's commanding general. Those failing to follow this order were supposedly subject to arrest and having their horses and vehicles seized, but everyone who was anyone seemingly could wrangle a legitimate permit signed by someone in uniform that would get them past the provost marshal's guards. Many simply ignored the order. The throngs of the curious were so large that the *Evening Star* reported on 11 July, "Early in the evening thousands of persons could be seen passing out Seventh street by every conceivable means of conveyance, while the road was literally lined with pedestrians. The hills, trees and fences within sight of Fort Stevens were covered with human beings, quite a number of whom were ladies. Quietly seated in a carriage, at a commanding point, was Secretary Seward, viewing the progress of affairs."

Other lesser notables tried to find the best vantage points possible to witness what was happening. Horatio Nelson Taft, for example, went up onto the roof of the Patent Office building, though he couldn't see much from there.

The theater continued even after the Rebels fled. Onlookers combed over the area long after the raid had ended, looking for keepsakes. The human remnants of the Rebel action remained on display in Washington's suburbs for most of the month. Tourists were confronted with the sickening sights and smells of the Southern dead or the wounded who were too hurt to be moved.

On the evening of 13 July Mary Henry went for a drive with her father. Passing the railway yards near the Smithsonian's Castle building, she was struck by the large numbers of rolling stock assembled there. When the

Mary Henry, the daughter of Smithsonian Secretary Joseph Henry, went up into the main tower of the Smithsonian's Castle building, which provided a good vista of the Washington skyline, especially when she used her father's telescope. Earlier in the war, when Joseph Henry used his telescope in the tower, he was accused of being a Confederate spy. (National Archives and Record Administration)

Confederates descended upon Washington, President Lincoln had ordered all railway locomotives in the city moved to Alexandria, Virginia, for safe keeping, but when word reached Washington that Confederate raider John Mosby was marauding around Falls Church, Virginia, Lincoln ordered the engines and cars brought back across the Potomac. During her drive out Fourteenth Street, 30-year-old Mary Henry and her father passed a column of about 75 Confederate prisoners being marched into town. The men were dirty and dressed in butternut tatters. Despite their physical condition, "many of them were exceedingly fine looking," Henry recorded in her diary. One in particular attracted her attention. He was a tall Virginian who demonstrated great nobility, she thought. In her diary she noted, "he moved sturdily alone in dignified disdain without one look of the curiousity [sic] indulged in by his companions."

As her carriage moved towards Campbell Hospital, on Boundary Street between Fifth and Sixth Streets, near Columbia College (now Gallaudet University), Henry and her father were confronted by the sight of injured Union soldiers lining both sides of the street.

Several of these invalids evoked particular pity from the Smithsonian secretary's daughter. "One or two pale sad young faces excited my warm sympathy, they looked so much in need of home kindness & affection," she wrote. At this point, mounted Union sentries turned the Henry party back. The secretary asked one of the soldiers at the guard post if he knew any details about the battle. It wasn't a battle, clarified the sentry, it was a skirmish. Shocked by that comment, the secretary asked how it was possible for 300 Union men to be causalities in just a skirmish. "Oh, that is nothing, we don't consider that anything of a battle these days," wrote the younger Henry of the soldier's reply. (Assistant Secretary of War Dana informed General Grant on 14 July that the Union causalities were 500 killed and wounded. The Union causality count reported in 1902 was 319, of which 54 were killed. Forty-one of those killed were interred in a small national cemetery dedicated by President Lincoln shortly after the battle. The Battleground National Cemetery, one of the smallest in the nation, is a short distance from Fort Stevens.)

Mary Henry also spent 15 July sightseeing. Again, she was stunned by what she saw. Everywhere beyond Fort Stevens she found signs of the Rebel presence. As she came onto the Rockville Turnpike, she saw a group of other sightseers in a nearby grove. She joined them and saw a number of Rebel graves. Several large square pits filled with straw had been prepared to receive the dead but were left unoccupied in the rushed departure. Further up the road she found some of the Rebel wounded sheltered under a few miserable tents. In the first of these, she found a Confederate surgeon, describing him as "a fine looking officer." A willing sacrifice, he had volunteered to stay behind to care for his wounded and dying comrades. His frank, unbowed bearing intrigued Miss Henry. She asked him if he was a prisoner. He told her that he thought he ought not to be considered such, as he had volunteered to remain with the wounded. (Medical personnel left by the enemy to care for their wounded were not treated as combatants.) His uniform was rough and worn, but his manners and bearing was noble. This greatly impressed the young woman. Clearly, she thought, a haberdasher doesn't make a gentleman. She asked whether he and his charges had sufficient food. He answered proudly that his companions had left enough to meet their needs, at least up to this point. In the next tent, she discovered two poor fellows shot through the head. One clearly seemed to be dying. He lay with his eyes closed, breathing heavily. His features were delicate and regular and his forehead, where the sun had not deeply tanned him, was, she thought, "as fair as a girls." Both men lay on the ground with only a little straw for bedding. A young boy served as their attendant. He was swatting away flies. Again, the young lady asked the boy whether he had enough to eat. Yes, he politely answered. She left the two poor unconscious lads with a heavy heart. In the next tent were 8 to 10 more causalities. One had a bad leg wound but otherwise seemed glad to be alive. He was lying on the grass swatting away flies with a tree switch. Near the next tent, a poor fellow was pouring water over a head wound. Besides

This is why Mary Henry described the Confederate field hospital at the third tollgate at Sligo, Maryland, as consisting of a few miserable tents. This view is of a similar field hospital at Antietam in 1862. (Library of Congress)

him was another of the volunteer nurses. He had remained because he was unwilling to leave his lieutenant, who was in the next tent. The young attendant asked Henry to look in on his superior officer, almost as if he was afraid to do so himself for fear of what he might find. She obliged. She found the officer lying on a blanket with clean linen. He was neatly shaved. His appearance was in stark contrast with those who surrounded him. He was clearly deeply cared for. In writing about her travels that day, she didn't record whether the lieutenant was dead or alive. She may not have known. Nor does she record whether she said anything further to the lieutenant's attendant, but the human carnage she witnessed in that visit clearly left an indelible impression on her.

The wounded seen by Mary Henry on 15 July were among a larger group that had totaled 63 soldiers the day before. That group had been left in the care of 1 surgeon, 2 assistant surgeons, and 12 attendants. The Confederates also left a chaplain to minister to the wounded. On 13 and 14 July, about 40 of these Rebel wounded, many from Ramseur's brigade, were moved to Lincoln General Hospital for better care. This left the small group of wounded seen by Henry near the third tollgate of the Seventh Street Pike. At the time, this was commonly known as the Sligo tollgate. It was at the intersection of Colesville Road and the Seventh Street Pike, the site of the Sligo post office, which served as a Confederate aid station. Most of the wounded were from Georgia and North Carolina units. It is highly likely that the soldiers buried in this area were ultimately relocated to the Grace Church graveyard. The

One of the wards of Harewood Hospital in Washington in 1864. The care furnished at facilities such as this was a far cry from the attention received at a field aid station, such as Mary Henry witnessed. (National Archives and Records Administration)

roughly 40 hospitalized Rebels admitted that they never really believed they could capture the capital, but they put up a good show of it so they could pillage most of Maryland unmolested while the Union army was distracted in fortifying and defending Washington, Baltimore, and cities in Pennsylvania. The wounded were happy that they had obviously done such a good job plundering the region.

On her 15 July journey, Henry would have also seen the Union pickets, including Union Corporal Christian Hook of the 151st Ohio Infantry, who was still posted in front of the forts. As a precaution, they remained on the skirmishing line and at the forts until 18 July.

The Rebels took what they wanted, and the battlefield sightseers walked off with a variety of keepsakes, too. Marylanders were becoming no strangers to such looting. Union troops also took what they wanted in the state. If confronted by an irate farmer or shopkeeper demanding payment, the common bluecoat reply was, "get it from Uncle Sam." Alfred S. Roe, a veteran of the 39th Massachusetts, would write about how around Poolesville, Maryland, in December 1862, "Nothing that was edible and transportable was safe from the predatory hands of the men and boys who, a very few months before, had been conspicuous in their own localities for their sterling honesty and straightforwardness." The war, and what passed at the time as "necessity," had transformed these pious New Englanders into petty criminals. For soldiers accustomed to eating salt beef, which bluecoats insisted was actually "salt horse," because a horseshoe was said to have been found in a barrel of what was purported to be beef, anything fresh was stolen if the chance arose. "The marvel," Roe wrote, "is that the natives had anything left to subsist upon." Coming from New England, Roe was also struck by the sparseness of Maryland. The villages north of the Washington and Rockville Turnpike weren't much to look at and didn't have much to offer soldiers trudging past. Dawsonville had one house, a blacksmith's shop, and a few other ramshackle buildings. Roe said Darnstown was appropriately named: it was a darn shame it was even there. He was struck by the beauty of Rockville, which he thought was the prettiest village he'd seen south of New Jersey. At Rockville his regiment picked up the paved turnpike into Washington. It lacked the muddy potholes Roe and his regimental brothers had become accustomed to, but he said the stone-covered surfaces of the turnpike were actually harder to walk over. It was clearly paved for horse-drawn traffic rather than for sore marching feet. The Rebels found it tough going too, in 1864, worsened by the fact that many of them had received new shoes on 7 July. The need for those shoes was made abundantly clear nearly a month earlier, while John C. Breckinridge's troops were still in Virginia. From Lynchburg Confederate Quartermaster Edward McMahon requested the quartermaster general at Richmond to dispatch 2,000 pairs at once. "The men are almost destitute of shoes…. There are no shoes here," he begged.

The Southerners were said to be jubilant that so many Marylanders had joined them in July 1864 while they were rampaging through the state, insisting that more than 1,700 recruits rallied to the Rebel cause during their raids. According to the *Washington Star*, 200 of those recruits came from Frederick and 1,500 from Baltimore. That number, however, like all the others being bantered about, was likely largely wishful thinking. The *Fayetteville Weekly Intelligencer* went even further, claiming, "our troops, with the aid of 15,000 Maryland Secessionists, had taken and now occupied the city of Baltimore."

As for Mary Henry, she found, standing outside the third hospital tent, a second officer, another of those who had temporarily risked their freedom to stay with the wounded. Realizing that most of the hospital's visitors that day were souvenir seekers, he cut off his uniform buttons and freely handed them out as mementos, joking that he could always replace them with captured Union buttons in the foreseeable future. Under the circumstances, he knew that was actually impossible, since he would soon likely be going into captivity, but his comment lightened the mood of the moment, and perhaps he was hoping for something in trade.

While the threat to Washington was minimal, the Federal idleness presented the Rebels with an excellent opportunity to steal horses, thought Navy Secretary Welles. At a time when the Confederate government valued useable horses at $1,200 each Early's army made off with tens of thousands of dollars' worth of Northern horseflesh. The *Washington Chronicle* couldn't have agreed more. Its view was, "Most of the troops came into Maryland on foot, but went back on horseback."

Welles also thought the Confederate foray was an ideal excuse for destroying personal property, and he was right. Such destruction was fully justified, thought John M. Daniel, a proslavery firebrand and the owner of the Richmond *Examiner*. In June 1864 he wrote,

> One of the greatest compliments that the Yankees can pay us is their thankfulness for the small favors which they receive at our hands. Of course, a real success makes them delirious, but any kind of success is welcome. A haystack reduced, a corn bin shelled out, a water-tank forced to evacuate, a pig-sty compelled to surrender unconditionally, a few yards of railway routed, the center of a bridge broken, libraries gutted, plate-boxes emptied, furniture ground into its ultimate atoms; any kind, every kind of devastation and plunder; anything, everything, seems as a matter of rejoicing, as a theme for future Thanksgiving Dinner orations. However, these are exploits more to the taste of the genuine Yankee than the rude work of actual combat, and we do them wrong in depreciating the achievements, which, of all others, they will remember with most satisfaction in after years. And well they may; for, besides stolen spoons, pilfered pictures, and confiscated books, they will have little to show in their own country for the oceans of blood and the mint of money which they have lavished on their grand speculation, their great South Land Bubble; and they will hardly choose to come to our blood-stained soil, to our desolated fields, in order to revive the memories of Manassas and Chickahominy, of the Wilderness and the Southside.

The following month, Daniel justified Early's army's actions outside Washington, saying, "if our people are to be treated as Rebels against their enemies, and thus visited with military execution, by fire and sword—and if either cannot or will not, when we have it in our own power, to pay slaughter with slaughter, pillage with pillage, conflagration with conflagration, then we fear that our doom is sealed." To Daniel's way of thinking, Southern men were duty bound to repay the North, slight for slight, if possible, but he feared that was not within their very nature. He continued,

> To Confederate troops the duty of retaliation is hard and odious; to retaliate everything in kind, would be altogether impossible for them; and no orders could make them outrage women or insult old men. Neither would any Confederate officer bring the dresses of Yankee women home as "trophies;" nor would Virginia girls like to wear such spoils. Retaliation, however, was a real and urgent duty, and the most essential business which our troops had in the enemy's country, if they had any business there at all.

Early's men took all that to heart, and knowingly or not, they made vengeance a real part of their essential business while in the North. And many extracted a great deal of personal satisfaction from their retribution. For many, it was as though it became a Southern obligation. And contrary to Daniel's vision of Southern manhood, the Rebel raiders of Washington stole many dresses, destroyed countless others, and scrawled suggestive messages on bedroom walls to the female occupants of some homes. "Our complements to the ladies," one said. "Sorry not to find them at home." Another apologized for the damage done to a young ladies' wardrobe. One Confederate soldier carved his personal justification for his damage into the top of a parlor table, explaining that he had ransacked the house as payback for Union's devastation of many such homes in Virginia. Inside another tossed house, a raider wrote on the flyleaf of a rare book, "On examination of this house you may form a faint idea of the suffering of 50,000 Virginians." Another book was nailed to a tree opposite the front of Montgomery Blair's burned-out mansion. The flyleaf displayed a threatening note addressed to President Lincoln.

During the raid, extorting, looting, burning, and ransoming was pervasive. Some of this was deeply personal, as when Postmaster General Blair's son's little pet donkey was taken, twice. The first time a Confederate officer ordered it returned to the family's housekeeper, but it was snatched away again later.

Union forces deliberately started fires around Washington a few days earlier. They had shelled a number of houses used by Confederate sharpshooters opposite Fort Stevens, setting ablaze properties belonging to Richard Butts, Abuer Shoemaker, William Bell, the late William M. Morrison, and J. H. McChisney. The Morrison residence was occupied by the Reverend Macueheimer, who was forced to flee the home from his sickbed. He lost his furniture, clothes, library of 800 books, and clerical robes. These were unfortunate colleterial damage.

As Robert E. Lee had hoped, Grant hastily sent a relief force to protect Washington. With the arrival of Federal troops in strength, Jubal Early realized it was time to go. He had gotten to within 6 miles of the White House and had caused significant havoc in the Maryland countryside, burning bridges, cutting telegraph lines, and threatening rail lines. He had done what he'd come for. Grant had withdrawn forces from Virginia, at least temporarily easing pressure on the defenses of Richmond. And Washington had been truly threatened for the first time in the war.

The withdrawal the night before allowed time for dissipation of the dust clouds that could have revealed the direction the Confederates took. On the 13th, the city held its breath wondering where the Rebels might be and whether they might attack somewhere else. Several days later, Mary Henry wrote in her diary, "Some fears are entertained that the force of Southerners which alarmed us will unite with those at Falls Church & attack us from the South."

During the evening hours of 13 July, President and Mrs. Lincoln visited many of the fortifications along Military Road, encouraging and congratulating all those who had served so ably in defending the city. That night the soldiers and civilians standing watch were fascinated by the brilliant lightshow emanating from the signal tower at the Soldiers' Home as signals flashed for miles in all directions in the moonlight sky. The signaling was being done by calcium lights that projected long and short flashes of intense light to mimic Morse code. Early had seen the signal tower when he first arrived outside Washington and knew that wherever he moved his men, they would be observed by the signalmen in the tower. From that observation point, Union troops could be successfully deployed to checkmate his every maneuver.

By the afternoon of 14 July, Early's army was once again in Virginia, after his cavalry had fought a rearguard action in Maryland with reluctant Union cavalry units cautiously following the Rebel force.

By 14 July mail and rail services were minimally restored, albeit somewhat impeded by a number of key burned bridges and torn-up tracks that still required repairs. Wire communications was also reestablished.

Given the disappointing performance of the War Department's clerks a few days earlier, Secretary of War Stanton ordered on 15 July that all the employees in every one of his various bureaus in Washington henceforth had to meet every afternoon, except on Sundays, for an hour's worth of military drill. Announcing this order, one local newspaper reported, "This

A butcher and his family at Fort Slocum. (Library of Congress)

will render the large clerical force in the War Department immediately available in an emergency, and will likewise give each of them an appetite for his dinner." While the reference to the appetite might have been true, the overarching premise was false. Clerks, commonly dubbed "counter jumpers" by the soldiers, were no substitute for battle-hardened bluecoats. They were clearly never intended to be soldiers, and the public's sentiment was that Washington's safety should never have been dependent upon office workers, payroll clerks, and scribes. An adequate defense of the Federal city was the army's responsibility, and in that regard the military showed that, for at least a few critical days that July, it had failed. Any attempt to portray overage and out-of-shape office workers as suitable backstops for defending the nation's capital in case of a repeat attack was purely ludicrous.

In the days following the raid, many senior-level government officials deplored the military's mismanagement of the attack on Washington. Most of the blame focused on General Halleck and Secretary Stanton. Stanton deflected fault by pointing the finger for the failure at Halleck, but was clearly shaken by the whole episode. There were rumors that Stanton offered to resign, but they were swiftly denied. Still, they persisted. Stanton was to be replaced by Senator John Sherman of Ohio, the brother of William Tecumseh Sherman, or General Benjamin Butler. All this grumbling had a negative effect on Stanton. Gideon Welles remarked on this as much in his diary entry on 15 July, writing, "The deportment of Stanton has been wholly different during this raid from any former one. He has been quiet, subdued, and apparently

Armory Square Hospital. (Library of Congress)

oppressed with some matter that gave him disquiet. On former occasions he has been active, earnest, violent, alarmed, apprehensive of danger from every quarter. It may be that he and Halleck have disagreed. Neither of them has done himself credit at this time."

For Captain Edward Hill, recovering in his Armory Square Hospital bed on 15 July, he penned in his diary, "The day is dull nothing new." Calm had returned to Washington.

CHAPTER 17

Early's Exit

According to Alanson Haines's history of the 15th New Jersey Volunteers, the end began in the late afternoon of 12 July. "It was about four p.m. when the guns of Fort Stevens opened upon the enemy stationed within the grounds of the Rives house…" he recorded. "The enemy fell back to a stronger position on a second ridge. At dusk Early threw out a picket line. After this feeble demonstration, he began his retreat under cover of night."

In withdrawing from the city, the Confederates couldn't go back the way they had come. Union forces were thought to have seized the passes at South Mountain. Early knew those passes could be held by a small Union force, one that might turn his retreat into an American Thermopylae. Union troops were also thought to have blocked the fords on the upper Potomac. The closest place the Rebels could cross the river was 45 miles away at White's Ferry. That was the quickest escape route into Virginia, and Early opted to take it.

In a 16 July news flash headlined "The Very Latest," the *Richmond Examiner* erroneously reported the fall of Washington. The news was based upon a wishful letter from a Marylander, who reported, "Washington is invested from the Potomac to the eastern branch of the Anacostia river. Every railroad north of Baltimore has been cut, and the telegraph wires destroyed. Today [the 13th] everything has been unusually quiet. Not a gun has been heard up to this time—twenty-five minutes past six o'clock a.m. It is believed they are negotiating for the surrender of Washington or giving time for the removal of women and children. Two forts that defend Washington—Forts Lincoln and Stevens—have been taken." Subsequent reports published in the *Examiner* on 16 July proclaimed that Baltimore had been captured thanks to "15,000 of the natives, armed with brickbats and bowie knives, having assisted our troops in the assault." With great glee the paper also reported the rumored fall of Washington and the capture of President Lincoln and his entire Cabinet. For good measure it added that 26 transports were taking Grant's army up the Potomac and that New Orleans had been retaken by Confederate forces.

Nothing was further from the truth. By daylight on 13 July the majority of Early's force was at Rockville. By noon it was at Seneca Creek, where it rested until dusk. By midnight the Rebel army was at White's Ferry, where it waited until dawn on 14 July to cross into Virginia with what was reported in one newspaper to include over 2,000 head of cattle. The Washington correspondent for the *New York Tribune* mockingly observed that "the third annual raid into Maryland is at an end, and that every man concerned in it, and every horse, wagon, mule, ox, cow, sheep, and hog that make part of it, objectively or subjectively, is safely on the Virginia side of the Potomac." The *New York World* wasn't really any more newsworthy in its reporting, telling readers that the raid was "to seize in the North the supplies which the cutting of the Danville road had temporarily interrupted from the South, and so convert an apparent loss into an advantage."

In making good their escape, the *Washington Evening Star* reported, "There can be no doubt that the force of Rebels that came into Maryland was about 30,000 strong." Based on the inflated estimates of the army, the number of cattle stolen may also need to be taken with a grain of salt. The Southerners also herded a mass of prisoners along with them as well, including those captured at Monocacy and taken elsewhere in Maryland.

The grossly inflated estimates of the Rebel army's numbers appear to have added to the timidity of any Union pursuit. The newspapers continued to encourage this misperception. The press wasn't ready to admit it was so wrong in accepting that this had been just a raiding party. The *Evening Star* reasoned that the number of senior Southern officers on the field during the past few days pointed to a far larger force. The *Star*'s opinion was, "a raiding party of 5,000 men, indeed, with two Major Generals and half dozen Brigadier Generals!" (Actually, there were four major generals.) There was some heavy cavalry skirmishing on the Georgetown and the Washington and Rockville Turnpikes about noon on 13 July that forced the Confederate rearguard to retire, but there was no immediate massed movement of Federal troops attempting to catch and crush the invaders before they crossed into Virginia for fear of the size of the Rebel force. Another major issue with any pursuit was the fact that as late as 11:00 a.m. on the 13th, Union military leaders weren't sure which way they went.

The fact that the Confederates were allowed to retreat in perfect order and with so much booty didn't sit well with Washingtonians. To Horatio Nelson Taft, it was an outrage. He recorded his disgust in diary, saying,

Very little has been heard of the rebels in this vicinity for the last three or four days. They seem to have departed with their plunder. No information has as yet been published that we have succeeded in recapturing a horse or cow or a rebel since they crossed the Potomac on their return. If this rebel 'raid' does not prove the ruin of this Administration, it will be Owing to successes in other quarters. More stupidity could not well be manifested than it has been shown in this matter, with Washington in a defenceless [sic] condition and inviting the invader. No body [sic] was on the alert, and all were in stupid ignorance until an army of Twenty or Thirty Thousand were found knocking at our gates. If they did not come in it was their own fault. They might have done it during three or four days.

As it was, Early, after retreating from Washington, led an unsuccessful series of attempts to keep the Federals out of the Shenandoah Valley. His ineffectiveness resulted in his ultimate dismissal from command. He had offered to step aside after his defeat at Cedar Creek on 19 October 1864. That battle eliminated further Confederate offensive operations in the valley and led to the ultimate destruction of the "Breadbasket of the Confederacy" in a campaign by Philip Sheridan known as "the Burning." According to the *Staunton (Virginia) Vindicator*, Sheridan, in his wrath, reportedly burned 30 homes, destroyed 31 gristmills, torched 45 barns, set fire to thousands of tons of hay, and made off with or killed about 1,750 head of cattle, 4,200 sheep, 3,550 hogs, and 3,770 horses in one county alone. While Early had been no angel around Washington, he hadn't been nearly as vengeful as Sheridan. Lee pondered Early's offer, and Early was notified of Lee's final decision, to send him home, on 30 March 1865. While Lee insisted that he still personally had every confidence in Early's abilities to lead, he claimed that the public and his soldiers no longer felt the same. "Your reverses in the Valley, of which the public and the army judge chiefly by the results, have, I fear, impaired your influence both with the people and the soldiers, and would add greatly to the difficulties which will, under any circumstances, attend our military operations in S.W. Virginia," Lee told his old friend.[1]

Lee replaced Early with Brigadier General John W. Echols, who had been one of Early's brigade commanders in the Maryland campaign. There were many differences between Early and Echols, not the least of which was physical stature. Echols was a giant of a man. He was 6 feet, 4 inches tall and weighed roughly 260 pounds. Early, who by the end of the war was being referred to by his men as "Old Jubilee" because of his stooped stature, was lucky if he weighed 170 pounds soaking wet. Echols's first task as the new head of the Confederate Department of Western Virginia and East Tennessee was to unite his force of 7,000 with Lee's army. Before he could accomplish that linkup, Lee surrendered. Echols and his men then accompanied Jefferson Davis partway on his escape to North Carolina following the loss of Richmond. Echols's men joined the forces of General Joseph E. Johnston, which surrendered at Augusta, Georgia.

Early was on his way home when Lee surrendered his army at Appomattox. Because Early was no longer a part of that army by then, he hadn't actually surrendered, avoiding the related personal humiliation. As soon as he was fit to travel, he set out to join Kirby Smith and the Confederate Army in the West to continue the fight. However, before he could reach Smith, that Western army also surrendered. Having never surrendered an army, received a parole, taken the amnesty oath, or received a presidential pardon, Early fled the country.[2] Disguised as a modest Southern farmer, he made his way to Mexico in 1865 and then sailed to Cuba. From there he ultimately moved on to Canada, where he remained until 1869. While in Toronto he penned his *Memoir of the Last Year of the War for Independence, in the Confederate States of America,* which particularly tried to justify his actions in Maryland, at Chambersburg and in the Shenandoah Valley.

Although totally unrepentant, Jubal Early finally received a presidential pardon in 1869. He returned to Virginia, where he practiced law. Throughout much of the remainder of his life, he dressed predominantly in Confederate gray.

John C. Breckinridge, Early's second in command, would go on to briefly serve as the South's secretary of war before the war ended and he too fled to Canada. Breckinridge's exile would last about as long as Early's. Bradley Johnson, who had led the Confederate cavalry on its ill-fated trek towards Point Lookout, was arrested in Baltimore in March 1866 on a charge of treason. At the urging of General Grant, the charge was dismissed by President Andrew Johnson. (Ironically, for the citizens of Bradley Johnson's hometown, Frederick, Maryland, whose town Early ransomed for $200,000, which it borrowed from five local banks, wouldn't be paid off until 1951. With interest, the town's cumulative repayments amounted to $600,000.)

In a postwar Congressional document concerning the need to save Fort Stevens as a historic site and install a monument there, the sentiment was, "Lincoln's presence at Fort Stevens proved a grand inspiration to the troops defending the capital. The Army recognized him as the foremost of the men who were alive to the great question of the hour, and watching the development of minds and of events." In hindsight, the framers of that document, which included Dr. Cornelius V. Crawford, expressed the opinion that Early's army that July had a chance to occupy the city, disperse the government, and destroy its archives, "all of which could have been completed by a single day's possession." The group concluded, "The historic battlefield of Fort Stevens should ever stand well to the front in the memory of the people; and for all time it should be a sacred place of inspiration to the generation of people who have reached the stage of action since July, 1864. Fort Stevens should be perpetuated in granite; and be a base for figures, in bronze, of Lincoln and Wright!"

Part of the resulting 1902 legislation to make Fort Stevens a historic site included the stipulation, "A further object of the bill is to mark the exact location where Abraham Lincoln in the midst of the consternation, trials, and confusion attending the threatened capital July 11 and 12, 1864, stood a noble spectator…." The resulting granite and bronze marker was originally installed on top of the battlements, a prominent place of honor, though perhaps not actually where Lincoln stood.

Some of the Union dead from the fighting at Fort Stevens were interred at Battleground National Cemetery, a short distance from what remains of Fort Stevens.

Fort Stevens Battleground National Cemetery. (Library of Congress)

CHAPTER 18

Early's Later Regrets

Towards the end of the war, Early relished his "Bad Old Man" personae. He exploited his irascible reputation. It added to his persona as a feared and fiesty commander, but in July 1864 he acquired another identity—fire-breathing terrorist. After that he was known more for threatening or visiting vengeance on the helpless, and that was a reputation he didn't want. He hated what he'd become.

While Early's action outside Washington likely prolonged the war by as much as a half a year because of the food he rustled up, but in doing so he found himself placed on the Patheon of arsonists alongside of William T. Sherman and Philip Sheridan. In truth, Early wasn't nearly as bad as these two Federal generals. He didn't believe in "total war" on civilians.

Sherman burned places like Atlanta because he said he never wanted to garrison any place that he captured. Sherman's and Sheridan's strategy meant taking whatever their armies needed, burning the rest, and moving on, inflicting as much carnage as possible. Early wasn't a grim reaper in this regard. He wouldn't become the South's avenging angel to the degree Sherman and Sheridan became the North's. He wasn't nearly as zealous with flammables, but he was still branded as though he were. For him, the bluff of burning was enough. The South needed money for supplies, and ransoming Northern towns was the easiest way to raise it.

Another characteristic about Early was that while he could be aggressive, he basically possessed more of a defensive military mind. This made him less than ideal for an actual assault on Washington, because he was more likely as not to hold back on pressing an attack, but if the raid was a ploy, then he was the ideal candidate to lead it.

Despite, or perhaps because of, his propensity for defense, Early was chosen in the summer of 1864 to carry out a cautious, yet audacious plan to lead a raiding party in force into the heart of Maryland and, if possible, threatening Washington, DC, or any other targets of opportunity that might prove opportune. He relished this assignment. He would be the only Southern commander to lead Confederate soldiers to Lincoln's very threshold. He would become the instrument of the South's respectable fury in front of the Nation's Capital, and possibly, just possibly, if successful he would have become the South's greatest field commander.

As he'd hoped, his coming caused Washingtonians to panic. Even Secretary of War Stanton hid his valuables under his mattress. Solomon G. Brown, the transportation clerk and caretaker of the Smithsonian Institution, hid a box of assistant secretary Spencer Baird's valuables under the center of the stone floor of the coal cellar in the south tower of the Smithsonian's Castle. The hiding place was to be covered over by the pile of coal at the very last moment should the Rebels break into Washington. Because the Smithsonian's assistant secretary was out of town at the time, Brown, the institution's first African American employee, wrote him a letter that advised him of the whereabouts of this secret space, saying, "This you will remember should anything turn up to prevent them being shipped to a place of safty [sic] outside of town, but at present [the valuables] remain where you last saw them."[1] Others buried prized possessions in backyards or hid them in garden plots.

Garden plots couldn't protect everything, especially Montgomery Blair's possessions in his summer house. He was a marked man. Blair had served as the mayor of Saint Louis in the 1840s and was appointed solicitor of the US Court of Claims in 1855. During this period Blair served as a counsel for Dred Scott, a runaway slave who became the focus of the nation's most infamous cases pertaining to the Fugitive Slave Act. Blair also assisted in the defense of abolitionist John Brown, charged in his attempt to incite a slave insurrection with an 1859 raid on Harpers Ferry. In Maryland, Blair became a stalwart of the Republican Party, serving as the president of the Maryland State Republican Convention. Lincoln selected Blair as his postmaster general, and Blair served with great distinction, creating postal money order service so soldiers and sailors could safely send money home from their closest post office. He also introduced free delivery to homes in the city, so that if patrons had to receive bad news of a soldier's death, they would not have to read it at their local post office.

Blair's house would be burned as the final act of Early's attack on Washington. Early swore that he had nothing to do with the act, claiming it was likely vagrants. His *Memoirs* contain a special footnote to this effect, as if his conscience still pained him for somehow being to blame.

After Blair's summer home was burned down during the Rebel raid, Gideon Welles decided to see the damage for himself. Falkland, the palatial, multistory mansion at Silver Spring, was only about 3,000 yards from Fort Stevens. The carriage ride passed sites of the fighting. "The chimneys of the burnt houses, the still barricaded road, the trampled fields, and other evidences bear testimony to what had occurred," he recorded in his diary.[2]

Montgomery Blair's father's summer home and farm, Silver Spring, located a short distance away from his son's house, fared much better. The senior Blair's house, begun in 1842, was at the heart of his roughly 1,000-acre farm. "The place was less injured than I had supposed," wrote Gideon Welles in his diary after visiting. "What depredation or plunder had been committed in the house I could not tell, for it was closed."[3] Welles's son Thomas, who had commanded the Federal pickets under Major General Alexander M. McCook a few days prior and had been among the first to reach the house after the Rebels withdrew, described it to his father. He said that other than papers scattered about, the floors the house appeared to be in good shape. He said he found the house full of vagabonds sleeping on the floors and prying into the family's personal papers and possessions, but that these vagrants were dutifully dispersed.

The senior Blair's house had briefly served as Early's headquarters and as a Rebel hospital for about 100 wounded, and though it was ransacked and the silverware and plates were stolen, and its extensive wine cellar was greatly diminished, it wasn't torched, thanks to the personal intervention of Confederate General John Breckenridge, Blair's cousin. That July he repaid the hospitality previously shown to him here by saving the house and most of its contents from destruction. Welles was struck by the fact that the grounds and shrubbery were so well preserved and that the crops, which he described as "the best corn I have seen this year," appeared to have been untouched.[4] When the Rebels withdrew, they left some of the worst of their wounded behind at Francis Preston Blair's house, including 19 who were too severe to travel. These wounded were attended by 11 Rebels who remained behind to look after their comrades. The house's use as a hospital ensured that it wouldn't be burned.

Moorings, the house of Montgomery Blair's brother, James, a naval officer, located at Jessup-Blair Park in Silver Spring, was largely unmolested.

Adam Gurowski was another of those who toured Silver Spring after the Rebel departure. What struck him was the fact that Rebel camp wasn't what he expected. If the invaders really numbered 30,000, he thought, why did their encampment seem so small? From what he was seeing, he they might have had scarcely half that number. None of what he read in the newspapers or heard on the streets of Washington made much sense. With 30,000 men and heavy artillery, the Rebels should have "swept us out of Washington," he wrote. "It seems that the Rebels faltered. Doubtless during the night of last Saturday [9 July] they could have pierced through and burned Washington, provided they were as strong as our frightened commanders believe. If so, then Washington was saved by a moral terror in the hearts of the Rebel matricides."

In retrospect, Welles thought that perhaps such damage was no worse than Union soldiers might have done had the tables been turned. In fact he knew better. He was aware of what Major General Sherman was already doing in Georgia at about that time. What Welles couldn't have known was something that would have certainly turned his stomach. On 7 July 1864 Sherman's men had captured Roswell, Georgia, a mill town on the outskirts of Atlanta. The cotton mills were being used to produce cloth for Confederate uniforms and other war material. While Early was approaching Washington, Sherman was approving a request to destroy the mills at Roswell *and* deporting all its workers to Northern prisons on charges of treason. Most of the mill workers were women. Approximately 400 women and their children were forcibly transported north by train with whatever meager possessions they could physically carry. Few of these women ever returned to Georgia.

As Early might have done to Washington had he gotten the chance that July, Sherman burned his target, Atlanta, that September because he knew he couldn't garrison the city if he ever expected to march to the sea and "make Georgia howl." And just as Early's forces had done in living off the land as they marched through Maryland, Sherman and his "bummers" would carry foraging in the South to the extreme in a few months. Despite

Jubal Early late in life. (Library of Congress)

that Sherman wanted to keep his movements secret, it was said that anyone could plot his progress through Georgia and the Carolina's from the smoke rising from all the burning homes, barns, businesses, and fields. If Early had selectively dabbled in "total war" on his way to Washington, Sherman clearly was to demonstrate that he was its principal practitioner for the remainder of the war.

Rectifying the physical, fiscal, martial, and political consequences of the raid were varied and would consume years on both sides.

Crabby to the bitter end, Jubal Anderson Early tripped while on the stairs of the Lynchburg post office on 15 February 1894 and appears to have suffered internal injuries in his fall. These resulted in his death on 2 March 1894.

The burning of Chambersburg haunted Jubal Early. It was the one thing he did that he feared would lead to his imprisonment for war crimes. This view of the destruction is from the corner of Main and East King Streets. (Library of Congress)

Epilogue

Following Early's flight from the Washington, General Grant suggested to use the city's forts as boot camps for the training of Federal troops, to help calm fears. This would ensure that ample bluecoats were available to protect the nation's capital if the need ever arose again.

Endnotes

Preface

1 Antietam on the web, https://antietam.aotw.org/, accessed 19 May 2021.
2 *Letters from a Civil War Surgeon: The Letters of Dr. William Child of the Fifth New Hampshire Volunteers,* Polar Bear & Company (1995).
3 Robert E. Lee's *General Order Number 73,* 27 June 1863.
4 Benjamin Franklin Cooling III, *Jubal Early: Robert E. Lee's "Bad Old Man,"* p. 89, Rowman & Littlefield, New York (2014).
5 Slave Narratives Project, National Writers Program, Works Project Administration, 1938–1939, Library of Congress. This is a remarkably rich source of oral histories of former enslaved Americans recorded late in their lives. A number of these, like Shepherd Rhone, said they had accompanied their masters or their masters' sons to war, serving them as cooks and valets. They suffered the same privations as their owners, including food shortages, which they recounted during their interviews.
6 Ibid. Gus Brown claimed he enlisted in the Confederate army, but it was perhaps more likely that he served as a personal butler to an officer.

Introduction

1 John Bell Gordon, *Reminiscences of the Civil War,* p. 314, Andesite Press (2015).
2 Jubal Early, *Jubal Early's Memoirs: Autobiographical Sketch and Narrative of the War Between the States,* p. 159, Nautical and Aviation Publishing Company, Baltimore (1989).

Chapter 1. The Confederates Turn the Tables

1 Jubal Early, *Memoir*, p. 293, Nautical and Aviation Publishing Company, Baltimore (1989).
2 Ibid., p. 294.
3 Ibid., p. 295.
4 Ibid., p. 294.
5 The papers of Union soldier Samuel J. Gibson (1833–1878) consist of a diary kept by Gibson in 1864 while serving with Company B, 103rd Pennsylvania Infantry, and archived at the Library of Congress.
6 Robert J. Schneller, Jr., *A Quest for Glory*, p. 279, Naval Institute Press, Annapolis (1996).
7 Ibid., p. 280.
8 Alvin and Marjorie Kanter, *Sanitary Fairs*, p. 235, SF Publishing, Glencoe, Illinois (1992).
9 Ibid., p. 233.
10 Ibid., p. 241.
11 Ibid., p. 238.
12 From a letter reprinted in the Washington, DC, *Daily National Republican*, p. 2, col 1. (extra edition), 19 July 1865.
13 Gideon Welles, *Diary*, vol. 1, p. 534, edited by Howard K. Beale, W. W. Norton & Company (1960).
14 Robert J. Schneller, Jr., *A Quest for Glory*, p. 283–84, Naval Institute Press, Annapolis, MD (1996).
15 Daily Richmond Examiner, vol. 17, no. 300 (March 3, 1864).
16 Mary E. Thropp, "Fourth of July in Richmond in 1865," letter to her father, National Park Service.

Chapter 2. Into the Valley

1 Jubal Early, *Memoirs*, p. i, Nautical and Aviation Publishing Company, Baltimore (1989).
2 Ibid., xlvii.
3 Ibid., xlviii.
4 Ibid., 378.
5 Ibid., 388.
6 Ibid., 385.

Chapter 3. Defending Washington

1 J. G. Barnard, *A Report on the Defenses of Washington*, p. 16, Government Printing Office, Washington, DC (1871).

2 Benjamin Franklin Cooling III and Walton H. Owen II, *Mr. Lincoln's Forts: A Guide to the Civil War Defenses of Washington*, pp. 3–15, White Mane Press, Shippinsburg, PA (1988).
3 Ibid., p. 159.
4 Gideon Welles, *Diary*, vol. 2, p. 68, edited by Howard K. Beale, W. W. Norton & Company (1960).

Chapter 4. The Rebels Are Coming

1 Abraham Lincoln Papers, Library of Congress.
2 Ibid.
3 Ibid.
4 Gideon Welles, *Diary*, vol. 2, p. 71, edited by Howard K. Beale, W. W. Norton & Company (1960).
5 Ibid., p. 70.
6 Diary of US patent clerk Horatio Nelson Taft, dotcw.com, accessed 19 May 2021.
7 Abraham Lincoln Papers, Library of Congress
8 Ibid.
9 Gideon Welles, *Diary*, vol. 2, p. 68, edited by Howard K. Beale, W. W. Norton & Company (1960).
10 Adam Gurowski, Diary from November 12, 1862, to October 18, 1863, Project Gutenburg.
11 Robert J. Schneller, Jr., *A Quest for Glory*, p. 185, Naval Institute Press, Annapolis, MD (1996).

Chapter 5. Across the Potomac

1 Jubal Early, *Memoirs*, p. 159, Nautical and Aviation Publishing Company, Baltimore, MD (1989).
2 Dr. Robert E. Oshel, *Silver Spring and the Civil War*, p. 32, the History Press, Charleston, SC (2014).

Chapter 6. 9 July—Monocacy Junction

1 Abraham Lincoln Papers, Library of Congress.
2 Ibid.
3 Ibid.
4 Ibid.
5 Ibid.

6   Thomas Lewis, "When Washington, D.C. Came Close to Being Conquered by the Confederacy," *Smithsonian*, July 1988.

7   Abraham Lincoln Papers, Library of Congress.

Chapter 7. 9 and 10 July—Taking Shelter

1   Adam Gurowski, Diary from November 12, 1862, to October 18, 1863, Project Gutenburg.

2   Ibid.

3   Ibid.

4   Abraham Lincoln Papers, Library of Congress.

5   Charles Willoughby, Dayton Diaries, vol. 2, January 1–December 31, 1864, New-York Historical Society.

6   Abraham Lincoln Papers, Library of Congress.

7   Ibid.

8   Charles Willoughby, Dayton Diaries, vol. 2, January 1–December 31, 1864, New-York Historical Society.

9   Ibid., p. 145.

10   Diary of US patent clerk Horatio Nelson Taft, dotcw.com, accessed 19 May 2021.

11   Ibid., p.66.

12   Ibid., p. 68.

13   Ibid., p. 70.

14   Ibid., p. 72.

Chapter 8. The Way to Washington

1   Jubal Early, *Memoirs*, p. 389, Nautical and Aviation Publishing Company, Baltimore, MD (1989).

2   Dr. Robert E. Oshel, *Silver Spring and the Civil War*, p. 76, the History Press, Charleston, SC (2014).

3   Dennis Hart Mahan, *A treatise on field fortification, containing instructions on the methods of laying out, constructing, defending, and attacking intrenchments, with the general outlines also of the arrangement, the attack and defence* [sic] *of permanent fortifications*, p. vi, Preface (1856).

4   Jubal Early, *Memoirs*, p. 390, Nautical and Aviation Publishing Company, Baltimore, MD (1989).

5   Dr. Robert E. Oshel, *Silver Spring and the Civil War*, p. 54, the History Press, Charleston, SC (2014).

6   John G. Barnard, *A Report on the Defenses of Washington*, p. 10, Government Printing Office, Washington, DC (1871).

7   Ibid., p. 136.
8   Benjamin Franklin Cooling III and Walton H. Owen II, *Mr. Lincoln's Forts: A Guide to the Civil War Defenses of Washington*, p. 38, White Mane Press, Shippensburg, PA (1988).
9   Jubal Early, *Memoirs*, p. 385, Nautical and Aviation Publishing Company, Baltimore, MD (1989).
10 Ibid., p. 394.
11 Frank E. Vandiver, *Jubal's Raid: General Early's Famous Attack on Washington in 1864*, p. 171, University of Nebraska Press (originally published by McGraw-Hill, New York, 1960) and reprinted by Bison Books in 1992. This remark was to Major Kyd Douglas ,who had been assigned to guard Preston Blair's mansion Silver Spring and was given the task of covering Early's withdrawal. Douglas and his 200-man rearguard force was to withdraw at midnight unless otherwise engaged by Federal forces. Early tried to encourage Douglas by assuring him that "Major, we haven't taken Washington, but we've scared Abe Lincoln like hell!"

Chapter 9. The Rebels Take Their Toll

1   Scotty E. Kirkland, Mobile Bread Riot, Encyclopedia of Alabama, http://www.encyclopediaofalabama.org/article/h-3536, accessed 19 May 2021.
2   Joseph Wheelan, *Libby Prison Breakout*, p. 134, PublicAffairs, New York (2010).
3   Mary Henry's Diary, Smithsonian Institution Archives.

Chapter 10. Outside Baltimore

1   Gideon Welles, *Diary*, vol. 2, p. 71, edited by Howard K. Beale, W. W. Norton & Company (1960).
2   *New York Times*, "Ishmael Day, the Old Loyalist who shot a Rebel," 17 July 1864, front page (reprint from the *Baltimore American*, July 13, 1864).
3   Ibid.
4   Mary Henry's Diary, Smithsonian Institution Archives.

Chapter 11. 11 July—Around Washington

1   Benjamin Franklin Cooling III, *Jubal Early: Robert E. Lee's "Bad Old Man,"* p. 91, Rowman & Littlefield, New York (2014).
2   Transcription of the Diary of Edward Hill, 11 July 1864 entry, St. Mary's College.

3   Gideon Welles, *Diary*, vol. 2, p. 72, edited by Howard K. Beale, W. W. Norton & Company (1960).

4   Transcription of the Diary of Edward Hill, 11 July 1864 entry, St. Mary's College.

5   Gideon Welles, *Diary*, vol. 2, p. 72, edited by Howard K. Beale, W. W. Norton & Company (1960).

6   Transcription of the Diary of Edward Hill, 11 July 1864 entry, St. Mary's College.

7   Abraham Lincoln Papers, Library of Congress.

8   Ibid.

9   Mary Henry's Diary, Smithsonian Institution Archives.

10   Gideon Welles, *Diary*, vol. 2, p. 73, edited by Howard K. Beale, W. W. Norton & Company (1960).

11   Transcription of the Diary of Edward Hill, 11 July 1864 entry, St. Mary's College.

12   Dr. Robert E. Oshel, *Silver Spring and the Civil War*, p. 149, the History Press, Charleston, SC (2014).

13   Gideon Welles, *Diary*, pp. 390–391, edited by Howard K. Beale, W. W. Norton & Company (1960).

14   Ibid., p. 390.

15   Gideon Welles, *Diary*, vol. 2, p. 72, edited by Howard K. Beale, W. W. Norton & Company (1960).

Chapter 12. 12 and 13 July

1   Gideon Welles, *Diary*, p. 391, edited by Howard K. Beale, W. W. Norton & Company (1960).

2   Dr. Robert E. Oshel, *Silver Spring and the Civil War*, p. 52, the History Press, Charleston, SC (2014).

3   J. G. Barnard, *A Report on the Defenses of Washington*, addendum to appendix A, Government Printing Office, Washington, DC (1871).

4   Gideon Welles, *Diary*, vol. 2, p. 73, edited by Howard K. Beale, W. W. Norton & Company (1960).

5   Ibid., pp. 75–76.

6   Ibid., p. 75.

7   B. A. Botkin, *A Civil War Treasury of Tales, Legends and folklore*, pp. 359–360, the Blue and Grey Press, Secaucus, NJ (1960).

8   James I. Robertson, Jr., *Soldiers Blue and Gray*, p. 143, University of South Carolina Press (1988).

9   J. G. Barnard, *A Report on the Defenses of Washington*, addendum to appendix A, Government Printing Office, Washington, DC (1871).

10 Christian Hook Diary 1864, Virginia Polytechnic Institute Special Collections.

11 Abraham Lincoln Papers, Library of Congress.

12 Gideon Welles, *Diary*, vol. 2, p. 75, edited by Howard K. Beale, W. W. Norton & Company (1960).

13 Ibid., pp. 75–76.

14 Dudley Taylor Cornish and Virginia Jeans Laas, *Lincoln's Lee*, pp. 134–135, University Press of Kansas, Lawrence, KS (1986).

15 Ibid.

16 Virginia Jeans Laas, editor, *The Civil War Letters of Elizabeth Blair Lee*, p. 410, University of Illinois Press, Chicago (1991).

Chapter 13. 14 July

1 J. G. Barnard, *A Report on the Defenses of Washington*, addendum to appendix A, Government Printing Office, Washington, DC (1871).

2 Gideon Welles, *Diary*, vol. 2, p. 76, edited by Howard K. Beale, W. W. Norton & Company (1960).

3 Abraham Lincoln Papers, Library of Congress.

4 Fred Pelka, editor, *The Civil War Letters of Colonel Charles F. Johnson, Invalid Corps*, p. 258, University of Massachusetts Press, Boston (2004).

5 Ibid., p. 4.

6 Mary Henry's Diary, Smithsonian Institution Archives.

7 Benjamin Franklin Cooling III and Walton H. Owen II, *Mr. Lincoln's Forts: A Guide to the Civil War Defenses of Washington*, p. 208, White Mane Press, Shippensburg, PA (1988).

8 Jubal Early, *Memoirs*, p. 395, Nautical and Aviation Publishing Company, Baltimore, MD (1989).

9 Fred Pelka, editor, *The Civil War Letters of Colonel Charles F. Johnson, Invalid Corps*, p. 259, University of Massachusetts Press, Boston (2004).

10 Mary Henry's Diary, Smithsonian Institution Archives.

11 "Office Provost Marshal, Frederick, Md., July 22, 1864," Duke University Libraries, https://repository.duke.edu/dc/broadsides/bdsmd51003, accessed 19 May 2021.

Chapter 14. Back Again

1 Jubal Early, *Memoirs*, p. 401, Nautical and Aviation Publishing Company, Baltimore, MD (1989).

2 Gideon Welles, *Diary*, vol. 2, p. 76, edited by Howard K. Beale, W. W. Norton & Company (1960).

3 Gideon Welles, *Diary*, vol. 2, p. 80, edited by Howard K. Beale, W. W. Norton & Company (1960).
4 Ibid., p. 73.
5 Abraham Lincoln Papers, Library of Congress.
6 Abraham Lincoln Papers, Library of Congress.
7 Gideon Welles, *Diary*, vol. 2, p. 80, edited by Howard K. Beale, W. W. Norton & Company (1960).
8 Ibid., p. 156.

Chapter 15. Point Lookout

1 Gideon Welles, *Diary*, vol. 2, p. 80, edited by Howard K. Beale, W. W. Norton & Company (1960).
2 Benjamin Franklin Cooling III and Walton H. Owen II, *Mr. Lincoln's Forts: A Guide to the Civil War Defenses of Washington*, p. 229, White Mane Press, Shippensburg, PA (1988).
3 Gideon Welles, *Diary*, vol. 1, p. 474, edited by Howard K. Beale, W. W. Norton & Company (1960).
4 David Dixon Porter, *The Naval History of the Civil War*, reprint, p. 472, Castle, Secaucus, NJ (1984).
5 Ibid., p. 472.
6 Gideon Welles, *Diary*, vol. 2, p. 111, edited by Howard K. Beale, W. W. Norton & Company (1960).
7 Ibid., p. 111.
8 Ibid.
9 Ibid., p. 146.
10 Mary Henry's Diary, Smithsonian Institution Archives.
11 Ibid.
12 Jubal Early, *Memoirs*, p. 385, Nautical and Aviation Publishing Company, Baltimore, MD (1989).
13 Ibid., p. 382.
14 Ibid., p. 394.
15 Ibid.
16 James I. Robertson, Jr., *Soldiers Blue and Gray*, p. 69, University of South Carolina Press (1988).
17 Ibid., p. 199.

Chapter 16. Fort Stevens

1 Adam Gurowski, Diary from November 12, 1862, to October 18, 1863, Project Gutenburg.

2   Gideon Welles, *Diary*, vol. 2, p. 101, edited by Howard K. Beale, W. W. Norton & Company (1960).
3   Edward Porter Alexander, *Military Memoirs of a Confederate*, p.563, Charles Scribner's Sons, New York (1907).
4   Ibid., p. 563.
5   Gideon Welles, *Diary*, vol. 2, p. 43, edited by Howard K. Beale, W. W. Norton & Company (1960).
6   Ibid., p. 44.
7   Ibid., p. 313.
8   David Dixon Porter, *The Naval History of the Civil War*, reprint, p. 794, Castle, Secaucus, NJ (1984).
9   Jubal Early, *Memoirs*, p. 390, Nautical and Aviation Publishing Company, Baltimore, MD (1989).
10 Ibid., p 390.
11 Ibid., p 391.
12 Ibid.
13 Ibid.
14 Ibid.
15 Chris Mackowski and Kristopher White, *Simply Murder*, p. 23, Savas Beatie, El Dorado, CA (2013).
16 Ibid., 23.

Chapter 17. Early's Exit

1   Jubal Early, *Memoirs*, p. 468, Nautical and Aviation Publishing Company, Baltimore, MD (1989).
2   Ibid., p. 468.

Chapter 18. Early's Later Regrets

1   Smithsonian Institution Archives.
2   Gideon Welles, *Diary*, vol. 2, p. 80, edited by Howard K. Beale, W. W. Norton & Company (1960).
3   Ibid.
4   Ibid.

Additional Reading

There are a number of highly readable books that compliment this work that readers may enjoy, including:

Bloody Autumn: The Shenandoah Valley Campaign in 1864 by Daniel T. Davis and Phillip S. Greenwalt, published by Savas Beatie (El Dorado Hills, California) in 2013.

Jubal's Raid: General Early's Famous Attack on Washington in 1864 by Frank E. Vandiver, published by the University of Nebraska Press (originally published by McGraw-Hill (New York, New York, in 1960) and reprinted by Bison Books in 1992.

Jubal Early: Robert E. Lee's "Bad Old Man" by Benjamin Franklin Cooling III, published by Rowman & Littlefield (Lanham, Maryland) in 2014.

Silver Spring and the Civil War by Dr. Robert E. Oshel, published by the History Press (Charleston, South Carolina) in 2014.

Index